Lone Traveller
One Woman, Two Wheels
and the World

Lone Traveller

One Woman, Two Wheels and the World

Anne Mustoe

This edition first published in Great Britain in 2000 by
Virgin Publishing Ltd
Thames Wharf Studios
Rainville Road
London W6 9HA

Reprinted 2000

First published in Great Britain in 1998 by
Swan Hill Press
An imprint of Airlife Publishing Ltd
101 Longden Road
Shrewsbury SY3 9EB

A catalogue record for this book is available from the British Library.

ISBN 0 7535 0426 X

Typeset by TW Typesetting, Plymouth, Devon
Printed and bound by Mackays of Chatham PLC

To all the people around the world
who gave me their time,
their friendship and their hospitality

Contents

Prologue

Liberavi animam meam
(I have freed my spirit)

St Bernard of Clairvaux

In 1987 I cycled alone round the world. I gave up my job as a headmistress, got a bicycle and set out from London one May afternoon. I was not a cyclist and I was full of uncertainties. At first I found it very hard going. France was rain-swept, cold and windy. I wobbled on my new bicycle and struggled up the hills. But once I'd puffed my way over the Alps into the warmth and ease of the Po Valley, I found that I was not just managing the ride – I was actually beginning to enjoy it.

I discovered that cycling was the perfect way to travel. It was faster than walking, but slow enough to appreciate all the sights and scents of the countryside. With no possessions to speak of, no complicated mechanisms to go wrong and no timetables, my days were wonderfully carefree and my only duty in life was to get myself safely from one shelter to the next before nightfall. Everything I needed was to hand, in two small bags on the back of the world's greenest and most energy-efficient machine. My life was simplicity itself. After years of responsibility, I just couldn't believe my luck.

To add an extra dimension to my travels, I followed historical routes around the world: the Romans, Alexander the Great, the Moguls, the British Raj and the North American settlers. Old roads echo with the footsteps of those who have trodden them throughout the ages, and to ride those roads slowly and sometimes painfully on a bicycle is to get a glimpse of the struggles, the hopes and the dreams of the people who built our world. On a practical level, the old roads are comfortable. Unlike modern motorways, which stride over hill tops, bridge rivers and gorges and tunnel under mountains in dazzling feats of engineering, the old roads meander along valleys and take the gradients gently, with due regard to the frailties of the men and beasts of burden who have to use them. I found them perfect roads for cycling. And as they passed through all the small villages, I talked to more people than I'd ever done in the days when I'd hurtled along in a car. Everyone finds time for a lone cyclist; and in countries where the bicycle is the chief form of transport, there's a fellow-feeling which transcends barriers of race and wealth. The travelling cyclist is a guest, not a tourist to be exploited.

Solitary long-distance travel is addictive. I came back home after fifteen months and wrote a full account of my journey in *A Bike Ride*. Then I itched to be on the move again. I'd cycled the world from West to East, London to London, and now the Yin was crying out for the Yang. The other circuit had to be completed, this time from East to West.

Looking for historical routes again, I found the ideal set which hardly overlapped at all with my first round-trip. I would start this time from the Forum in Rome and follow the Roman road network across Europe to Lisbon, picking up the great explorers and conquistadors as I went. I would travel in their wake across the Atlantic to Salvador, the first Portuguese capital of Brazil, and follow the expansion of Portuguese power northwards up the coast to the mouth of the Amazon. As a change from cycling, and because roads are scarce in the rainforest, I would take a succession of cargo boats up the navigable length of the world's mightiest river, then cycle the trail of Spanish Pizarro, the conqueror of the Incas, over the Andes and down the Pacific Coast of Peru to Chile. From Santiago I would fly, via Easter Island and Tahiti, to the south-east corner of Australia, cycle up the east coast and across the Outback to Darwin. From there I would fly to Indonesia and cycle across Bali and Java to Jakarta. My heroes on that stretch would be Captain Cook and the Australian settlers, who struggled to find paths across the wastes of their inhospitable continent. Finally, I would fly to China and cycle the fabled Silk Road from the ancient capital, Xi'an (which is on roughly the same line of longitude as Jakarta) back to Rome. At the end of that second circuit, I would write another book.

The second journey was longer than the first and far more

arduous, but I tackled it in a more leisurely way. I'd made the first round-trip in one continuous circuit, moving relentlessly on from country to country, cycling every inch of the way. The journey had been a challenge which I'd met head-on, losing more than 10 kilos in weight in the process and returning home triumphant, but gaunt and weary. The second circuit I took in three stages, with breaks between. I cycled this time purely for pleasure, choosing the season to suit the climate.

The first winter, I did the idyllic ride round the Mediterranean coast from Rome to Valencia, then over the Sierras to Lisbon. It was a winter of orange, lemon and olive groves, of magical Christmas hoarfrost on the Cathedral in Pisa, of sunshine on brilliant blue seas and empty beaches, of roses, carnations and mimosa along the Riviera, of stunning Roman monuments, vineyards in Provence and civilised evenings over excellent food and robust local wine. Out of season, it was all remarkably inexpensive and I couldn't imagine why all the retired people in Europe weren't out there with me, drifting along on their bicycles in the balmy air of that beautiful coast.

Three winters later, I flew out on Christmas Eve to Brazil and spent almost a year crossing South America, Australia and Indonesia. It was October when I reached Jakarta and my next country, China, was far too bleak and mountainous for winter cycling. So I came home to sit out the bad weather in London before flying to Beijing in the Spring, to begin the last leg. When I finally reached the Roman Forum again, the whole circuit, with time off between rides, had taken me five years.

There were more political problems the second time round. I could not get visas to cycle in Iran and parts of Central Asia; there were the Shining Path guerrillas in Peru, the PKK in Eastern Turkey and ethnic conflict in Xinjiang; there were hassles with police, border guards and officialdom generally. Then there were drug-runners, pirates, robbers and wild dogs. And on top of all these animate obstacles, I had to cross some of the world's most punishing terrain – the mountain passes of the Andes, Pamirs and Karakorams, and the Atacama, Gobi and Taklimakan deserts. It was not a ride to be undertaken lightly and there were a few occasions when I feared for my life.

Had I not gained confidence on the first circuit and learned a multitude of tactical wiles, I could never have coped with the dangers and rigours of the second.

When I got around to thinking of the book I should write, I was at a loss. As an experienced cyclist, I never really doubted that I should be able to complete the tour, so that a straightforward narrative account, on the lines of *A Bike Ride*, would lack the element of uncertainty and possibly some of the freshness and excitement which gave the first book its edge. And then, the second circuit was so grandiose in its sweep, the landscape so colossal, the extremes of climate so great. There were so many incidents, so many interesting people along the way, so much history and art, that it seemed impossible to cram it all into one volume. A different approach was needed.

When I give talks on my travels, audiences always home in on the logistics. They're fascinated to know what I pack, how I organise my daily routine, how I manage to wash my socks in the desert, how I change my money and how I mend my punctures. Above all, they want to know how I overcome the loneliness and inherent dangers of solitary travel, particularly for a woman.

So in this book I've decided that practicalities will take precedence over history and landscape. The central section consists of four narrative chapters, which give a detailed day-to-day account of the four most challenging parts of the journey – crossing the Australian Outback, the Gobi Desert and the Karakorams, and sailing the length of the Amazon in Brazilian cargo boats. In the other chapters, I've tried to make sense of the mass of incidents, problems, people and predicaments by grouping them together under subject headings.

Cycling round the world may seem a bold, almost heroic enterprise, but it's still composed of a series of individual days, each one full of very ordinary happenings. Crossing Rawalpindi on a bicycle is no more amazing than crossing London. So this is an honest book, written without exaggeration or embellishment, to show what it was really like. Some incidents may seem trivial, but such is the stuff of our lives.

Occasionally, things get rough but I've dealt with 'Terrible Terrain' at length, to show that even the harshest places are manageable. They present few problems which can't be avoided at the planning-stage, or solved at the time with a bit of ingenuity and a dash of optimism. In a grim sort of way, the difficult bits can sometimes be enjoyable, or at least satisfying. And afterwards, in the comfort of home, they can even seem amusing. For the rest of the journey, I've scarcely mentioned the landscape. That's because it was usually a pleasure to cycle through and I can't go on indefinitely about sunshine, blue skies and stunning views.

The practicalities are easy to list. What I find more difficult to deal with are the more personal topics. As a Classicist both by temperament and training, I find it uncomfortable to emote all over the page. I don't like revealing too much of my inner feelings, my hopes and disappointments, or holding forth on my own personal likes and dislikes. That sort of writing strikes me as too self-indulgent by far. But I'm asked so often about my response to solitude, danger and illness, that I've finally screwed myself up to discuss it.

This book is written for everyone who would dearly love to go on an adventure, but teeters on the brink, full of self-doubt. It's a book for the unfit, the unathletic, the clumsy and the comfort-loving of any age and either sex. You don't have to be twenty, male and an ace mechanic to set out on a great journey. I've cycled round the world twice now. I'm not young, I'm not sporty, I never train, I appreciate good food and wine, and I still can't tell a sprocket from a chainring or mend a puncture! If such an unsuitable candidate can circle the globe on a bicycle and live to tell the tale, there's hope for everyone.

1 Good Days

When I was at home I was in a better place; but travellers must be content.

Shakespeare, *As You Like It.*

Travelling contentedly is an art which takes practice, optimism and patience. Nothing on a journey is ever quite as comfortable or convenient as it is at home, but we know that before we set out. As soon as we close our front doors behind us, we leave the security of our daily routine and begin the struggle to lead normal lives in abnormal circumstances.

Optimism and patience are gifts of temperament. Some people are born with a sunny disposition and the ability to take the unexpected calmly, while others find it hard to stop worrying. But the logistics of easy travel boil down to a set of simple skills, which anyone can acquire with practice. Even the longest, most exotic journey is made up of single days, and each of those days can be a good day or a bad one. But good days don't come by accident. They come because we've avoided most of the troubles that lie in wait by careful planning beforehand and plain common sense at the time.

So many people have asked me how I go about planning a long trip and how I organise my life when I'm far away from home, that I think the time has come for me to set it all down. At the risk of appearing to preach, or to state what must be obvious to the seasoned traveller, here goes!

The first essential is meticulous planning. After two world tours on a bicycle, I've had so much practice that I could take a doctorate in luggage lists, schedules and budgets. I love them all! To me, they're almost as exciting as the journeys themselves.

Packing for a bicycle-ride is a particular challenge, as two small panniers leave little room for error or frivolity. (I've attached my luggage lists as an appendix). Some items, like prescription medicines and camera batteries, are difficult to find in the East and have to be carried from home. Clothes, which can be bought anywhere in the world, are less important. When choosing the ones to take, I particularly look for items with more than one use – slip-on sandals which double up as bedroom slippers, and a large cotton square which serves as scarf, beach-wrap, dressing gown, laundry bag, pillowcase or tropical sheet. I take drip-dry cottons which dry overnight, so that I don't need many spares; and I rely on lightweight layers, which I can pile on top of one another to suit the climate. They are warmer and more flexible than heavy woollens. I often take clothes which are wearing thin and discard them as I travel. There are parts of the world where tailors still make a living out of turning collars and cuffs, and my cast-off shirt may be some poor sweeper's treasure.

Every item weighs and it makes for easier cycling to get rid of the heaviest. Glass is the worst culprit. If I can't find the cosmetics I need in plastic pots or tubes, I transfer the contents of glass jars to the plastic pots I hoard for just that purpose. I transfer my antibiotics and aspirins from glass bottles to plastic. My Nescafé goes from a glass jar into a tin; and I always buy my duty-free whisky in two half-litre plastic bottles, one for each pannier, even if it means contenting myself with a brand I like less. I resist the temptation to buy bumper bargains. A succession of small tubes of toothpaste, for instance, may cost a few pence more, but they are infinitely preferable to one giant tube the size and weight of a policeman's truncheon. My bags of medicines, sunscreens and toiletries are usually the heaviest items I have to pack, but it's possible, with a little thought, to reduce their weight by as much as a kilo, and that really counts on hills.

The same applies to books and maps. The *Lonely Planet Guide to China* was 1,060 pages long, so I tore out the 380 pages I needed and discarded the rest, saving over half a kilo. In Western countries, I can rely on picking up accurate maps as I go along, but for the East and South America, I have to carry them from London. It goes against the grain to cannibalise printed matter, but I force myself to save weight and space by cutting out my route and about 200 km either side of it. Then

I roll up the resulting strips and unwind them as I go along, throwing them away when I come to the end.

About a week before I leave on a trip, I lay out on my spare bed all the items I'm thinking of taking – and I'm usually horrified when I see the size of the pile! I go and look through it every day, subtracting a pair of socks here and a book there. By the end of the week, it's amazing how the pile has shrunk and how easily I can fit the remainder into my panniers.

Planning the route takes longer, as I always follow historical roads which have to be researched. But the great advantage of poring over maps and texts is that I know exactly where I want to go before I set out and can make a detailed schedule of the journey. I'm never overambitious. I work on an easy average of 80 km a day, five days a week (i.e. 1,600 km or 1,000 miles a month) leaving myself with plenty of spare time for sightseeing, meeting people, sheltering in bad weather and taking short holidays from cycling. Plotting my probable progress on my maps, I can make a rough estimate of the dates on which I'm likely to arrive in major cities. This enables me to give correspondence addresses to my family and friends. (I use American Express, where possible, as their customer mail service tends to be more reliable than the *poste restante* counters of Third World post offices). Given time, and accurate maps and guide-books, I can sometimes do more detailed route-planning in advance, but it's usually better to wait until I can talk to the locals and I've seen the state of the roads. What looks on a map like a comfortable day's cycling can in practice be two or three days' toil.

I'm a fair weather cyclist, so I plan my seasons as carefully as my routes. Some cyclists belong to the school of endurance, even masochism, but I cycle for pleasure. I don't go out in the rain, snow or searing heat if I can avoid it. I've never understood why Dervla Murphy chose to cross Europe in the depths of winter, then boiled through the Persian summer. Europe in spring is delightful and the Eastern autumn is sunny and dry. She could have had beautiful weather throughout, if she'd started a few months later.

On my first ride round the world, I managed the seasons

perfectly: Europe in the spring and summer, the Levant in the autumn, the Indian subcontinent, Thailand and Malaysia in the warm tropical winter and the USA in the following spring and summer. The second circuit was more difficult. If I chose the right season for South America, it would be wrong for Australia, and the Gobi Desert would be harsh, whatever the season. But I chose with care and was only uncomfortably hot on my cycle-ride up the Brazilian coast in midsummer and cold at the start of the Chinese spring.

I've never run into financial problems on a trip, because I make a budget and stick to it. The first time I cycled round the world, I worked on £125 a week for food and accommodation (£15 a day, plus £20 extra, in case I had to spend a night in a more expensive hotel). On my second circuit, I allowed for inflation and raised my budget to £150 (£20 a day, with £10 to spare). On both tours, my normal expenditure fell far short of those limits when I was cycling across South America and Asia; just about level in Australia; and well over the top in the United States and Northern Europe. But averaged over the journeys as a whole, my expenditure worked out within budget, even allowing for occasional treats. London is an expensive city and cycling the world is cheaper for me than staying at home. It would work out even cheaper if I let my flat, or took to a tent.

Hotels are my biggest single item of expenditure, so I have to choose carefully. Fortunately, my bicycle is a great help here. I'm not at the mercy of touts and taxi-drivers and I'm not weighed down with a suitcase. I can cruise at my leisure past all the more modest hotels, rejecting the ones that look seedy and pricing the rest. In the West, I have to be content with two stars or a room in a bed and breakfast. On the budget I set myself, there would be no money left for a good meal if I chose a smart hotel – and I'm sure that one of the reasons I stay so well on my travels is that I never compromise on food. Better a spartan bedroom than no dinner. In eastern cities, I live more stylishly. I still couldn't afford five star luxury every night, even if I wanted it, but I can afford the top end of the local market. These are usually very good hotels, with every amenity that a normal person could wish for, and my fellow-guests are families and business people from the country itself, not gangs of westerners on package tours. I enjoy staying in those hotels and make lots of useful contacts.

Less comfortable are the hotels along the highways, where I have to stay between towns. In remoter parts of China, for instance, I had to stay in the *lüshes*, the overnight stops for lorry-drivers. These were fascinating places, as they were the direct descendants of the Silk Road caravanserais. They were rectangular complexes, built round a central courtyard and their only entrance was a wide double gate of iron or steel. In the great days of the silk trade, the merchants used to drive their animals into the yard, where they were stabled in one of the surrounding buildings. The great gates were locked behind them and their masters slept easily in another wing, confident that they themselves, their precious wares and their livestock were safe from bandits. Today, there are heavy lorries in the courtyards instead of camels and the goods are more prosaic – electric toasters, timber and rock from the quarries – but the drivers still count on the security of these overnight stops. They are proof against robbers on the outskirts of towns and havens of comfort in the wilderness. The truck-drivers sleep in dormitories, but there are always a few double or triple rooms. I would take one of these, paying somewhere between 5 and 10 yuan (40–80 pence) for the exclusive use of all the beds. They had clean sheets and warm quilts, and there was usually a large colour television in the corner. The floors were bare, but in countries without vacuum cleaners, I actually prefer washed concrete to stained and fluff-covered carpets where little creatures lurk. Sometimes there was a communal washroom down the corridor, with cold running water and a foul trench with planks across it. But more often, bowls of warm water for washing were brought to my room and the lavatory was a walk into the Gobi sands.

I'm not sure that these *lüshes* were licensed to take foreigners, but their keepers could hardly turn me away into the desert. Transactions were in cash, no forms were filled in and my bicycle and I were swiftly tucked away out of sight. I was made most welcome and charged the same rate as the lorry-drivers –

unlike licensed hotels, which had three prices for identical rooms. There was one price for citizens of the Chinese People's Republic, one for Overseas Chinese and another for foreigners. No prizes for guessing who paid the most!

Across country is where I save my money. Sometimes there are no hotels of any description and I have to depend on a village bed. I'm constantly embarrassed by the generous hospitality I receive from people who are so much poorer than I am. Yet they are proud to share what little they have and would be offended if I offered them payment. The way round that problem, I've found, is to press them into accepting money for their children, to buy them shoes or school books.

I carry my money in dollar traveller's cheques, in a mixture of American Express and Thomas Cook, the most acceptable cheques worldwide. It's wise to carry two sorts, especially in South America, where forgery is rife and the banks sometimes go through spells of refusing to accept a particular brand. I also carry a supply of small denomination dollar bills to use as tips or to change at airports, when I just need a cup of coffee before a flight. Sterling notes are much less useful, with their minimum value of £5. Drawing out money on credit cards is obviously possible in developed economies, but it's unwise to rely on it. I got quite excited in Kuqa, a town on the edge of the Taklimakan desert. I walked into the Bank of China and saw a Mastercard sign. 'Can I draw out some money on my Mastercard?' I asked. 'Certainly – if it's a Great Wall Mastercard' was the reply!

I don't stint on travel insurance for myself. It's a great comfort to know that I have enough medical insurance to pay for a helicopter and a flight home, should I have a serious accident. But I don't insure my bicycle. The premiums quoted are so high that I could replace it with a satisfactory model abroad for little more than the cost of the insurance. I've saved hundreds of pounds so far.

Some people do serious training as part of their journey preparation, but I hate taking exercise and riding round in small circles. I just fix the departure date, load up my bicycle and go. I train on the journey, doing shorter distances at first and gradually building up to my normal 80–100 km a day. It's a system (or lack of it) which always seems to work.

Where I do expend a bit of energy in advance is in brushing up, or learning from scratch, the languages I shall need on the journey. I wash up with my Walkman plugged into my ears and sit on the Tube memorising lists of vocabulary. In western China, high in the Andes, and even in some rural parts of Europe, it would be difficult to get by without a smattering of the local language. Even in Australia, where the language is supposed to be the same, I found my bit of Oz invaluable. (When the sun in the *arvo* made me *crook*, I did a *U-ey* into a *servo* and bought some *sunnies*, a *chook sammo* and a bag of *mandies*.) The Australians never use a syllable more than they need and every abbreviation ends in a vowel sound. Perhaps the Romance languages have got it right and the vowel is the natural word-end? Everywhere in the world, people respond warmly to travellers who try. A simple 'Good Morning' in their own language can be the ice-breaker which opens hospitable doors.

When I've finished all this forward-planning, I set out with confidence. I know that most of my days will be good days and I fall easily into a stress-free travelling routine.

I sleep with my curtains open, so that I wake with the sun. In hot climates, I like to brew a quick mug of Nescafé (I wouldn't be without my electric boiler) and get on the road in the cool of the dawn, so that I've finished my day's cycling before the midday heat starts to addle my brains. In the Brazilian summer, we thought we had a problem, as the hotel charge included a splendid breakfast of tropical fruits, which we were loath to miss. It was too hot to hang around in the hotel waiting for the restaurant to open, so we hit on the idea of demanding breakfast immediately we had checked in, at about 10 a.m., instead of waiting till the following morning. A plate of chilled pineapple, papaya and mango, with brioches and a pot of good Brazilian coffee, was just perfect after 80 km of relentless sun.

Exercise is an appetite suppressant and I find that I fare better on fruit and frequent small snacks during the day than on hearty lunches. When I reach my destination, I take a shower and a siesta, and by 5 o'clock I'm ready to enjoy the best part of the day – a stroll round the town, a little sightseeing and shopping, a newspaper, a coffee or a glass of wine as I write up my notes, and finally dinner. Italy has the best cyclists' food: a plate of pasta to top up the carbohydrates, grilled meat or fish for protein, and salad and fruit for vitamins, all washed down with a carafe of delicious chilled wine.

I don't book my hotels in advance, because cycling is unpredictable and I can never be sure of arriving. I might get a puncture, it might pour with rain, I might feel tired and decide to finish early, or I might pass the most wonderful hotel and succumb to temptation. One day in Indonesia, though I'd only just started out, I passed Hotel Anne, which advertised 'Good Food and Ecstasy'. It was irresistible.

Working on my average daily distance, I consult my map and find a sizeable conurbation about 80–100 km along the road, where I feel fairly confident of finding a hotel or guest house. In thinly populated areas I go to the local police for advice before I set out and I consult the hotel manager, who always knows his rivals within a day's cycling distance. I've never yet failed to find a room for the night, except in the middle of the Australian Outback, where I knew in advance that I should need a tent. I've slept in some funny places. Pilgrim accommodation in Indian temples, station waiting-rooms, gymnasium floors, army barracks and mud huts. The comforts may have been minimal, but at least I've had a roof over my head and people around to keep an eye on me. I've slept in peace, knowing that my bicycle and I were safe.

My evenings are not exciting. Men who travel alone can drop into a bar or nightclub and spice up their travel-writing with racy anecdotes and fascinating local colour. But if I strode alone into a nightclub in Salvador or Bangkok, my presence would certainly be misconstrued!

Fortunately, satellite television has brought programmes in English to most screens and I've spent many happy Indian evenings watching test matches. Sometimes the situation seems quite unreal. In Pasuran, a small and undistinguished town in

Java, I lay on my bed watching *LA Law*, while the geckos clicked above my head. In Chilete, a poor mining town high up in the Peruvian Andes, I watched the Oscar Presentations over my dinner of *lomito saltado* and beer. The men of Chilete, all Hispanics or *mestizos*, crowded into the restaurant with me, dividing their attention between the stars of the screen and the strange cycling *gringa*. Hollywood had never seemed so far away.

In China, I was forced to improve my Mandarin, as that was the only language on offer. I sat riveted to the screen as a hefty middle-aged woman in spectacles and an army uniform screeched patriotic songs, while twelve girls paraded behind her in red evening dresses, twirling pink fans. Another night, three hefty women officers screeched in trio, while the twelve girls pirouetted behind them in army caps, long black boots and khaki tutus. Then there was a pipe band from Scotland, which swirled its kilts every night for a week to rapturous studio audiences. Advertisers displayed the latest washing machines, in a country where most households don't have running water. And the Chinese preoccupation with health was reflected in all the advertisements for tonics and pills. If you believed the state-controlled television, everything in China was wonderful. British television, by contrast, seems determined to depress us with reports of sleaze, dishonesty, violence and incompetence. I wish our respective countries could find some sort of mean.

Dinner is the highlight of my day. I find a good restaurant and reward myself for all my cycling. I usually pass the time between courses, and ward off unwanted company, by working on a crossword puzzle. Then there are chores to be done and letters to be written. I have to be in bed early if I'm to make an early start, so my solitary evenings are never too long. I go to bed with a book and soon drift off to sleep, reflecting on one good day and looking forward to the next.

I'm lucky to be an optimist by nature. Things generally go right and I start each day with the assumption that they will. There's no point at all in worrying about the scores of things that might go wrong. If problems occur, they have to be dealt with at the time they occur and in their own particular set of circumstances. Until then, they are best put out of mind. That doesn't mean being improvident. I always start out across a desert with plenty of extra water. What I don't do is pedal along worrying about what might happen to me if I ran out – or, even worse, decide not to cross the desert at all in case I died of thirst. A certain amount of risk is inevitable, whatever we do, and I cheer myself up in difficult times with the statistic that most accidents happen in the home. The desert may in fact be a safer place than my kitchen!

I love my wandering life. It has its small discomforts, but I've learned to accept what comes and I couldn't be more content.

I'd just finished my Australian 'tea' of beer and a barracuda barbie in the Wayside Inn at Larrimah. Larrimah was an important communications centre in World War II, but the railway no longer runs and the glory days are over. Today the town consists of the Wayside Inn, a tea room (in the former gaol), a dusty little museum and two filling stations with camp-sites attached. The night I stayed there, the inn was run by a Mr Bolton from Bolton and his temporary assistant, Mark from Maidenhead, who was over in Australia on a working holiday. A parrot sat on Mark's shoulder as he pulled the drinks, seven peacocks screamed in the yard and a larger than life-sized Pink Panther fished in an ornamental pond out front. It was an engagingly eccentric pub. I was sitting on a sofa in the corner of the bar (Highest Bar in the Northern Territory: 181.04 m), working my way greedily through a pile of women's magazines. I'd had nothing to read for over a week. The hotel cat was asleep on my lap and I was looking forward to my comfortable bed. There was one other guest in the hotel. I'd been chatting to him over tea and now he came over and joined me.

'I know why you're so happy,' he said. 'I've just worked it out. You can sit down and relax, take things as they come and make yourself at home wherever you happen to be in the world. That's your secret.' He was a perspicacious man.

2 Bad Days

The best laid schemes o' mice an' men
Gang aft a-gley.

Robert Burns

Most of my days on the move are pleasantly trouble-free. There have been some moments of high drama, when I've feared for my safety – when I've been arrested, robbed or attacked by wild dogs – but those frights appear elsewhere in the book. This chapter deals with the everyday problems, the small frustrations which turn good days into bad and make me wonder why I ever left home.

Take route-planning, for example. I usually get it right, but in parts of the world where maps are inaccurate, or I've been given silly advice, I can find myself in quite alarming difficulties. In Queensland (in Gympie, Widgee-shire, the Home of the Mighty Cats), I was warned by the woman in the tourist office to avoid the stretch of the Bruce Highway between Gympie and Maryborough, as it was dangerously busy. She recommended a detour through Tin Can Bay: it was a little longer, but the road was quieter, more scenic and flatter. I learned that day not to take the advice of non-cyclists! There were back-breaking hills for the first 30 km and to make it even harder, I was cycling towards the coast into a strong east wind. When the road turned north towards Tin Can Bay, it ran for 60 km through state forests of scots pine, gloomy and forbidding under a lowering sky. I had to survive all day on an apple and a tangerine, as I'd expected to be able to buy food and there was not a single café, filling station or shop along the entire 100 km of the route. The 'quieter road' turned out to be totally deserted. I'm not a nervous cyclist, but I was nervous that afternoon. I was alone, in the middle of a vast, black forest, with no habitation for hours in any direction. I was vulnerable to attack and no one would have driven by to help. Even a mechanical problem would have been a disaster, with no passer-by to give me a hand or a lift. And to crown all my miseries, it began to rain at midday and poured all afternoon. Night fell and just as I was on the verge of panic, I saw the red and yellow lights of a Shell service station looming through the darkness on the outskirts of Maryborough.

In Maryborough's Federal Hotel, the chaps in the bar were horrified to hear that I'd cycled that road on my own. 'Who on earth told you to bike along there? It's not safe!' And a bearded David Bellamy lookalike, who even had a David Bellamy voice, spoilt the illusion with his very unbotanical remark: 'Trees, trees! There's nothing but bloody trees along that road!' He bought me a whisky to calm my nerves.

Being overtaken by darkness in desolate places is one of my worst fears and I try to err on the safe side. Given a choice between a day's run across difficult terrain of 35 km and 100 km, I tend to choose the distance that's shorter, rather than risk a late-night finish. But sometimes there's no choice at all – and sometimes my maps get it wrong.

When I left Chilete in Peru, halfway down the Andes, I judged from the map that my day's run to Pacasmayo on the Pacific coast would be about 95 km. They assured me in the café that it was all downhill and 'only two hours in a *combi* (minibus)'. I should manage the journey with ease; but if I didn't make it, there were hotels along the way, in Guadalupe. I set out with confidence.

The road along the Jequetepeque River turned out to be undulating, with a few steep climbs, rather than 'all downhill', but I enjoyed my early morning ride in the shade of the mango trees. At Trembladera, the river had been dammed to form a giant reservoir, drowning the malarial marshes which had given the village its name of 'Trembling Place'. I cycled 15 km round the perimeter road and found a policeman guarding the engine house. 'You'll never make it to Pacasmayo today. It's two hours in a *combi* and there are no hotels on the way'.

It had been 'two hours in a *combi*' from Chilete – and that was five hours ago! Someone must be mistaken. The policeman was so worried that he offered to drive me to Pacasmayo in his pick-up truck but accepting lifts is cheating and I cycled on. I had left the green of the river valley and was now struggling with a burning cross-wind past sand quarries and barren mountains. Then came fields of maize and watermeadows, where horses grazed and women and children sat, fully clothed, up to their necks in the irrigation canals, trying to keep cool.

At 4 o'clock, exhausted by the heat and the buffeting wind, I pulled into a cool grove for a rest. I was immediately joined by three talkative teenagers. In my weary state, it took a great deal of effort to respond to their eager questioning, but they had their uses. They were on bicycles too and knew exactly how long it took to Pacasmayo. It was not 'two hours in a *combi*', but 'on a *bici*, about an hour – a bit more, if the wind's against you'. Then they looked at my loaded panniers and looked at me and added, with great tact, 'or perhaps two hours at your age, with all that gear'. I felt that I finally had a reliable assessment.

It was another 18 km to Guadalupe and I decided to end the day there, instead of battling on to Pacasmayo. But Guadalupe turned out to be a desolate, fume-ridden bomb-site of a crossroads, milling with trucks, buses, the famous *combis* and frenetic people. It had everything, in fact, but a hotel. I emptied two cans of Sprite in quick succession, then turned wearily onto the Pan American Highway for the last lap. It was the worst lap of all. The ribbon of tarmac was patchy, the road hilly and the wind, which was now directly against me, was blowing at near gale-force. In every direction lay grey grit desert, littered with rusting drink cans and black plastic bags. It was so desolate that I even began to long for a few lorries to break the isolation. The sun sank ominously low. At only 6° south of the Equator, I knew it would set very fast, but I had no strength left to hurry into the wind. My imagination ran riot. If night overtook me, there was nowhere I could hide until morning, not so much as a bush or a sand dune to cower behind – and the wild dogs were starting to prowl. I peered anxiously ahead through the swirling dust and there, to my immense relief, was a road junction and a side road leading down to the lights of Pacasmayo. I ended the day with a wonderful downhill swoop to the Pacific.

Even then, my problems were not quite over. There was a fiesta on in town, with merry-go-rounds, stalls and a Ferris wheel. The streets were jammed with holidaymakers and I feared for my bed. But luck was with me. There was just one room left in the Hostal Ferrocarril and it was the best room, with a superb view of the ocean through the palms of a flowery park. I collapsed on my bed, just in time to watch the nightly spectacle of the crimson sky and the swift dive of the sun into the blood-red Pacific.

It had been a run of 110 km, not the 95 km indicated by my map, and that extra hour's cycling into a headwind at the end of the day had almost led me into danger. Julio, the hotel manager, came up with a bottle of Pepsi. He was a strapping prize-fighter of a man in a vest (English underwear, not an American waistcoat), but his huge muscular torso hid the heart of a fussy nanny. 'Here's your Pepsi. I know you're thirsty, but don't drink it too fast. Have a glass now, then wait five minutes. And don't take a shower until you've cooled down, or you'll catch cold. Cycling all that way! What a stupid thing to do.' He went on muttering indignantly as he clattered down the spiral staircase.

Fear is irrational. Though a pre-dawn arrival is just as dark as a late evening one, it has an entirely different feel to it. When I got off the bus in Cajamarca, high up in the Cordillera Central, it was 3 a.m. The bus station was a dirt yard on the outskirts, with no waiting-room, so I had to move into the city. A mysterious stranger swathed in shawls and scarves approached me with great gallantry and offered to escort me to my destination, but I didn't know where I was going. I pedalled off alone. The hotels were all bolted and barred, so I cycled slowly round the frosty city, waiting for it to come to life. It was a magical night. Moonlight and brilliant Andean stars lit up the rich façades of the churches, throwing their intricate stone carvings into high relief, and topiary bushes cast fantastic shadows across the monumental main square, the Plaza de Armas. Without people or traffic to link me to the twentieth century, I drifted down the cobbled Spanish alleyways into a dreaming time-warp. Strangely, I wandered through the deserted city, in a foreign land with a reputation for violence, and yet I never felt a moment's anxiety. It was all so beautiful in the silence, as unreal as a Baroque stage-set, and fear was somehow inappropriate.

Cajamarca had a wide range of hotels and I was soon very comfortably ensconced in the Hostal Atahualpa, named after the last great Inca. Accommodation in cities is hardly ever a problem, but I've had to develop techniques for dealing with the bad days in small places where nothing is available.

I always carry a sleeping mat and a sleeping bag, but I hope that I never have to use them. If I arrive in the late afternoon to find that there's no hotel and the next village is too far along the road to reach by nightfall, I go straight to the central café or tea-house. I order a cup of something and wait. A strange woman on a bicycle is bound to draw the crowds and they soon gather round. Its cost and all its special features provide the ideal conversational opening. Then, even if I can't speak the language, I can recite the list of the places I've travelled through and mime my age, marital status and number of children. (I never confess to being a widow. Widows are thought to be unlucky in some societies, while in others, the local men get over-optimistic ideas.) Someone is bound to offer me another cup of tea and we all become sociable together. At that point, I ask innocently if there's a hotel in the village, knowing full well that there isn't. Animated conversation ensues and I'm soon swept along by an eager group to a house where an old lady has a spare room, or a café with a guest room upstairs, or a grass-roofed hut, where I'm offered the marital bed, while the extended family of seventeen sleep on the floor. The technique not only works; it's safe. At least half the village has been involved in finding my accommodation and I am, in a sense, their guest. I know I shall come to no harm. It's much safer than turning for help to a chance stranger in the street.

My sleeping bag and mat have come in useful on waiting-room tables and in basic accommodation, where the bed has been nothing but three planks of wood or a concrete slab. They've been useful in hammocks, as supplementary covers on freezing nights, and in hotels where the sheets have been grey with grime. Sometimes I go for months without using them and start to resent the extra burden, but when I next spread my mat over filthy blankets and zip myself into my own clean space, I know why I drag them round the world.

In Australia I acquired a tent. I don't think it's very sensible for a lone woman to spend the night in a tent by the roadside, and in any case I loathe camping, but when I crossed the Karakorams, I found a useful ploy. If I asked permission to pitch my tent outside, people invited me in and offered me a bed. It was a much gentler approach to shy locals than a brazen request for accommodation, which would probably have been refused.

The only night when I thought I had absolutely nowhere to sleep, in the days before I owned a tent, was my New Year's Eve on the Italian Riviera. I tried every hotel as I cycled through Finale Ligure, Borghetto and Albenga, but without success. At first, I was panicky, but then I became philosophical. The next town was Alassio and I knew there was an important railway station there. Failing a bed in the town, I would dine late and long in the best restaurant I could find, then tuck myself into my sleeping-bag on a station bench. There was a sliver of new moon, the air was balmy and I even began to look forward to my adventure. Just to fill in the time before dinner, and with no hope of success, I tried a few hotels. The Hotel Cairo, a small *pensione* in a side street, was my seventh.

'You must be pretty desperate if you've got nowhere to stay at 9 o'clock – and on New Year's Eve too!'

'I *am* pretty desperate. I expect I shall end up at the railway station.'

'The railway station! We can't have that.' The proprietor looked very concerned. 'Of course, I don't have a proper room. We've been booked up for months. But it just happens that one of the chambermaids has had to go home. Her mother's ill. It's only a tiny room, no bigger than a mousehole. But it's got a bed and a washbasin – and it beats the railway station.'

If you have to spend New Year's Eve alone, a small family *pensione* in Italy is probably the happiest place to do it. For the grand New Year's Eve Dinner, *il Cenone*, I was placed at a table with Alberto and Maria, a newly married couple from Bergamo, where Alberto worked in a lift factory. Undaunted by the presence of a foreign woman cyclist almost three times their age, and quite without resentment at the imposition of a gooseberry, they went out of their way to give me a nice evening. What football team did I support? What about Liverpool? Alberto reeled off the names of all the players. And which Italian pop group did I like best. I struggled to think of a name, any name. 'Who are your favourites?' I asked cunningly. 'Zucchero.' 'They're my favourites too' I lied, never having heard of them before. We all beamed. As soon as dinner was over, I pleaded tiredness and retired to my mousehole with a book, leaving my kind companions to celebrate their first New Year's Eve together. They were modest young factory hands, who had never travelled outside Italy, yet they had coped magnificently with a testing social situation. I couldn't help wondering how well a solitary Italian cyclist would have fared, had she been forced on their English counterparts in similar circumstances. Not nearly so well, I suspect.

My bicycle is usually welcome in hotels and some safe place (often my bedroom) is found for it at night. Only five times in all my travels has it caused me a problem. In Seville, the owner of a small hotel slammed the door in my face as soon as he saw it. Three hotels have charged me for it. When I was arguing with their managers, I told them that their behaviour was outrageous and threatened to name their hotels in one of my books. So here is the list. Other cyclists beware!

Hotel Plaza, Taranto, Italy
Hotel Miramare, Arenzano, Italy
Bayinguoleng Binguan, Korla, Xinjiang, China.

In China, where the thought-processes of the locals often left me bewildered, I had my strangest experience. We had just got through the lengthy booking procedure at my hotel in Zhangye. The receptionist had filled in the last of her forms in triplicate and entered my details in the last of her registers. I had handed over my payment in advance, plus my deposit against breakages, the receptionist had written out separate receipts for the two amounts, again in triplicate, and we had both signed all the copies. (Checking-in in China is never swift!) She was ready to hand me my key.

'Where shall I put my bicycle?' I asked. Her face registered profound shock.

'You can't bring a bicycle in here,' she said indignantly. 'This is a hotel for people and cars, not bicycles. You must leave it in the street.'

I looked across the hotel car park and saw a large cycle-shed. 'What about that shed? Can't I put my bicycle in there?'

'That shed is for employees' bicycles. You are not an employee, so you must leave yours in the street.'

There was certainly logic in this line of argument, but it was leading to a most unsatisfactory conclusion as far as Cube (my bicycle) and I were concerned. The old ladies who guarded bicycles in the streets for a few yuan presumably went home to sleep and I wasn't prepared to leave my bicycle unattended all night on a main road. I got out my phrase book to look for 'Send for the manager!' then thought better of it. If the manager came and he too banned the bicycle, I should have boxed myself into a corner. I had to be more cunning than that.

With no more argument, as if I were accepting the veto graciously, I went out and unhooked my panniers. Then, quick as a flash, I sprinted across the car park, wheeled the bicycle into the employees' shed, chained it to a cycle-rack and dropped the key down the front of my blouse. The Chinese are extremely modest people and I knew it would be quite safe there.

All this time, the receptionist had been watching me through her window and now she came clicking across the car park on her stiletto heels. I waited unconcerned for the onslaught. I would simply look bewildered and take the foreigner's easy way out. '*Bu dong*' (I don't understand), I would say, followed by a very apologetic '*Dui bu qi*' (I'm so sorry). But to my astonishment, she smiled warmly. 'Why don't you chain your bicycle to that railing at the back? It will be safer there.'

I hesitated. Was this sudden turn-around just a crafty ruse to get me to undo the lock? While I was still trying to decide, she tottered off to the main gate and I heard her telling the commissionaire to keep a special eye on my bicycle, as I was a guest in the hotel. I fished out my carefully hidden key and made the transfer.

The receptionist helped me upstairs with my panniers, chatting amiably about the weather, my journey and the size of our families. Not a word was said about the bicycle. I'm still trying to explain such bizarre behaviour.

In retrospect, perhaps the funniest bit was the sequel. I was just finishing my packing the next morning when there was a banging on my door and in rushed the staff of the Zhangye Tourist Office, with the hotel manager, the assistant manager, the receptionist, a dozen chambermaids, the local press and sundry excited hangers-on. I was the first independent tourist since the city had been opened to foreigners and they had decided to make a big promotion of my visit. There were to be articles about me in the newspapers and they wanted photographs for a new Tourist Office brochure. The shot which really amused me was the one of the hotel manager, the receptionist and myself in a beaming group around Cube, taken in the very car park from which Cube had been so ignominiously banned the day before!

Mechanically, my bicycles are never a problem. If anything goes wrong with them, I just wheel them to the nearest cycle-shop. I don't mend my car, so I don't see why I should have to turn mechanic for a bike. In these days of Kevlar tyres and thorn-proof inner tubes, I ride across whole continents without a single puncture, even on stony nightmares of roads. I had seven punctures on my first world tour and only two on my second. I've had one broken spoke, up in the Andes, and my chain snapped once, in Berkeley, California. The bicycle is such a straightforward machine that it can be mended anywhere in the world. In countries where everyone cycles, there's a repairer on every street corner, and every wayside tree has a tyre hanging down to advertise bicycle services.

If I put my mind to it, I expect I could learn cycle mechanics. But I have a wonderful excuse for not trying. A puncture repair in many parts of the world costs as little as 10p. For me, that's a negligible sum, but for the man who does the repair, it's enough to feed his family for the day. It makes sense to help the local people help themselves.

Before I perfected my luggage list, I spent some of my worst days shopping. In Lanzhou I spent two days combing the shops for a replacement camera battery. There were splendid arrays of new Japanese cameras but no spare parts. When friends say, 'Send me a postcard,' they have no idea that I can use up a whole day in tracking down the card, a morning finding a post office, and an afternoon standing in one queue to buy stamps, another to stick them on with glue from the one available glue-pot and another to have them franked. Small chores and small purchases, which are a moment's job in the West, can take days in the East. And people sometimes wonder how I fill my time!

My greatest frustration is shopping for shoes. I take a size 8 (Continental 42) and few countries make such large women's shoes. In China, my trainers started to wear thin in Gansu Province and I made a number of unsuccessful attempts to replace them. By the time I reached Xinjiang, they were in holes and I knew that my last chance of finding any to fit was probably in Hami, a major city where the shops were comparatively well stocked.

I began with the street markets, where ranks of attractive trainers lined the pavements. I knew that the dainty women's shoes would never fit me, but I was surprised to be turned away from the men's stalls too. There were a number of department stores in town, but they all carried the same stock and the assistants were indifferent. They laughed at the idea of a size 42 and turned their backs on me, refusing even to look. I decided to gain their attention by clowning. The Chinese like nothing better than a ridiculous foreigner.

I went into the next store. Its sparse stock was unimaginative-ly arranged in dirty glass cases, there were no electric lights and the floor was bare, dusty concrete. It was a typical Chinese department store. I went up to the shoe counter and stuck my foot on top of it. 'My feet are too big,' I announced. The startled assistants stared at my foot and a crowd of wide-eyed shoppers gathered round. A woman started to giggle, others joined in and soon I was surrounded by a shrieking mob, helpless with laughter and all pointing at my feet. In a country where small feet were so prized that little girls traditionally had their feet broken and bound (a cruel practice which the Communists have succeeded in stamping out), my own great pasties were clearly regarded as grotesque. I spread out my arms, like a fisherman exaggerating his catch, and repeated, 'Too big. Too big'. The shoppers provided the chorus. 'Her feet are too big,' they cried.

By now, the assistants were on their mettle. They would show this crazy foreigner that no feet were too big for *their* shoes. Cartons were rapidly rummaged through and discarded, until finally one pair of size 42 trainers was found at the bottom of a stack. There were no seats in the store, so I was given a sheet of newspaper to stand on. I tried the right foot. The crowd pressed closer to watch and I felt like Cinderella when I heard their gasps of delight. The trainer fitted! It was a white Japanese model, with transparent plastic soles, inside which little coloured marbles could be seen to dance when I walked. They were real 'airs', which the coolest dudes of Battersea or Lambeth would have been proud to wear. My street cred was short-lived, because they soon dropped to pieces, but they got me through the rest of China. I've made a note to take reserve footwear in future.

I was told in China that Deng Xiao Ping had freed the economy and the consumer revolution had arrived, but compared with shops in the capitalist world, there was still very little choice. For instance, I went there in cycling mittens and almost suffered frostbite on a pass in the Qilian Shan. I needed warm gloves. But when I toured the department stores, I was offered the same two pairs: elbow-length white nylon, with ruched wrists and silver embroidery, or a cheap pair of beige knitted cotton. Neither was ideal. As a rich westerner, I was obviously expected to go for the expensive white nylon and the assistants were most disappointed when I admired them, but said they were not exactly what I needed for cycling! I bought the thin knitted cotton and wore them under my mittens.

Fortunately, I enjoy rude health and have the digestion of an ostrich. In all my travels, I've only twice had an upset stomach, once in the middle of India and once on the way to Rome Airport. In India, I drank black tea and rested for a day. In Rome, I had a plane to catch and there was nothing for it but to keep on pedalling between violent roadside vomits. The secret is slow travel. People who fly out to foreign parts straight from their own hygienic homes are invariably sick, simply because the composition of the water has changed. I move from one region to the next so gradually that my body has time to adjust to the new microbes.

Colds take a long time to clear up on a bicycle, as the dust and traffic fumes irritate the sinuses. I get the occasional strained back, knee or thigh, and once I was on the verge of sunstroke. In Praia do Frances, a beautiful resort on the Brazilian coast, I sat on the golden sand admiring the brilliance of the young Adonises on their surf-boards till I could resist it no longer. I hired a board – and within two minutes a powerful Atlantic roller had dashed it into my ribs and broken one of them. I felt distinctly foolish. How stupid to think that I could take up such a dazzling sport at my age! But these were all minor problems, easily cured with aspirin and a few days' break from cycling.

Only once was I seriously ill. I flew out to India and arrived in Delhi with such a stiff neck that I got shooting pains in my head every time I moved it. Resting in bed only made the pain worse, as my neck and shoulders seized up completely. I soldiered on. I took my bicycle on the train to Chandīgarh, to begin my planned cycle-ride south through India. Although I found that I could ride my bicycle without too much discomfort, the head pains became more agonising every night. I crawled out of bed in the mornings, put on dark glasses and ordered a tray of tea. Two aspirin and half an hour later, my shoulders began to loosen up, my head began to clear and I could start to face the day. I tried resting, exercising, sunbathing and hot showers, but none of them made any difference. Alone and far from reliable medical help, my imagination ran riot. Suppose I had a brain tumour?

The low point came one night in a particularly squalid village guest house. The pain was so bad that I didn't even go out to dinner. I zipped myself early into my sleeping-bag and lay there in misery, watching the cockroaches crawl over the furniture. They were as big as armoured personnel carriers and I suddenly felt that I couldn't cope with India a moment longer. I struggled back to Delhi and took the first flight home.

By that time, my legs had stiffened too. I was in despair. I'd given up my job in order to travel the world and now it seemed as if my cycling days were over. If I didn't die of a brain tumour, what would I do with the rest of my life, when I was so immobile that I couldn't even climb onto a London bus?

But a miracle cure was at hand. My doctor soon diagnosed polymyalgia rheumatica, a rheumatic condition easily treated with corticosteroids. Just three hours after taking the first tablets, I was nipping around as if the problem had never existed. The polymyalgia is still there, but it's gradually burning itself out and the steroid dosage needed to control it gets smaller every year. Since those terrifying three weeks in India, it's never interfered with any of my plans. If anything, those bad, despairing days have made me even more determined to get on with my life. There are so many places I still want to see in the time that's left to me – and you never know what lies in wait just around the corner.

3 Solitude

One of the pleasantest things in the world is going on a journey; but I like to go by myself.

William Hazlitt

I love solitary travel. I've loved it since the age of fifteen, when I got caught up in a French rail strike. I was on my way to Bordeaux to spend Easter with Marcelle, my French exchange. My father put me on the morning boat train at London Victoria, but services on the French side were disrupted and I didn't reach the Gare du Nord until well after midnight, by which time my French family had given me up. I had no Paris address for them and I might have been in great difficulties, but I wasn't. A kind French boy scooped me up from the station, along with two other English girls in the same predicament, and helped us to find a triple room in a cheap, respectable hotel. For an over-protected only child, it was the start of a magical week.

The Metro was free, as the ticket-collectors were on strike, and the Army had been called in to service the suburbs, so I could travel anywhere I liked in the city, without counting the cost. I tramped the streets and museums of Paris till I dropped and rode to Versailles in the back of an Army lorry. I lived on bread and chocolate, sat in cafés, dressed as I pleased, strolled through Pigalle and stayed out till midnight – all the things I should never have been allowed to do at home. It was my first real taste of freedom.

My money just stretched to the hotel bill and I had my onward ticket. Some days after the strike ended, I took the night train to Bordeaux and landed in the morning on Marcelle's doorstep. '*Que les anglais sont flegmatiques!*' said her father. Needless to say, they had been frantic with worry, but my own parents knew nothing of my adventure until it was safely over. It was so much easier to slip through the net in the days before everyone had phones.

No solitary journey since has quite matched the exhilaration of that first trip. Boarding the Heathrow bus on a frosty morning for a flight to the tropics, or slipping the car into gear and pointing the bonnet to Dover are still high on the list of excitements. But the nearest thing to those heady days in Paris is loading up one of my bicycles and cycling off alone into freedom and anonymity. No schedule, no holiday address, no telephone numbers. I go where the fancy takes me and all possibilities are open.

Travelling is different from taking a holiday. When I'm on holiday, I like company. There's nothing sadder than sitting alone in a holiday hotel, when everyone else has a husband or friend. I've never taken a whole holiday on my own, but I've spent the occasional night on my travels in a holiday hotel and found it immensely depressing. Once in Turkey, I checked into a five star seaside hotel. I'd been travelling across country, managing on cold water for three weeks. My clothes were grimy, my hair was stiff with dust and I was desperate for a proper bathroom with hot water. I spent a happy afternoon washing myself and my clothes, but my evening was profoundly miserable. I dressed myself up and went for a solitary drink in the bar, where everyone else was in laughing holiday groups, then I sat alone at my table, eating a dull package-tour meal, while my neighbours, a group from Germany, glided across the floor to romantic music. I took my loneliness early to bed. I should have been much better off, in every way, if I'd checked into a local Turkish hotel, handed my clothes to the laundry, gone to the *hamam* and the hairdressers, then found the best restaurant in town for a really good Turkish dinner. I'd made an expensive mistake.

Real travel can be quite stressful and stress can lead to arguments, or smouldering resentments. (How many perfect friendships have ended on a motoring holiday?) I'm not a quarrelsome person. In fact, I'm so anxious to avoid conflict that I weakly allow myself to be talked into things against my better judgment. When I'm working on a project, the only way I can be sure of carrying out my plans precisely is by travelling alone. Then I can follow small leads, even if they take all week; I can change my plans at a whim, with no one to say, 'But I

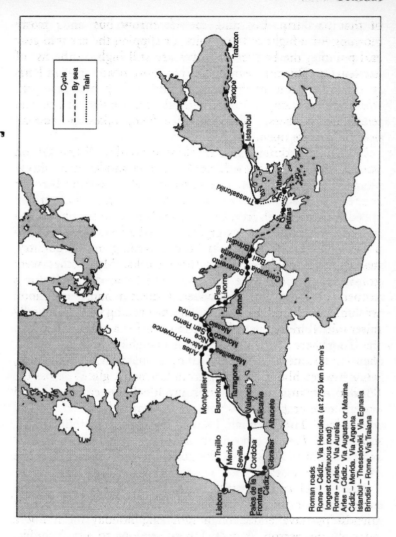

Cycle

By sea

Train

Roman roads
Rome – Cádiz. Via Herculea (at 2750 km Rome's
longest continuous road)
Rome – Arles. Via Aurelia
Arles – Cádiz. Via Augusta or Maxima
Cádiz – Merida. Via Argenta
Istanbul – Thessaloniki. Via Egnatia
Brindisi – Rome. Via Traiana

thought you wanted to stay another day' or 'I thought you
wanted to go via Bologna'; and I can even abandon the trip
altogether and go home if I feel like it.

Cycling has all the usual travel pitfalls, plus a few extra.
Finding a companion who goes at the same speed is one of

them. I'm a slow cyclist, and I hate to have to puff and pant to keep up with all those people who are fitter than I am. I like to cruise along, singing to myself and looking around at the scenery. On the other hand, I don't like going with cyclists who are really slow and hold me back. Then there are off days and on days. If I'm having one of those days when turning the pedals seems a monumental effort, I like to stop early. I see no point in pushing myself when I don't feel like it. But my bad day might be my companion's good day, or vice versa, and that can lead to friction. The other problem is circadian. Even if our average speed is the same, the rhythm of our days may be different. I have friends who are early risers, larks who leap out of bed full of vigour and ride at their fastest and cheeriest in the early mornings. But I'm a night owl by nature and perhaps I get a smaller or later dose of epinephrine in the mornings than most. It takes me a long time to get started. I go slowly in the mornings and speed up gradually. By the afternoon, when my early-rising friends are beginning to wilt, I'm just getting into my stride. And the crown of my day is the cool of the evening, when I bowl along merrily with the prospect of dinner before me. That's always a solitary pleasure. If I'm cycling in the company of larks, I've succumbed to pressure and found a hotel hours before.

I like to follow historical routes on my bicycle and they are sometimes hard to find. No matter how much research I do in advance and how carefully I study my maps, I sometimes lose the trail and have to poke about for hours until I get back onto it. For me, that's a part of the fascination of the trip, but for others, I can see it's a bore. They want to get on!

When I followed the Roman road-builders from their capital to Lisbon, I cycled the majestically scenic Via Aurelia, which took me along the Italian and French Rivieras, then turned inland to Provence. Halfway between St Maximin la Sainte Baume and Aix-en-Provence, my map showed the tomb of Marius. I had never much cared for Marius in my student days, as the history books concentrated on his struggle for power in Rome against the patrician Sulla. It was all very dull constitutional stuff and Marius seemed a stolid, lacklustre character. But I suspected hidden colour. Why else would Marius still be a popular name in Provence, even to this day?

My research revealed a great benefactor. When northern tribes swept down from the Baltic towards the Mediterranean, it was Marius who was appointed to defend the coast. He needed to raise troops quickly, so he waived the usual property qualification for military service and recruited a large proletarian army. They were untrained in battle, so to build up their stamina, he set them a brilliant fatigue-task – excavating a canal from Arles to Fos, to by-pass the silted Rhône estuary and open the way to Roman shipping, straight from the Mediterranean into the heart of France. It was the start of the region's prosperity. And when his fatigue-hardened soldiers had wiped out those northern invaders in 102 BC, at the battle of *Aquae Sextiae* (Aix-en-Provence) Marius rewarded them with grants of farmland in that rich and beautiful area. I could see why this straightforward, practical soldier, who was despised in Rome for his lack of political finesse, should be regarded with such affection in Provence. It was the right place for his memorial and I was determined to find it.

I cycled to the crossroads where the tomb was marked on my map. They were deserted. I searched the scrubby fields and found nothing. When I asked at a local farmhouse, the farmer's daughter had never heard of Marius and was much keener to fire questions at me than to answer mine. 'Why don't you look in the cemetery? Perhaps he's buried there.' I doubted it. I roamed around till late afternoon, asking everyone I met along the road. They were all fascinated to talk to a solitary Englishwoman on a bicycle, but hadn't a clue about the tomb of Marius. I finally got the information I needed from an old woman pruning her vines.

The tomb was in ruins. It was just a few stones under an oak tree, but its situation, on a vast plain bounded by the white cliffs of the *Croix de Provence*, was superb. I sat in the railed enclosure, looking at the sweep of the land and thinking about Marius. I was relieved to be alone. A companion who didn't share my enthusiasm would have found it a great trial – a whole afternoon wasted on a pathetic heap of stones! But for me, it was a kind of pilgrimage. I had found the tomb of Marius and my solitude under the darkening sky lent romance to his monument. I cycled into Aix-en-Provence and celebrated my find with a luscious, gold-crowned Epiphany cake, *une Galette des Rois*.

I enjoy my solitary cycling, though the evenings in Europe can hang heavy and I often wish I had someone to talk to over dinner. The antidote to loneliness is to go on the trip armed with a project. My main one is always the history of the road I'm travelling, but learning the language of the country is also a good discipline. I take a grammar book and study a page or two every night. Sometimes I take a Latin or Greek text to re-read, a work like Horace's *Odes*, which I studied as a student and no longer find very easy. As I'm a fast reader, novels scarcely justify their pannier-space. I read them in a couple of evenings. A book of poetry or a substantial work of non-fiction, which is slow to digest and benefits from re-reading, gives many more hours of enjoyment for the same weight. I crossed Spain on *The Complete Works of Shakespeare*. I'd never read many of the historical plays and I got so involved in them that I couldn't wait to finish my day's cycling and go on to the next gripping instalment of *King Henry the Sixth, Part Three*, or similar. I was surprised to find the plays so absorbing. I brooded on the intrigues and murders as I rode along and even had gory Plantaganet nightmares. When I tire of reading, there are *The Times* crosswords, which I cut out at home and carry abroad in sheafs, along with copies of *Tough Puzzles*.

Outside Europe, I have a more sociable time. Australians and Americans are very friendly and eager to talk, while the people out East are consumed by curiosity. Everyone talks to a cyclist and I'm often invited to make up a party in a restaurant or visit a family at home. In fact, my problem in some places is how to get a bit of time to myself. I've been known to buy a take-away pizza and hide in my bedroom, or to look bewildered and say '*Bu dong*' (I don't understand) to eager Chinamen inviting me out to dinner.

An Australian girl came up to me, when I was pushing my bicycle across the Avenida B. O'Higgins in Santiago. She was taking a holiday with friends in Chile before flying to London to embark on a long cycle-tour. As soon as she heard that I was bound for Australia, she urged me to go and stay with her parents in Sydney. In the course of conversation, she said she was a little worried about going off on her own, in case she was lonely. 'You're not often lonely on a bicycle,' I said. 'Just look at us now. You would never have come up to me in the street, if I'd been just another tourist. But I was pushing a bicycle, so you came over for a chat – and you even offered me a bed with your parents in Sydney. You wouldn't have done that to a non-cyclist. Cycling is a wonderful way to meet people.' She went on her way feeling much more cheerful.

Cities are good places for lone travellers. They have cinemas and well-lit thoroughfares, where it's safe to walk at night. In Santiago, it was such a delight, after weeks of cultural starvation, to put on my best silk suit and high-heeled sandals and go to the National Theatre for *A Thousand and One Nights*, to music by Rimsky-Korsakov. Ballet is tremendously popular in Santiago and the theatre was crowded with people of all ages and classes, dressed in everything from dinner jackets to jeans and T-shirts. On the way back to my hotel, I called in at a delicatessen and picked up a splendid array of mouth-watering goodies and a bottle of excellent Chilean wine. It was a good evening out. The country, abroad as in England, has less to offer and I try to avoid it. It is, as the Rev. Sydney Smith so aptly put it, 'a healthy grave'. My cycling consists of a quick sprint from one city to the next.

There are, of course, many practical advantages to travelling in company. You can save a great deal of money by sharing a bedroom and at dinner you can share a bottle of wine and a wider choice of dishes. The Indians, Chinese and Thais are not used to dining alone. There's no such thing as an individual portion; people go out to restaurants in groups and order communal dishes. This is a great problem for the solitary eater. If I order a chicken dish, a vegetable dish and rice, I get enough in each bowl to feed at least three people. Eating with a friend is cheaper and much less wasteful.

Another advantage is that there's always someone to keep an

eye on your bicycle at airports and railway stations. One can queue for the tickets, shop for a picnic lunch or look for the lavatory, while the other guards the baggage.

Then, there's relief from being stared at. A foreigner on a bicycle is an extraordinary sight in some countries. In Xinjiang, a junior cyclist was so fascinated that he turned right round to gaze at me and crashed into a donkey-cart, upsetting himself and a load of walnuts. Somehow, being the object of such curiosity seems less irritating when you're in company. You are often so busy talking to each other that you don't notice the gaping crowds around you.

But, despite these advantages, I prefer to cycle alone. I can focus my attention on the Silk Road or the Conquistadors and write up my notes with no responsibility for another person's amusement or safety.

I took up solitary cycling partly because I wanted to explore ancient roads, and the bicycle seemed the perfect vehicle for it, and partly because I wanted to escape from an over-full schedule. We all need contrast in our lives. At home I have plenty of company and I know that my friends and family will always be there for me when I get back from my travels. I'm very lucky. Solitude would be much less attractive if it were a permanent state. Then it would turn to loneliness.

There are days when I do feel lonely and bored with my own company. But I have a remedy for that, which works just as well at home as it does on my travels. I read an article once in a French magazine about the use of yoga in stress control. It began by describing a yoga camp for neurotic cats. (Imagine trying to make a cat do yoga!) Then it went on to suggest remedies for neurotic people. In the middle of all the lunacy, I discovered one gem. If I felt low at the end of a dreary day, I should lie in bed and think of ten good things which had happened to me. On really bad days, the ten take a bit of unearthing, but I find them in the end, even if they're as trivial as a nice cup of tea. It's a simple exercise in positive thinking but, as the article claimed, it makes me appreciate the good which surrounds me and I go to sleep content. It has only failed me once – on Easter Island.

When I was a headmistress, I used to tell my girls that there was no such thing as a boring place or a boring situation. There were only boring people. Anyone with a spark of spirit could find something interesting to do, whatever the circumstances. Stirring words, and I spoke them with conviction, but Easter Island almost made me eat them!

I arrived in the dark on the tiny dot in the Pacific which is further away from the nearest land-mass than any other island on our planet. Easter Island lies utterly alone, 3,790 km west of Chile. Its original inhabitants called it 'The Navel of the World', which just shows what a difference perspective can make to one's scale of importance.

The twice-weekly arrival of the Santiago plane was an event which crowded the ramshackle airport buildings, even at midnight. There were minibus drivers and couriers with placards lining up for their tour-groups, while hopeful landladies hovered around the edges, waiting for the polyglot 'fixers' to fill their spare rooms. I did my deal with a smiling, rotund Polynesian and was soon rattling along a dirt road in Señora Inez' car, with my Condor bicycle (which I rode from Rome to Jakarta) roped to the roof, going I knew not where. I gazed gloomily out of the window, thinking for the hundredth time how much I preferred to arrive in a new place on my bicycle, when I could cruise around in daylight and choose my hotel. Being bundled into cars in the middle of the night was always unnerving.

In the event, my 'fixer' had done me proud. I was in a well-appointed bungalow at the bottom of Señora Inez' garden and I walked over to her poky little dining room for my breakfast and dinner. I never met her husband, who was the chef up at the Hanga Roa Hotel and worked early and late, but there was a silent teenage daughter and a whole menagerie of peaceable animals. When it rained, which it did most of the time, the dogs, cats, kittens, hens and chickens all huddled together for shelter under the same rickety garden table. It was a charmingly biblical scene, like the wolf dwelling with the lamb and the leopard lying down with the kid.

Señora Inez was a thin, nervy little woman, who saw it as her duty to sit with me while I ate my meals. When I had passed the expected compliments on her cooking, conversation began to flag and I wished that my Spanish were up to suggesting, without giving offence, that she leave me to dine on my own. But I dared not risk it, so we sat together among the china knick-knacks and polished brasses, like two prisoners sharing a cell, until the last drop of coffee was drained.

Her grandfather was a Chilean seaman, who had settled on Easter Island. That was all I could find out about her background, and she was most unforthcoming about life on the island. I hit on only one topic which aroused some animation.

'It must be difficult for you,' I said, 'picking up people at the airport in the middle of the night. You bring them home with you, and you've no idea who they are or what they're like. They could give you all sorts of problems.'

'Don't talk to me about problems! I've had every sort of problem in the book.'

'What sort of problems?' I prompted, when she seemed to be drying up.

'I had an American woman staying here on her own. She got up in the morning and she'd lost her memory – just like that! She couldn't even remember her name. And she'd only come for three days, so she'd left her passport and all her papers in Santiago. What a business that was!'

I clucked in sympathy. 'What else?'

'There was an English girl. She went mad. She started smashing the crockery and I had to call the police.'

I had to spend four days on Easter Island waiting for the next flight out. Had it been longer, I might have started smashing the crockery myself! I went on a guided tour and learned more about the *moai*, the giant stone statues, than I'd ever wanted know. There were some six hundred of them, some standing some fallen and some half-hewn in the quarries. There was to be development from the earliest to the latest AD 800–1,400), but to the inexpert eye they all looked I felt like the apocryphal Texan: 'When you've seen one seen them all!'

Captain Cook landed on Easter Island in the course

Second Voyage. He was not impressed. In his spare, matter-of-fact style, he wrote in his journal, 'No nation need contend for the honour of the discovery of this island, as there can be few places which afford less convenience for shipping than it does. Here is no safe anchorage, no wood for fuel, nor any fresh water worth taking on board. Nature has been exceedingly sparing of her favours to this spot . . . nothing but necessity will induce anyone to touch at this island, unless it can be done without going much out of the way.'

Tourists go very much out of the way to reach it these days, though I found it much as Cook had described, except that it had sheep, cattle and horses, whereas Cook had seen only chickens and edible rats. It was an island of low, round, eroded hills, cold, wet and windy. The roads of tamped red earth turned out to be easier for cycling than I'd expected, so I was able to spend the one fine afternoon of my stay visiting Cook's Bay, the petroglyphs and the volcano of Rano Kau with a reed-fringed lake at its heart. But that was all I found to do. The history of the island, or the theories which pass for history, was all too shadowy for my taste. Was the original culture brought across from South America, as Thor Heyerdahl claimed in *Aku Aku*, or did it come from the Marquesas Islands? I saw no way of telling and soon lost interest in the debate.

I can never understand the appeal of islands. To me they are claustrophobic. I need the excitement of distance, of fresh possibilities round every corner as highways unwind – the wonder of standing on the quayside at Calais and knowing that I could cycle on and on, without sea to hinder me, until I reached the port of Shanghai. I was pleased to have found my way to such an inaccessible spot as Easter Island, but there was a limit to the length of time I could spend watching ultramarine waves breaking along 24 km of rainy shore. Time hung heavy. If I was not exactly bored, I was tottering precariously on the edge of that shameful abyss. What would my students have said?

Strangely enough, when I started to write these paragraphs, I remembered the huge, smiling roly-poly Polynesian men, zooming along in flowered shirts on their motorcycles; I remembered the tall, thin, swarthy men, like gypsies, whose waist-length hair flowed free in the wind as they galloped bare-back over the green hills on splendid half-wild chestnuts. But apart from Señora Inez, I remembered nothing at all of the Easter Island women, who must have stayed firmly indoors. I later found that Captain Cook had made the same observation: 'They either have but few females among them, or else many were restrained from making their appearance during our stay; for though we saw nothing to induce us to believe the men were of a jealous disposition, or the women afraid to appear in public, something of this kind was probably the case.'

I was glad to leave Easter Island for the liveliness of Tahiti.

4 Company

How a little love and good company improves a woman!
Farquhar *The Beaux' Stratagem*

In the last chapter, I ran the risk of offending my friends. In this one, I hope to make amends.

If I had to describe my ideal trip, it would be one where the serious travel was a solo effort, but I had company for the holiday bits. When I go on a world tour, or cycle from one end of India to the other, I'm away from home for months at a time. It can be weary work, riding a bicycle across difficult terrain, scratching around for acceptable accommodation and writing up my notes in the evenings. I sometimes need a break – and that's where my friends are wonderful. They fly across continents, without bicycles, to join me in Thailand, Colombia or India, and we spend Christmas and Easter together in pleasant hotels, sightseeing for the fun of it, like normal holiday-makers.

On rare occasions, I've been pleased to have the company of cycling friends. When I cycled across South America, for instance, I was travelling round the world from East to West, so the ride northwards up the Brazilian coast, from Salvador to Belém at the mouth of the Amazon, was not strictly a part of the circuit. There was no historical highway for me to research, though there were fascinating fifteenth-century Portuguese cities along the way. It was more a holiday than work and I wanted to have company, particularly as I'd never cycled in South America before and was slightly nervous about its shady reputation. So Katherine joined me for the ride along that idyllic coast, possibly the most beautiful in the world. We stayed in seaside hotels, bathed from pure white beaches, explored the local markets and feasted on mangos. Dining with a friend is always more agreeable. In Brazil, it was essential. The portions in restaurants were gargantuan and were meant to be shared. If the diner was eating alone, the street children hung around waiting for the inevitable leftovers. Even with two hungry cyclists, they rarely left empty-handed.

In Turkey, I was joined by Shirley, who lives in Ankara, for the leg of the Silk Road from Erzurum to Trabzon on the Black Sea. After my long, solitary crossing of China, it was wonderful to have someone to talk to. There was the added advantage that Shirley's Turkish was fluent and that opened many doors which would otherwise have been closed.

But on the whole, I prefer to do my serious cycle-rides alone and rely for company on chance meetings with strangers. It's amazing how many people come up for a chat when you're travelling on your own. Two people sitting together in a café are left to their own devices, but one person sitting alone has company within moments. The bicycle too is a great conversation-starter, as it always draws the curious, particularly shy people and children, who would normally be too timid to accost a stranger.

It was the bicycle and my western face which attracted Shang Weng Sheng. I was strolling in the gardens of the Buddhist temple in Zhangye, when he came up and offered to be my guide for the day in return for English conversation. I needed advice on accommodation between Zhangye and Jiuquan, so I took Shang along with me to the Prefectural Tourist Bureau. It was helpful to have him there, as the manager spoke no English. But he knew the road well and told me of *lüshes* in places which weren't even marked on the map. He was so delighted to have his first western tourist (Zhangye had only just become an 'open' city), that he invited me home for lunch, with Shang to act as interpreter.

We went in bicycle convoy to the bright new flat on the outskirts, which was the Duos' pride and joy. The approach was a filthy concrete stairway and we sat all afternoon in our coats, because there was no heating. But with two bedrooms, a living room, a kitchen/dining room, a bathroom and a balcony, they were awash with living space compared with most people in China. Beside their block, a row of windowless brick boxes was under construction.

'Are those your storage sheds?' I asked. Duo looked puzzled.

'They are new houses – for the workers. In China it is the policy for everyone to have somewhere decent to live,' he added proudly.

Duo Hongbin and his wife were victims of the Cultural Revolution. Duo was a published author and the winner of national trophies for Classical Chinese singing. His wife taught Classical Chinese Literature at a Zhangye middle school (16–21 years). They were clever professional people, yet neither of them spoke a word of anything but Chinese. They had grown up in the nightmare years when foreign languages were denounced as 'counter-revolutionary', the tools of capitalist lackeys, and were swept from the curriculum. Linguists had to conceal their facility or be banished to pig farms. Shang Weng Sheng's generation was luckier.

Shang worked in the local pesticide factory. He spoke competent, everyday English, but he was no intellectual. This was a terrible frustration. There was so much we all wanted to know, I about China and the Duos about the West, and here was an ideal opportunity to learn from like-minded people. But poor Shang lacked both the vocabulary and the background. Conversations went something like this:

'This is a lovely new flat. Have there been many improvements in your standard of living since Deng Xiao Ping took over?'

The Duos gave a ten-minute answer, interrupting each other in their eagerness to explain.

Shang: 'There have been many changes.'

'Were you in Zhangye during the Cultural Revolution?'

Another ten minutes of earnest reply.

Shang: 'It was a difficult time.'

My own answers on the future of the EEC, the monarchy and the British electoral system were similarly telescoped. So we gave up in despair and simply exchanged facts about our everyday lives.

I was amazed to learn from Mrs Duo that, although she was a full-time teacher, she taught only two 45-minute lessons a day. No doubt she was paid a pittance for such a light timetable and that is how employment is spread around in the Chinese

People's Republic. She had classes of sixty pupils. I tried to discuss the feasibility of halving class-sizes, so that she would teach four lessons a day to groups of thirty, with the same marking load, but Shang was unused to educational debate and got in a terrible tangle. He tried to extricate himself by changing the subject.

'Duo Hongbin asked us to lunch because you were on your own and he thought you looked a nice old woman.'

Sensing that I was less than thrilled at this remark, he added hastily, 'I like your spectacles. They are good for you. You look young for your age.'

Despite the difficulties in communication and my embarrassment when I gagged at the special delicacy produced in my honour – emerald green and indigo duck eggs in aspic, with the texture of cold eyeballs – it was an afternoon of bonhomie. When the Duos' twelve-year-old daughter came home from school, they got out the Yamaha keyboard and she was ordered to sing for us. Standing straight up in her navy blue track-suit with her hair in neat bunches, she was overcome with shyness and kept forgetting the words. But Chinese children are remarkably obedient and it never occurred to her to refuse, or even to complain. She and fifty-nine like her would be quite easy to teach in one class, unlike sixty British teenagers!

We ended with a photo session, all of us in various permutations with our arms around one another on the settee. It was one of my happiest days in China. Shang was delighted too. He escorted me back to my hotel and told me of his ambition to go into the travel business. Contacts *(guanxi)* are vital in a country where goods and services are scarce and nepotism reigns. Thanks to me, he had made his first all-important contact. He invited me to help him celebrate that evening in his favourite karaoke bar.

When I followed the Roman roads across Europe to Lisbon, I was not just marching with the legions; I was out to find the roots of the men who 'discovered' (that politically incorrect word!) and conquered South America. I picked up Christopher Columbus in his home-town near Genoa and followed him to the ports of Southern Spain, where he embarked on his three voyages of discovery. Columbus, who first set foot in the New World, and Amerigo Vespucci, who gave his name to it, were both Italians. But the men who exploited it were Iberians, most of them from the harsh, sun-baked plains of Spain's Extremadura. I was particularly keen to go to Trujillo, the birthplace of Francisco Pizarro, the Conqueror of Peru. His was a real rags-to-riches story. The illegitimate, illiterate son of a minor Spanish nobleman, he joined the South American gold-rush in 1502, rose to power in Panama, sailed to present-day Peru and took on the mighty Inca Empire with a puny force of 180 men and 27 horses. With a mixture of luck, treachery and sheer audacity, he won a startling victory and wealth beyond the dreams of avarice. He returned to Trujillo in triumph, as Marques de la Conquista, and flaunted his riches by building a splendid palace and living the life of a grandee. The conquistadors, unlike the North American migrants, were not 'settlers'. They did their conquering, took their loot and went back home to impress the neighbours, and that was South America's tragedy. North America, which began with fewer natural resources, became far more prosperous, because its settlers invested their work and stayed there to plough back their profits.

I had followed the Roman Via Argenta (Silver Road) from the southern port of Cádiz up to the city of Mérida, so hot in the summer that it's called 'Spain's frying-pan'. On the way, I'd passed the turning to Jerez de los Caballeros, where Balboa was born, and Medellín, the birthplace of Cortez. The region was littered with conquistadors, and I could see why. It was poverty-stricken, desolate and unbearably hot, even in early May – a land to escape from, if at all possible. I cycled out of Mérida and climbed to a vast, unpeopled plateau of cork oaks and ilex. It was too rough for farming. I passed donkeys, pigs and sheep grazing on stones, with egrets on their backs. The only traffic on the road was transporter-trucks taking livestock to market. When pigs rode by, the smell was overpowering, but the animals were quietly resigned. They slept in their little cages or sat watching the landscape rush by. Sheep were less smelly, but far less philosophical. I could hear their anguished bleating long before they overtook me. Trujillo, a spectacular sight on its hilltop, dominated them all.

I was pushing my bicycle up the final cobbled slope to the Plaza Mayor, when I overtook a woman with an easel on her back. 'You can't be Spanish,' she said. 'Not on a bike.' 'And you're American,' I said. 'Yes. From Santa Barbara.'

We fell into step together and climbed up to the square. It was a stunning space, a bowl of sheer theatricality, with castles, palaces and churches towering above it. In the middle pranced a dramatic equestrian statue of Pizarro, with plumes on his helmet and his hand on his sword. It was a fairly recent work (Rumsey, 1927), but it seemed so much at home there that the surrounding Gothic and Baroque might have been built just to form its backdrop.

Gloria Calamar was an artist with a special interest in buildings. We sat together in the square while she sketched and took photographs, to be worked up later in her studio. She showed me a set of postcards from her most recent exhibition in California. Her pictures were architectural drawings of great accuracy, softened to the edge of romanticism with a light watercolour wash. She let me choose one of the cards as a souvenir.

We spent a companionable afternoon in Trujillo, both of us delighted to have found another English-speaker of similar tastes in the middle of Extremadura. Gloria was travelling around by bus, which was so inconvenient when she was carrying her paints and easel as well as her luggage, that she had made up her mind to buy a campervan. For an artist, it would be ideal. She could travel the world in her own mobile studio – and I could see that she was determined to do just that. She was quite a bit older than I was and I admired her spirit. I've always hankered after a campervan myself and when I'm tired of cycling, I shall take it up as my next form of freedom on wheels.

It was not an eventful meeting, but it was richly rewarding. For me, sitting quietly in the Plaza Mayor and seeing it through an artist's eyes, there was an extra dimension to the view. I looked longer and absorbed more detail than I normally do, when I rush around, guide-book in hand. As my contribution,

I told the story of Pizarro and the fall of the Incas, to give Gloria some background to the heroic statue she was busily sketching. We parted with regret. We've never seen each other since, but Gloria was a passing stranger who enriched an afternoon. And had it not been for the bicycle, we should probably never have spoken.

At the other end of the world, there is another Trujillo, the Trujillo founded by Francisco Pizarro on the coast of Peru. In that Trujillo, I found a very different kind of company.

I was watching the evening *paseo* in the main square, the grandiose Plaza de Armas, and thinking how proud Pizarro would have been of his foundation. A bustling commercial centre of three-quarters of a million inhabitants, Trujillo had lost none of its Spanish colonial charm. Palaces had been cleverly adapted for use as banks, so that routine chores like changing a traveller's cheque were aesthetic experiences; and my hotel was a palace in Moorish style, where the windows of cool, dark bedrooms opened onto flowery courtyards. The only feature Pizarro would not have liked was the grotesquely inelegant monument to the heroes of the liberation from Spain, under which I was sitting in the Plaza.

'May I look at your bicycle?' It was Xavier, one of the army of shoeshine boys who haunted the square. 'How many gears has it got? Where did you get it from? How much did it cost?' Always the same questions. The technical ones were easy, but the cost was impossible. Even if I divided Condor's price by ten, it would still represent a lifetime's savings for a shoeshine boy. The minimum weekly wage in Peru at the time was 72 soles (about $33), but that was for workers in full-time employment, not for the likes of Xavier. I invented a modest figure. Encouraged by his reception, he asked me very politely if he could join me on the bench and talk to me for a while. I was wearing trainers, so there was no chance of custom for him. Like all Peruvians, he wanted to learn.

'Is there unemployment in England?' was his first question. To my amazement, he spoke with understanding of Peru's economic problems, blaming the Shining Path guerrillas for frightening off foreign investment. I asked him if he was still studying. He wasn't and, little by little, he told me his story. He was fourteen, the oldest of four children. His father had been out of work for so many years that he had finally, in desperation, left his family and gone off to Argentina to look for a job. He couldn't write and of course the family had no telephone, so they had had no news of him for six months and they were very worried. Xavier was the sole bread-winner and he was trying to earn enough money to keep his younger brothers and sister at school.

He was such a good boy and I wondered how I could help him. He was talking to me as an equal and I knew that his pride would be wounded by a crass offer of money. I had to be more subtle than that. Then I had an idea. I remembered my emergency rations for crossing the Andes, which were still in my pannier pockets. 'Do you like sardines?' I asked. 'I've no use for these any longer and they're heavy to carry around on a bicycle.' Like a magician pulling rabbits out of a hat, I produced two tins of sardines, a tin of tuna and a packet of coconut creams – and I managed to slip a few dollar bills unseen into the bag.

'O Anna, Anita! What a treat! My mother will be able to make us a wonderful dinner tonight. Sardines and tuna! And biscuits too!' Xavier was overjoyed. He stowed them away in his boot-box, shook my hand, wished me a safe journey and skipped away across the square.

Travelling by bicycle in South America, I was living in a masculine world. Buses, hotels and restaurants were staffed by men and it was invariably men and boys who came over to look at my bicycle and chat. Machismo reigned and the women were most retiring. Even in mixed gatherings they hardly opened their mouths. So it was a welcome change to sit next to the exuberant Maria one day on a bus. She had the dark face, high cheekbones and currant-black eyes of the Andean Indian, the *campesina*, but she was dressed in an immaculate grey tailored suit and a dazzlingly white frilly blouse. Her ankles gripped a linen shopping bag, from which an angry cockerel's head emerged. She was off to stay with her married daughter, 'my baby' as she called her, and the cockerel was to be their celebration dinner. Maria had been lady's maid to a Brazilian woman working in Peru. Although she was retired now, her Brazilian Senhora flew her to São Paulo every year and took her away on holiday, so she was well-travelled and bursting with confidence. I'd just been treated to a Pisco Sour by a man in the square, been serenaded at the bus station by an amorous Italian and had an earnest conversation with a handsome young dentist from Sydney. But for sheer good fun, my ride with Maria was in a class of its own. We joked in a mixture of Spanish, Portuguese and mime, and laughed all the way to Ica.

The Peruvians were sociable people and I was never short of a chat. They were courteous and formal, in a rather old-fashioned way, and I wondered what they made of some of the weirder tourists who converged on their ancient sites.

Nasca, with its mysterious Lines, was a mecca for cranks. It was a dusty town with a Wild West feel, no more than a desert stop on the Pan-American Highway, but international tourism was booming. It was not the opulent, mainstream type, but the tourism of dormitories and cheap cafés, where soulful Jesus-lookalikes and their crop-haired, combat-booted girl-friends chainsmoked over books on the paranormal.

I cycled out to the Lines, to see what attracted such seekers. There were thousands of them, extending over 500 square kilometres of the Nasca Desert. Some were geometric shapes, some took the form of animals and plants, and all had been formed by removing oxidised surface stones to expose the paler earth beneath. Their most intriguing feature was that they could be appreciated only from the air. Perfect triangles and rectangles extended for kilometres on end across the desert; the figure of the condor had a 130 m wing-span, the lizard was 180 m long and the monkey with its elegant convoluted tail was 90 m tall. As they were produced anywhere between 900 BC and AD 600, well before the days of air travel as we know it, wonderful theories have sprouted around them: the Nasca civilisation invented hot air balloons, for example, or even that the Lines were drawn to mark landing-strips for extra-terrestrial visitors!

I met Alan from Colorado at the Lines and we ate our

evening chicken and chips together in one of the sawdust cafés. Above his luxuriant beard, his eyes burned with messianic fervour.

'I was *found* in New Zealand by a group of pre-Maoris,' he said solemnly. 'They recognised me as The Pathfinder, the spiritual leader.'

'Did that make any difference to your life?' I asked.

'It transformed it. Since that day I've lived alone in the mountains, meditating and communing with the Spirit. And it's not just self-deception. It's not some sort of an ego-trip. I've been recognised by spiritual leaders from many tribes in many countries, including the head of the family of the Inca High Priest, who fled into the highest ranges of the Andes to escape the Spaniards. I go and stay with them often in their village and we commune together. They're my family now. I no longer own a family of birth.

'Now the Spirit has told me that I'm ready to leave the mountains. I must go back to the States, to Colorado and Arizona, to bring groups of seekers to the holy places of Peru, to the magnetic centres – Nasca, Machu Picchu, the Sacred Valley, Lake Titicaca – all the places where the power of the Spirit lies.'

'Is there any philosophy behind all this that I might recognise?' I asked.

'The Spirit I serve embraces all religions, all philosophy. But I suppose, of all of them, It inclines most to Taoism, the philosophy of gentleness, of flowing with the currents of life, not battling against them. If our planet is to survive,' said Alan, 'we must follow the Taoist Way. The environmentalists and the peace-makers are all unconscious followers of my Spirit.'

I thought, rather cynically, that Alan was onto a good thing. I could just see all those 'seekers' from Arizona and Colorado flocking to tour the magnetic centres of Peru with him. It was perfect alternative travel for the Millennium. Yet I had no doubts about his sincerity. He lived as he preached and, in the middle of the mumbo-jumbo, he talked a great deal of sense. We *are* too acquisitive, we are gobbling up the world's resources in our rush for gimcrack possessions. For Alan, the only thing worth possessing was his own soul.

Two months later, I met my next bunch of 'seekers'. They were hanging out in Byron Bay, New South Wales, and this time their gurus were the Indians of the subcontinent, not the Andean Indians. Ignoring the magnificent surfing beach, they sat around in vegan restaurants, swaying their beards and pony tails to Indian devotional music. They were all barefoot and the girls wore identical droopy skirts in dusty plum-coloured chenille with mirror-work trimmings. Palmistry and aromatherapy were on offer, and shops selling scented candles, tarot packs and incense carried posters for the Holy Goat Commune. Devotees of Hari Krishna shambled round the streets, banging their little drums and chanting, with a faraway look in their eyes and a big black dog in tow.

What with the surfing and the alternative lifestyle, Byron Bay was so fashionable that I couldn't find a hotel room anywhere and had to resort to a backpackers' hostel. My three room-mates, a noisy girl from Wrexham, a Dutch girl and a mysterious mulatto beauty, were not 'seekers after the inner light'. They came stumbling in, at three different hours of the morning, at three different stages of inebriation. It was my first experience of backpackers, many of whom lived for their drinking. They nursed their hangovers through the day and recovered in time for the next night's session. When the money ran out, they took casual work until they'd saved enough to move on to the next resort, the next hostel and the next round of drinking. I found this alcohol culture depressing.

Noosa Heads was another popular resort where I was doomed to a hostel. There I shared a room with two silent, abstemious Japanese girls and Linda, a Calamity Jane from Liverpool. Everything went wrong for Linda. She told me about her stay in Byron Bay, where she'd had to share a dormitory with Compassionate, a Hari Krishna devotee.

'She sat there burning incense, ringing bells and meditating, with the door and windows shut tight. In the end, I said to her, 'I'm not being funny or anything, Compassionate, but I've just had flu and I can't breathe in here with all that incense and no fresh air.' She turned really nasty. Compassionate! Not likely!'

Linda went out drinking that night and came reeling back to

the hostel at 3 a.m. She undressed and got into bed, only to find that she was in the wrong room and had climbed into bed with a pair of love-birds. They kicked her out, literally, and sent her running naked round the hostel, looking for the right room.

We were joined the next afternoon by the mulatto beauty from Byron Bay and a Chinese Canadian with no more than a centimetre of fuzz over her skull. I asked her if she was a Buddhist.

'No. I was going to be travelling round Australia and I thought it would make life easier if I didn't have any hair. So I had it all shaved off. But it was a mistake. I'm here on a working holiday and I've got to earn money, but no one will give me a job. They think I'm some sort of an oddball. I've bought a bottle of hair tonic and I keep rubbing it in. Do you think it's growing a bit?'

That night a man appeared in the early hours, stripped and climbed into the vacant bunk above mine. He seemed completely unfazed when he woke up the next morning to find himself in a bedroom with five women. He drank coffee and shovelled down aspirins with Linda and Sheena, as they nursed their hangovers together in companionable silence. It had been a night of cane-toad racing in the bar and even more alcohol than usual had been consumed in the excitement.

I spent an interesting couple of days there. The hostel seemed little more than a daycare centre for alcoholics, but it had one real plus factor – the genuine open friendliness of the backpackers. I was old enough to be their grandmother, but I was welcomed, included in the conversation and, inevitably, offered a share of the drink and cigarettes. Like the backpackers in other hostels, they seemed comfortable with me, happy to have someone older and a bit different to talk to. My bicycle and I were always the centres of attention and the recipients of confidences. Hostelling in Australia was non-ageism at its best.

My last hostel was in Cairns, where I did manage to get a double room to myself. I came in late from dinner and was swept up by Peter, Mark and Guy for a glass of wine in their dormitory. They were cheerful lads, but the conversation soon turned to their great passion in life, motorbikes and their maintenance. I returned to the privacy of my room. A few moments later, there was a knock at my door. Peter was feeling lonely and had come along for another chat.

'Do you smoke?' he asked. 'And I don't mean cigarettes.' He produced a little pipe and some pot. 'I got this today. It's real good stuff. I thought you might like to share it.'

That was my introduction to marijuana. We sat side by side on the bed, passing the little pipe back and forth, while Peter, who had had a great deal to drink, told me that I was the greatest woman he'd ever met, apart from his mum and his sister. I once smoked opium in Thailand and found it utterly nauseating, with a taste like bad meat. Pot was much more agreeable to smoke but, like nicotine, it did nothing for me. I decided to stick to my customary drugs, whisky and the pleasures of a smooth, full-bodied wine.

Peter was no exception. Wherever I go, I seem to fall into the company of handsome young men. I think they find me restful. Unlike the travelling girls, I'm not out to lure them into matrimony or a passionate relationship, so they feel quite safe with me. They're lively companions and sometimes we stick together for days.

I met Jim at the bus station in Artvin. I'd just fulfilled a lifetime's ambition and arrived in Rose Macaulay's Trebizond. ('"Take my camel, dear," said my aunt Dot, as she climbed down from this animal on her return from High Mass . . .') My Dutch friend, Mignon, who shared my romantic notions about the place, had arranged to fly from Amsterdam to meet me there, but she was not due for another week. While I waited, I decided to take a holiday from cycling and ride the buses to the far east of Turkey.

Artvin was a dull one-street town, but its dizzy situation, on top of a 600-metre crag, offered spectacular mountain views in all directions. After a night up there, I booked a seat on the bus bound for Kars near the Armenian border, another visit inspired by a book, Philip Glazebrook's *Journey to Kars*. Jim and I picked each other out as the only two westerners in the bus station and we boarded the rattletrap together. He was on sabbatical leave from his job as a housemaster and history teacher at an independent school in Massachusetts, so we had a shared background in education and plenty to talk about.

The journey to Kars took all day. First we ran along a ledge over the rushing brown Çoruh River, then emerged into steppe country, which looked more and more desolate as we travelled further east. The villages were walled enclosures, where the stone cottages were exactly like the ones described in Xenophon's *Anabasis*. Partly dug out of the ground, to protect them from the extremes of temperature in that inhospitable land, and partly built of grey stone, their low walls were topped with flat earth roofs. Nothing had changed since the fifth century BC, when Xenophon had led his troops out of Persia to the Black Sea and passed just such buildings as these. Perhaps they were ideal for the climate, or perhaps the people out on that grim plain were so depressed that they'd never worked up the energy to improve their housing. It was PKK territory and the army kept hauling us out at road-blocks to scrutinise our papers and search the bus for arms. We were finally dumped down, in the dark, in a grit yard way out of Kars. Was I glad to have Jim with me!

Jim was glad of my company too, as I spoke a little Turkish, which he didn't. I tracked down the local bus to the centre of town. Then a strange thing happened. I was used to western Turkey and the more sophisticated coasts, where men would talk to me in a perfectly straightforward manner. But in eastern Turkey, in the company of a man, I suddenly vanished. Every remark on the bus was addressed to Jim, who didn't understand a word and had to turn to me for a translation. I replied on our behalf in Turkish, but the men in the bus continued to look at Jim, as if he were the speaker and I simply wasn't there. It was the same in the hotel. I asked for the rooms and the man at reception replied to Jim and gave him the registration forms and keys for both of us.

The Turks are unashamedly nosey and it was clear that our relationship foxed them. Jim looked a bit too old to be my son, but he was too young to be my husband – and anyway, we weren't sharing a room. In a part of the world where friendship between the sexes is unheard of, the locals were utterly bewildered. A group of old men who were sitting around in the lobby drinking tea invited Jim (not me) to join them. He amused me over dinner with his account of the tea-party, where the old chaps were dying of curiosity and Jim had no Turkish to satisfy it.

The next day we went to Ani, the romantic ruin which was once the ancient Armenian capital. It was separated from present-day Armenia only by the narrow stream of the Arpa River, so it was a military zone and we had to get official permits to go there. We went along to the Tourist Office. They inspected Jim's American passport and gave him a form to fill in. I was ignored. Eventually, he was issued with a permission slip for two persons. An Englishman in a hired car happened to be in the office at the same time and he kindly offered us a lift to Ani. The road to the border bristled with road-blocks and the two men were constantly asked to produce their passports and permission slips. None of the soldiers so much as looked at me. I could have been a general in the PKK and no one would have been any the wiser. At one check-point, there was a car-load of Iranians, the women totally enveloped in black *shadars*. They too were ignored and I thought how easy it would be for terrorists disguised as women to slip through the army defences.

Ani was a forlorn ghost of a city, where the shells of Byzantine churches and the ruins of the first Seljuk mosque in Anatolia stood sadly among the weeds. Tourism was not a big industry there, though the Cathedral attempted to cater for the three of us with an English notice: 'This building's architect was Tridates mendet the dome of S. Sophia in Istanbul after the earthquaken, in 989.'

Kars was not much better. It was a town of grey stone buildings, more Russian than Turkish in style, grey rubble, grey streets and intrusive telegraph poles. The hotels were shabby and seemed to be retirement homes for lonely old men. Where were the famous eastern extended families? Working in Germany or Istanbul perhaps. There were police cars at every corner and security was particularly tight as it was *Zafer Bayrami*, the celebration of Turkish independence in 1922.

Flaming torches were paraded past our restaurant window and we heard what sounded like gunfire or firebombs. We felt uneasy and were glad to move on to Doğubayazit, affectionately known to travellers as 'Dog Biscuit'.

Doğubayazit was a Kurdish town and even more backward than Kars, but at least it was livelier. Farriers were shoeing horses in the main street, in the shadow of the armoured personnel carriers, and the shops were crowded with Iranian tourists stocking up on cigarettes, kitchenware and hideously gaudy china. But all this human activity was dwarfed by the snow-capped peaks of Mount Ararat, which towered in majesty over the town and surrounding steppes. Unfortunately, the mountain was out of bounds to civilians, because its foothills were a PKK stronghold.

Jim and I spent our last full day together climbing out of the town to the palace of Ishak Paşa. The hills were an arid multicoloured moonscape, where piles of beige, green and terracotta rocks were ranged like a selection of ores in a chemical factory yard. There were spot-checks (for Jim) along the road and helicopters circled overhead, but by this time we were so used to military activity that we thought nothing of it. The warm biscuit-coloured dome and the slender patterned minaret of Ishak Paşa Sarayi stood in their Kurdish strength on a peak commanding the road from Iran. We wandered through the ruins of the palace's 366 rooms, then sat for an hour gazing at it from the terrace of a café on the neighbouring hill. We'd spent five uncomfortable and rather risky days travelling across PKK territory to get there, so we were determined to have a really good look at it. It was an interesting building, but its main charm lay in its remoteness. We felt quite proud to have got there.

That evening, we were joined at dinner by two regular army lieutenants, one from Kaiseri, the other from Istanbul. They had served in Dog Biscuit for fourteen months and still had another twenty-two to go. They were bored out of their minds, and nervous. But at least they were regulars who had chosen the military life. The ones I felt really sorry for were the poor National Service boys, who were no match at all for the highly trained PKK guerrillas, but were drafted out to the frontier to contain them.

The bus station clerk issued Jim with one ticket for two passengers and we travelled together as far as Erzurum, where our ways divided. Jim took a bus from there to Malatya, while I went back to Trabzon. I felt bereft. Travelling together in some personal danger across harsh, alien territory is a bonding experience. Strangers who meet by chance and are unlikely to meet ever again usually trade confidences. They tell each other things they would never dream of telling even their closest friends. Jim and I had been totally inter-dependent for five days. If I hadn't had Mignon's company to look forward to, I should have felt very lonely indeed as I watched him board the Malatya bus.

Friends, acquaintances and ships that pass in the night can all be placed into categories. The one person who was a category all to himself was George Hunt. I had never met him, yet he travelled all the way to Leticia on the Amazon to take me out to dinner!

The saga began when George, who was an agronomist working on World Bank projects, picked up *A Bike Ride* at Heathrow on his way to Lagos. He wrote a letter to me echoing my own views on the tyranny of material possessions. He said that I would be proud of him, as he'd gone out to Nigeria on a year's assignment and everything he owned in the world, including his bicycle, had weighed less than the airline's baggage allowance. Later that year, he changed planes in London and gave me a ring. When he heard that I was setting off in December for South America, he invited me to dinner on the Amazon.

His home was in Canada and he was due to take up a new assignment in Venezuela. So he cycled from Ontario to Mexico City, which for a 70-year-old was no mean achievement, and flew from there to San Carlos. There followed a long struggle with the South American telephone system, interspersed with faxes to the American Express offices in Belém and Manaus, as we tried to fix the date and place for our dinner. George was travelling round the farms of Venezuela and I was out of touch for weeks on end on my Amazon boats. It was a great logistical challenge.

He finally managed to reach me on the phone at my hotel in Manaus. We were cut off halfway through the conversation, but not before we'd arranged to meet at the Hotel Colonial in Leticia at noon on Friday 4 March. To get there, George had to make what we labelled 'the incredible journey'. He left San Carlos on Wednesday afternoon and caught a bus to Valencia. The next morning, he took the 6 a.m. flight to San Antonio, still in Venezuela, and hired a taxi to take him across the Colombian border to Cúcata. There he found that his flight to Bogotá had been cancelled and he had a six-hour wait. To make matters worse, the later flight was on a different airline and he couldn't transfer his ticket, so he had to buy another ticket, in cash, and that used up all his ready money. He arrived late at night in Bogotá and combed the streets, looking for a hole-in-the-wall which would take one of his cards and dispense some cash. He succeeded at the fourteenth attempt. Finally, on Friday morning, he flew from Bogotá to Leticia, where he arrived at the hotel a good half-hour before the appointed time. He was carrying a bunch of red roses, which he'd bought on Thursday night from a stall in Bogotá and somehow kept fresh for the rest of the journey. George was a resourceful man.

On Friday night we duly ate the famous dinner. We had delicately flavoured Amazon fish and a few bottles of beer in a tropical garden, where we were the only customers. On Saturday morning, George hired a bicycle so that we could explore what bit of countryside there was. He left immediately after lunch, as he had Monday appointments in San Carlos and a two-day journey to get there. He'd spent four days and a small fortune on the trip. It was a truly magnificent gesture. I hope he thought I was worth it!

George was killed last year by a truck, as he was cycling through Wyoming on his way home to Canada. His 'incredible journey' was typical of his generosity and panache. I have set it down as a modest tribute to a most extraordinary man.

5 Police

Come, let's away to prison!

Shakespeare, *King Lear*

As a law-abiding citizen, I've never been afraid of the European police. British bobbies in their helmets; *gendarmes* in their *képis* and natty jumpers; *carabinieri* flicking the scarlet linings of their handsome winter cloaks like so many black-booted peacocks – all exist for no more sinister purpose than to set me on the right road at intersections and tell me where I can find a bank or a bed for the night. Whatever their nationality, they cluck over me. 'Aren't you cold in this weather? Are you sure you'll be all right on your own?' And when I leave their protection, they all show the greatest concern. 'Why don't you stay in Greece? You're safe here. We'll look after you. Over in Turkey, they're all robbers. It's a terrible country.' I cycle over the border and the Turkish police greet me with a glass of tea. 'It's a wonder you've still got that bicycle! They're all robbers in Greece. But you're safe now. We'll look after you.' Wherever I go, the European police are my friends.

South America was a different matter. I'd never cycled there before I stepped off the plane in Brazil and I had no idea what to expect. The guide-books I was carrying warned of the high-handedness of the South American police and I had read disturbing accounts of corruption, bullying, capricious behaviour and demands for bribes. Experienced travellers had been thrown into prison for minor breaches of visa regulations, or because they didn't hold a return flight ticket, or simply because they had the wrong haircut. More seriously, some had been arrested on trumped-up drug charges, for which the penalty was life imprisonment, and it had taken high-level help and the exchange of considerable sums of money to get them released. Even allowing for the flourishes of macho young travel writers, it was still a pretty daunting picture.

I travelled with Katherine for moral support and we both cheered up immediately we landed in Salvador. It was 1.15 on Christmas afternoon and everyone in the small airport was half-asleep, until our bicycles stirred them into action. A porter woke up and seized the pump from my hands, while another put back the chain which was dangling loose. The rest of the airport staff crowded round us to find out who we were and where we were going. People the world over are fascinated by travellers on bicycles and in Brazil we were a double novelty because, as we realised later, no Brazilian woman would ever dream of riding a bicycle. In the middle of all the fuss and excitement, an armed Airport Police officer swaggered over. We had no Brazilian cruzeiros and the bank was closed. To our amazement, the guard telephoned the Banco do Brasil, who opened up the airport branch specially for us – at siesta-time on Christmas afternoon! It was unfortunate for the poor bank clerk, who was dragged away from his family on Christmas Day, and the incident showed all too clearly the extent of police power. But if it was a sample of official behaviour towards foreigners, perhaps we had little to fear.

My only other encounter with the Brazilian police was in São Luis, where I was robbed. Theft is supposed to be a way of life in South America, but people had run after me in the streets with things I had dropped. Even my new top-of-the-range Pentax, which I'd foolishly left behind in a church in Salvador, had been handed in to the verger by a man who declined to give his name. Such simple honesty among destitute people was profoundly moving. I became careless.

When we arrived in São Luis, a poverty-stricken shadow of its former colonial glories, I didn't like the look of the hotel manager. He was a shifty character and I mistrusted his safe deposit arrangements, so I decided to keep my spare cash and traveller's cheques hidden in my padlocked panniers. It was a mistake. We went out on our bicycles the next morning and came back to find that my panniers had been rifled. It was obviously an inside job, as we had left the room-key at reception.

I went to report the theft to the police. They were a cheerful crew. Most were in uniform, but the detective in charge was wearing a hectic holiday shirt, emblazoned with the brand-names of all the world's favourite beers. Their English was worse than my Portuguese, so the manager of the Varig airline office was called upon to interpret. (He happened to be married to the Assistant Chief of Police.) We called in at the Varig office later in the day, to ask if any progress had been made. The manager telephoned his wife. 'The investigation is taking its course,' he told us. 'They've just finished beating the chambermaids.' My eyes opened wide and he noticed. Shrugging his shoulders, he spread out his hands in a gesture of resignation. 'This isn't England, you know.'

The police probably beat up the hotel manager too, because he turned decidedly unfriendly towards us. I never got my cash back, but I got the police report for my insurers, and all my traveller's cheques were replaced very promptly, by both American Express and Thomas Cook. I was annoyed with myself for not taking greater care, but it was some consolation to think that whoever took those dollars undoubtedly needed them more than I did. I hope the hotel staff and their families really enjoyed them – and I hope they didn't have to give a cut to their disagreeable boss!

My next country was Colombia. I had travelled by boat up the Amazon as far as Tabatinga, the port where Brazil meets Colombia and Peru. By that stage, I'd been in Brazil for well over two months and had come to like the place and feel comfortable in it. Now I was going to cross the Brazilian border to explore the 80-kilometre stretch of river-bank, which is all the Colombians own. The Brazilian frontier guards put the exit stamp in my passport. I was no longer officially in Brazil. I cycled up to the Colombian Immigration Office.

'How long are you staying in Colombia?'

'Four days.'

'It's not worth stamping your passport then. You'll be gone by Tuesday.'

My concern got me nowhere. The guard put his feet back up on the desk and I was dismissed. Of all the countries in South America, Colombia had the most unsavoury reputation. All I knew of it was what I'd seen on television, the shoot-outs in the streets of Medellín. It seemed a lawless place, run by the drug barons, where I might easily get caught in the cross-fire. And officially, I was not even there! I had no stamp in my passport and no tourist card. I could disappear and there would be no record of my existence.

But luck was on my side and my dodgy status did nothing to mar my pleasant weekend in Leticia with George. When I returned to Tabatinga to embark on my next boat, the Brazilians, with their customary correctness, stamped me back into Brazil, even though I would be leaving the country again at 4.30 the next morning. After four trouble-free days, I had come to terms with my statelessness – but it was still a great relief when I ceased to be a non-person.

Peru has a most efficient Tourist Police. I went along to their office in Iquitos to enquire about my onward journey. My aim was to find a small boat or boats plying between Iquitos and Yurimaguas, the last port of any size up the Amazon. From there, a road of sorts climbed steeply into the Andes and I planned to follow it on my bicycle through Tarapoto and Moyobamba to Cajamarca, where Pizarro ambushed the Inca, tricked him of his gold and finally burned him at the stake.

But the journey was vetoed. The Peruvian army was having a crack-down on drugs and terrorism, and the Province of San Martín, through which I had hoped to cycle, was a virtual war-zone. The situation was especially serious at the time, as a recent anti-narcotics campaign by the Colombian Government, assisted by the CIA, had driven the Colombian drug cartels across the border into Peru. There they had taken to growing opium poppies as well as the local coca. These Colombians were running a far more sophisticated operation than the Peruvians were used to, with well-armed troops and fleets of helicopter gun-ships. The Tourist Police said they could not be responsible for my safety either on the river or the road and I must fly over the Province to Cajamarca. I was a *gringa* and consequently a target. 'If they think you're an American, you're dead.'

I felt sorry for the Peruvians. They talked hopefully of

persuading coca-growers to turn to other crops, but what other crops can offer such profit to subsistence farmers? Coca and opium poppies are worth any risk. Meanwhile, drug production distorts the economy and prevents legitimate development in other directions. The problem is not unique to South America; I've met it on my travels in Pakistan and Thailand too. Second and Third World governments consume resources they can ill afford in doomed attempts to curb production at its source, while the moralising West continues to provide the ready market. Fortunes are made through drug-dealing, with its concomitants of organised crime and terrorism. Only by taking the Mafia money out of the trade can drug-production be halted – and if this has to be done by the legalisation of drugs in the West, so be it. We should at least be prepared to debate the issue. We should be ready, if necessary, to take our fair share of the danger, instead of heaping the burden of our drug addiction on impoverished peoples. We should put our own houses in order. And if altruism doesn't persuade us, perhaps the drug-warfare and the guns which are surfacing on the streets of our cities will.

The Tourist Police were taking no chances. When I cycled out to Iquitos Airport for the flight to Cajamarca, I found Juan waiting for me, just to make sure that I left as instructed. Juan was a handsome *mestizo*, who looked quite grown-up and dignified, until he took off his policeman's cap to smooth his hair and gave me a cheeky grin. He was twenty-two and had just graduated from Police College. While we waited for my flight to be called, he described the rigours of his boot camp – a hundred fast press-ups morning and evening, running round the track till he dropped, square-bashing, study day and night, all on scant, unpalatable rations. But it had been worth it. He now had a most comfortable life, with a leisurely job, siestas every afternoon, good dinners and a fat cheque at the end of the month to spend on whatever he liked. All he lacked for perfect happiness was a wife.

'What I should really like is a nice interesting girl from Europe or North America – German, Swiss, American, English – I don't mind where she comes from. There are flights every week, you know, direct from Iquitos to Miami, and I'm saving up to go there for my holidays. I'd love to see the States and I might even find myself an American fiancée while I'm there.'

'How much holiday do you get?'

'Two weeks.'

'You'll have to work fast then!'

'Oh I shall,' he assured me. 'I shall rush off the plane in my best suit, with my hair brushed and my eyes spinning round, looking, looking . . .' He gave me a spirited demonstration. 'I shall be so dashing, the girls won't be able to resist me! And you never know my luck. I might even captivate an air hostess on the flight out. That would save me a lot of bother.'

We joked about his matrimonial prospects. Then he became serious and warned me again about the 'bad boys' up in the Andes, which I thought was rather a mild description of the drug barons and their gun-toting gangs. He was an engaging lad with excellent English and I have seldom passed a more amusing hour at an airport.

Juan was a member of the Peruvian Tourist Police. My next encounter was with the more serious end of the force. I had cycled over the pass above Cajamarca and was beginning my descent from the watershed of the Andes down to the Pacific, when I came to a road-block. Although I was clear of the coca-growing regions on the eastern slopes, I was still in a sensitive area. The road was a possible drug-run down to the coast and the Shining Path guerrillas were still an active, if weakened, force in the mountains. The policeman on duty asked to see my passport. This was most inconvenient, as I had hidden it for safety at the bottom of one of my panniers. I explained my problem, but he was insistent. By this time, the entire village had gathered round to stare, so he led me into the police post, where I could unpack my belongings in private. Any *gringa* is a rarity high up in the Andes; but a *gringa* on a bicycle is the event of a lifetime!

The constable apologised for the trouble he was causing me. 'You see, I must have identification. It's the rules.'

That was the glimmer of light I needed. 'Identification? If that's what you need, perhaps this will do.' I opened my handlebar bag and produced a visiting card. The effect was magical. He took the card, holding it delicately at the edges so as not to dirty it. He read it, turned it over, turned it back, read it again and gazed at it in wonder. '*Que bonita!*' he exclaimed. 'Can I keep it?'

At this point the sergeant came out of his office. He was shown the card. 'It's mine. The señora says I can keep it.'

The sergeant looked at it longingly. '*Que bonita*! Can I have one too?'

They sat me down, the passport forgotten, and plied me with glasses of Pepsi. They asked me how I liked Peru, how I got on with the food and whether the people were kind to me. I replied with the usual compliments and delighted them by reeling off the names of all my favourite Peruvian dishes. I was making for Chilete and they assured me that I should reach the town quite easily by nightfall. 'And if you have any problems there, of any sort at all, go straight to the police station and say that we've sent you.' As I left, the constable stood to attention and saluted: 'Your friends, the Peruvian Police!'

The whole way through their country, the Peruvian Police were indeed my friends, giving me advice and offering me lifts across difficult terrain – which I never accepted, because that would have been cheating. As for Chile, the police force was so inconspicuous that I have no recollection of it at all. My only slight *contretemps* was with the immigration health officers, who insisted that I throw away a potentially contaminating Peruvian bun before I entered their hygienic land. It was a particularly nice bun, with currants and cinnamon, and I had no intention of throwing it away. So they sat me down under a striped umbrella at the border-post café and watched while I ate it. When it was consumed down to the last crumb, they allowed me into Chile.

I went to South America expecting the worst of officialdom and met only the best. Nowhere in Brazil, Peru or Chile was I treated with anything but the greatest courtesy. Perhaps my bicycle, or the fact that I was a woman, was responsible for this kindly attention. Perhaps the treatment of other travellers by the police is significantly different, but I have my doubts.

Corruption and crime are part of the folklore of the continent, and its unsavoury reputation is perpetuated by what I suspect is often picturesque embellishment. With a little common sense, a little common courtesy and a modicum of effort with Portuguese and Spanish, I'm sure that the traveller in the three countries I crossed can fare as well as the traveller anywhere else in the world. I can only speak from my own experience, but that's how it seemed to me.

Yet, despite my good South American experiences, I still boarded the Sydney-bound Qantas jumbo in Tahiti with that sense of relief which comes at the end of a tricky journey. I had been treated kindly in South America and had flown without accident in the South American planes over the Atlantic, the Andes and the South Pacific, but there had always been that edge of uncertainty. On the Qantas flight, I was home. These were my people, with my language, my food, my set of values and my standards of safety. For the first time in six months, I really relaxed.

That feeling of security never left me in Australia. Even when I inadvertently broke the highway code, I was totally unafraid.

I had cycled more than 800 km along the Pacific Highway from Sydney, with no complications, but just as I approached Brisbane, the highway turned unexpectedly into a freeway, where it was illegal for me to ride. It was the morning rush-hour and the traffic was ferocious. I had no idea how to get off the freeway, or what alternative route I could use. I struggled on along the hard shoulder, searching for an exit, and I was actually relieved to be flagged down by the Queensland Police.

The two officers on duty, a man and a woman, were dressed in identical blue bush-ranger hats, short-sleeved blue shirts and navy blue trousers with revolvers at the hip. I had to wait while they dealt with a motorcycle accident. Then they turned their complete, admiring attention on me. I was a sportswoman, a heroine in Australia! We discussed my plans for the ride to Darwin and propped up the roadside barrier while I told them about my crossing of South America. Then they escorted me to the nearest exit and provided me with a map of Brisbane, carefully marking out their recommended route across the city to the Bruce Highway. They were full of misplaced sympathy, based on an exaggerated idea of the winter cold in England. It was no wonder I had to come to Australia to enjoy my cycling, when Steve Ovett, they reliably informed me, had to go out for his training runs in *three* tracksuits. 'How do you motivate yourselves for sport in such a climate?' Of all the world's police forces, only the Australians would spend half an hour discussing sport with a law-breaker! The Chinese, I knew, would be far less relaxed about their duties.

Communist bureaucracy is notorious and my problems with China and Central Asia began long before I left home. I was planning to cycle along the Silk Road from Xi'an north-west across China to Kashgar. From there, I hoped to go over the Torugart Pass into Kirghizia, cross into Uzbekistan and follow the lush Fergana Valley to the legendary cities of Samarkand and Bokhara. It was to be the ride of dreams. But my dreams were soon shattered. Although the two former Soviet republics were now independent, in 1995 they had not yet set up their own consular services and Intourist was still their agent. As a private visitor, I needed an invitation from a citizen of each country, which had to be approved by the local police; I had to give definite entry and exit dates, which could not be altered *en route*; I had to produce a full itinerary, showing exactly where I should be travelling on every single day of my stay; and I had to pay in advance for three nights' accommodation out of every seven, in approved tourist hotels.

For a cyclist, these were impossible conditions. I had no detailed maps of the area and no lists of hotels. I couldn't even work out the probable date of my arrival at the Kirghizia frontier, as I had no idea how long it would take me to cycle across China. I had calculated the journey from Xi'an to Kashgar to be approximately 4,000 km, a ride of about ten weeks at my usual leisurely average of 1,600 km a month. But I knew nothing of the state of the roads, nor did I know if I should be physically capable of cycling across the Gobi and Taklimakan deserts. And even if I were, I was uncertain that the Public Security Bureau (the Chinese Police) would allow it. The Silk Road was now supposedly 'open', but I had read no accounts of cyclists who had travelled along it. I might be left in peace all the way to Kashgar – or I might be picked up by the police on my very first morning out of Xi'an and bundled into a truck bound for the nearest airport and home.

The Silk Road is not one single road, but an ancient network of routes linking the markets of China to the trading-posts of the Mediterranean. It crosses some of the world's most desolate and politically unstable country and travellers throughout the centuries have always had to take the branch of the road which was politically possible at any given time. In 1995, nothing had changed. It was clear that Kirghizia and Uzbekistan were out, thanks to Intourist, and so were Kazakhstan and the Russian Federation, for the same reason. Afghanistan was at war. Kashmir's Muslim insurrection against the Indian Government was continuing and was to progress that summer to the taking of western hostages. So I was left with only one overland exit from China, the Khūnjerāb Pass into Pakistan. The Pakistan High Commission in London produced a visa within the day and I thought my problems with officialdom were over. But more were to come.

My tried and trusted Condor had been lovingly prepared by Monty Young and his team in the Gray's Inn Road and was gleaming in my garage, complete with new Kevlar tyres and extra gears for the mountains. Just four days before I was due to leave, I had a phone call from a friend in the British Embassy in Beijing. On her advice, I put in a call to the Vice-Consul.

'You know it's illegal to import bicycles into China without a special permit, don't you?'

I didn't know and I pointed out that people did take their bicycles into China, because I'd read about them.

'Yes. Sometimes they're lucky with their Customs Official and he lets their bicycles through. But sometimes they're impounded, and that's the last they ever see of them. There's no compensation. Nothing. We do our best for them at the Consulate, but they've broken the law and there's really no redress. If your bike is a good one, you need to weigh the risks very carefully. You don't want to lose it.'

I rushed to the Chinese Embassy in London, where they

issued me with a printed document stating that foreigners were not allowed to take any vehicles, including bicycles, into China. With only four days left to put in an application, I had to accept that a special permit was out of the question. My Condor had been the constant companion of my travels and was far too precious to risk. So I left it behind reluctantly and took some extra dollars with me to buy a bicycle in Beijing.

Although I was admitting it to no one, I was scared – and my Beijing phonecalls had just added a few extra scares to the list. My concern was Chinese bureaucracy in all its manifestations and I was particularly worried about the provincial police who were too far away from Beijing to be controlled. They could be as erratic in their behaviour as they liked. I remembered a particularly chilling report by Amnesty International about 'administrative detainees', who were said to be held without charge or trial for anything up to four years, on the sole authority of those local police officers. Amnesty claimed that the official regulations were so vague and so little regarded that illegal detention was widespread; and the potential for ill-treatment, even torture, was increased by the lack of judicial supervision and safeguards for detainees' rights.

It was not a happy situation. In the daylight, I could convince myself that such injustices would never be perpetrated against a foreign traveller, but in the cowardly small hours my courage sometimes failed me. I should have felt even more insecure had it not been for my friend Joan. By a stroke of amazing good fortune for me, Joan had recently married the British Ambassador to China, so for once in my life I had someone to smooth my path, someone in Beijing who would care if I was thrown into prison and might even be able to do something about it.

I spent a week in Beijing, tracking down a suitable bicycle and exploring the city on it. My idea of Chinese bicycles was of heavyduty black jobs, which weighed a ton and had no gears. There were plenty of those around, but with persistence I managed to find a small specialist cycle shop in the diplomatic quarter, which had just the kind of hybrid machine I was looking for. For 1,780 yuan (about £140), a fortune in Chinese terms, I became the proud owner of Cube, a sturdy medium-weight, with medium-knobbly tyres and twenty-one gears. Assembled in China, it had a Chinese frame, American wheel-rims, Taiwanese tyres, Japanese gears and an Italian saddle – a truly international model for a world cyclist! It was sprayed in a dingy purple verging on puce, with funny grey squiggles all over in a shattered windscreen pattern. The word 'Cube', superimposed on a picture of three little cubes, was printed on each side of the crossbar. The two diagonal bars read, again on both sides, 'Geometric Line' and 'Kenhill', with a pink blob instead of a dot over one of the i's and a green blob over the other. A great deal of loving care had obviously been lavished on the design and the result was staggeringly ugly. But the bicycle went well and the saddle was comfortable. I came to love it dearly, squiggles, blobs and all.

I took it on the train to Xi'an, visited the terracotta warriors on it, then set off to ride it to Rome. I pedalled out through the city's Ming West Gate on a bright April morning, my spirits soaring as they always do at the start of a trip. At first, I was held up by flocks of sleepy workers on their heavy black bicycles. Their cruising speed was one-third of mine and their saddles were far too low, so that their knees and feet stuck out sideways. But once I was clear of this dreaming traffic, I found myself on a relatively empty highway with a good flat tarmac surface. I bowled merrily along in the sunshine between avenues of poplars. In the middle of the morning, four members of the Public Security Bureau rode by on a motorcycle. One policeman drove, one rode pillion, while a policeman and a policewoman sat in the sidecar. The quartet cruised slowly through a street market, exchanging greetings with the stall-holders. They were out among the people, close enough to be 'bobbies on the beat', yet they had the turn of speed of a panda car at their disposal, should they need it. It seemed an admirable arrangement and very economical. The policewoman gave me a smile and a wave as they rode by. I continued on my way undisturbed.

The weeks passed and I had no problems at all with the police. I was starting to feel very confident – until I came to San Dao Ling, a small industrial town at the far end of the Gobi Desert.

It had been a hard day's ride in wind and pelting rain, and I was drying off in my hotel room over a welcome pot of tea, when there was a knock at the door and in marched an odd couple. The uniformed policeman was amazingly untidy. His hair sprouted out in tufts from under his cap and he flapped across the room in battered sandals and bright green socks. Officials in China are given their uniform jackets, trousers and caps, but wear their own shirts, jumpers and shoes, so it's not unusual to see trainers, pairs of flip-flops, or even purple plastic wellingtons on the ends of smart military legs. By contrast, the plain-clothes officer was as dapper as a 1930's matinée idol in cream linen jacket, silk socks, expensive leather shoes and a straw hat with 'World Cup' printed round the ribbon. He wore the dark glasses beloved of plain-clothes policemen the world over. Neither of them spoke a word of English.

Before I set out for the wilder parts of China, I had been careful to get a letter of introduction, in Chinese as well as English, from the British Embassy in Beijing. It only gave my name and passport details and asked 'whoever it might concern' to help me on my cycle-ride along the Silk Road, but it carried a very impressive array of government stamps and seals. I had already used it to good effect in Hami. I had gone to the police station to renew my visa and the letter had made such a dazzling impression that the Head of the PSB had provided me with a chauffeur-driven car and an English interpreter to take me across town! So I now produced my letter with a flourish and a show of confidence which I didn't feel. These local clowns were a world away from the sophisticated Chief of Police in Hami and I was nervous of their reaction. But if you look like a victim, you soon become one.

The plain-clothes officer read the Chinese letter carefully, twice. He scrutinised the English version, which he couldn't understand, peered at my passport, read the letter a third time, then handed everything over to the constable. His bluster was gradually turning to deference and I began to breathe more easily.

PC Plod produced a notebook and laboriously copied the entire Embassy letter, while the officer questioned me. It was the usual Chinese catechism. 'How old are you? Are you alone? Where is your husband? How many children have you got? What is your profession? Do you like China?' I had answered all these questions so many times before that my Mandarin flowed and I thought everything was going smoothly. Then he said,

'You can't cycle in China. It's not safe.'

'But I've already cycled here from Xi'an and I've been perfectly safe. I've had no trouble at all.'

'This is the desert. The desert is not safe.'

'But I've just cycled across the Gobi, from Jiayuguan all the way here – nearly 800 km of desert.'

'There are bad men on the road. We cannot allow you to cycle. If there were three of you, you could go on your bicycles. But one, or even two, is out of the question. It's not safe. You must take the bus to Turfan.'

I argued my case. I offered them Marlboro cigarettes, the favourite foreign brand, which I had bought for just this sort of situation. I even smoked myself, because offering cigarettes without joining in might be interpreted as a bribe. I flattered them, waxed lyrical about China, made them tea and shared the last of my nice Hami biscuits with them, but all to no avail.

'There is a good bus service to Turfan. I will speak to the hotel manager and he will get you onto the bus tomorrow morning. He will look after you.'

He was taking no chances. He was arranging for me to be put on the bus, to make sure I did as I was told. I had no way of knowing if the 'bad men' and the dangers of the desert were the real reasons for his decision. But whatever his motives, he was clearly very worried about this foreign lady cyclist and determined to bundle her off his patch as fast as possible.

Early next morning, a bevy of giggling girls in emerald green jackets with brass buttons presented themselves at my door to escort me to the bus. They carried my panniers down the corridor which was lined, like all Chinese corridors, with rows of enamel spitoons on stands (these had the kitten pattern, not the roses) and pushed my bicycle down the road to the bus-stop. They were only the floor attendants from the hotel, not an armed escort, but it came to the same thing. They were obviously acting on police instructions and were not to be argued with.

Once they got me to the bus-stop, they relaxed and started to boast to the rapt crowd that I was sixty-one and had just cycled all the way from Xi'an on my own. There were gasps of astonishment. I was the first 'big nose' they had ever seen and I faced the usual barrage of questions. 'You are alone? Why? Where is your husband? Where are your children?' The Chinese never travel alone if they can help it and simply can't understand why anyone should wish to do such a peculiar thing.

When the bus arrived, it was a small overcrowded minibus with no rack on the top, so the driver refused to take the bicycle. I stood back while the green-jackets attacked him. My local admirers joined in the argument and in no time at all, the other passengers were shunted around and I was ushered into the front seat, with Cube in the aisle beside me.

We climbed the hill out of San Dao Ling and reached the junction with the highway. I looked for Stan and Ollie and spotted them, as I guessed I would, sitting in their PSB car watching the bus. Just checking.

Apart from the bore of having to take the bus, when I would rather have cycled the 400 km to Turfan, I thought my first encounter with the PSB had gone off fairly well. My next one was potentially more dangerous.

I was five days out of Turfan. They had been days of desperate cycling, with desert sandstorms and formidable passes in the foothills of the Heavenly Mountains, the Tian Shan. I had even climbed the dreaded Dry Ditch Gulley, gasping my painful way past the broken-down trucks which had scattered their fan-belts and died in the burning solitude. In such a wilderness, the accommodation had been primitive – no running water and plenty of rats. I was looking forward to a good hotel and a bath in Korla.

On the outskirts of the city I passed a *lüshe*. Its hospitable owners rushed out to the roadside to offer me lunch and a cheap room for the night. Had I accepted and stayed overnight with the lorry-drivers, I should have saved myself a great deal of trouble. I should have paid in cash without signing the register or filling in forms, and the PSB would not have known of my existence. But the thought of a bath and a comfortable rat-free room was irresistible. I checked in at the best hotel in town.

Mid-afternoon, the PSB did their daily inspection of the hotel registers and I was called down to Reception. There were two plain-clothes officers there, one of whom was proficient in English. He asked to see my passport and I handed it over, together with my Embassy letter.

'You know it's illegal for foreigners to cycle in China, don't you?'

I had been cycling in China for seven weeks and this was the first mention of illegality.

'But I understood that the Silk Road was open to foreigners all the way.'

'The cities of the Silk Road are open, but not the road itself. You must fly between the cities, or take the bus.'

'But the British Embassy checked for me in Beijing and . . .'

He interrupted me with an outburst of rage: 'This is not British Embassy business. This is Chinese Police business. It's nothing to do with the British Embassy.'

I decided to keep quiet about the British Embassy after that, so as not to provoke him further. Chinese telephones are hopelessly erratic, but the fax works, and there was a business centre with a fax in the hotel. If the police turned really nasty, I could probably manage to get a fax through to Beijing, to the British Consul. That thought gave me some confidence.

The officer then produced a notepad. 'You must write down all your movements since you entered China. Every journey, every hotel, every visit. I want to know exactly where you've been and exactly what you've been doing every day since 29 March.

I copied it all down from my log book and it took me almost two hours. The officer then wrote out an accompanying statement, in Chinese, which he said he would translate for me. He read out my passport details and said that I was exploring the Silk Road and cycling illegally. I was made to sign the document. Although I could speak some Chinese, I couldn't read the script, so I could have been putting my name to anything. But the police were standing over me and I had no choice but to sign.

The officer packed away the two documents in his briefcase, together with my passport and the British Embassy letter. The loss of my passport sent me into a panic, but all my protests were in vain. My passport had to go to headquarters, where the Chief of Police would decide on 'the appropriate punishment'. Meanwhile, I was to stay in the hotel. I was under house arrest.

Incongruously, at the end of all this unpleasantness, he asked, 'Are you having a nice time in China?' 'I *was* having a nice time, until this afternoon,' I replied tartly. He gave me an inscrutable smile and left me to my house arrest.

The PSB kept me waiting for three long, anxious days. Finally, the English-speaking officer returned, this time alone. To my relief, he handed back my passport.

'Yours has been a difficult case, but as it's your first offence, we have decided not to punish you on this occasion. Also, we are very proud of you. You have been cycling across China at an age when most people are staying at home keeping an eye on their grandchildren.'

With that somewhat backhanded compliment, he ordered tea. When he was not engaged in official harassment, he turned out to be quite a nice man and we spent a pleasant half-hour together. But he told me that I was on no account to cycle in China again. I must take the bus to the border at Tashkurgan.

'And don't think that you can jump on your bicycle again once you're out of Korla. The PSB will be keeping track of you and you will be severely punished if you break the law again.'

So I rode a relay of buses to the frontier, with Cube roped to the top. In Kashgar, I met a group of American students who had been picked up by those same Korla police and banned from cycling; and they had been 'punished' with a heavy fine. Yet other cyclists had apparently travelled the whole way across China and encountered no problems at all. It was one of the unnerving features of the system that so much seemed to depend on luck or the attitude of the local branch of the PSB. It was impossible to find out what the punishable offences were and all too easy to break the law unwittingly.

Hard news is difficult to come by in China, but when I reached Kashgar I was able to exchange information with travellers who had just crossed over from Pakistan. I learned from them that the Chinese had been testing nuclear devices in the Taklimakan Desert. Everything suddenly became clear. Both San Dao Ling and Korla lay on the rim of the Taklimakan, and I happened to be passing through them at the critical time. With nuclear bombs exploding around them, the last thing the PSB needed was a foreign woman poking about on a bicycle. No wonder they were jumpy!

6 Terrible Terrain I
The Australian Outback

And yonder all before us lie
Deserts of vast eternity.

Andrew Marvell

Imagine a desert. You will probably see in your mind's eye an infinite stretch of yellow sand with elegantly rounded dunes and a distant file of muffled Bedouin on camels. Such deserts are the stuff of Hollywood. They do exist in parts of Arabia and the Sahara, where I've crossed them in a four-wheel drive. But there are not many of them. Most of the world's deserts are far less picturesque. Grey grit, red dust, stones, camel thorn and telegraph-poles. Deserts are big, ugly, desolate places – and yet I love them.

I love them because I've crossed them slowly on my bicycle. People who have only flashed across deserts in cars have no idea of their infinite variety. It takes the slowly moving eye to see the subtle colour-changes in the sand, the changes of texture and strata in the rocks, and notice the tiny creatures and the sparse vegetation they feed on. Travelling on a bicycle brings awareness of every gradation in tone, every shift of light. There are changes in perspective too. A snow-capped mountain comes into view in the far distance, moves slowly alongside and finally disappears behind me, in counterpoint to my own forward motion. I creep across the vast, empty landscape, feeling no larger or more significant than an ant. There is nothing like the immensity of a desert for cutting human beings down to size, except perhaps the open sea. We are out there on our own, living on the edge of danger, with nothing but our own resources. Deserts are never boring, except to the speeding traveller.

When I crossed Australia from Sydney to Darwin, I met a desert unlike any other. I had followed the Pacific coast north from Sydney to Townsville. It had been a month of gloriously soft holiday cycling, of smooth roads, breathtaking scenery, comfortable hotels, good food and drink and cheerful company. But my life was to change at Townsville, when I headed off into the Outback.

There was one road, the Flinders Highway, which ran westwards out of the town to Cloncurry, where it changed its name to the Barkly Highway for the rest of its run to a speck on the map called Three Ways.

There, in the Red Centre of Australia, it met the north-south Stuart Highway. If I turned left at Three Ways, I could follow that single artery south, via Alice Springs, to Adelaide on the Southern Ocean. For Darwin, I had to turn right, through the Northern Territory. The paths of the early explorers and cattle-drovers had led across the central desert from creek to well, to billabong, from water source to water source – and even today, those same water sources are vital to the traveller. The Highways follow the water.

I loved telling the Australians that I was planning to cycle to Darwin, to hear their incredulous 'Dorween!' The sanguine ones added, 'Good on yer!' or 'Better take plenty of tucker. There's not much out there.' The rest were worried.

Few of the people I met in Sydney or Brisbane had ever been to the Northern Territory, but they were as sure of its dangers as the Brazilians had been of the perils of the Amazon. I should be molested, mugged, knocked off my bicycle by the road-trains, run out of water, die of dehydration.

'You'll never do it. The temperature gets up to 35°C out there.'

I tried to reassure them. 'I've cycled across a few deserts already – the Nevada, the Utah, the Great Thar. As long as you prepare for them, they're perfectly manageable. And I've cycled in 45°C before now.'

They were astonished, but in no way floored. 'You haven't cycled across *our* desert before. You wait till you see it!' For Australians, everything in Australia has to be the biggest, the best, the worst, the most difficult. Nothing would persuade them that the Outback was not the hottest, driest, most desolate land in creation, so I stopped trying and accepted their warnings as expressions of kind concern.

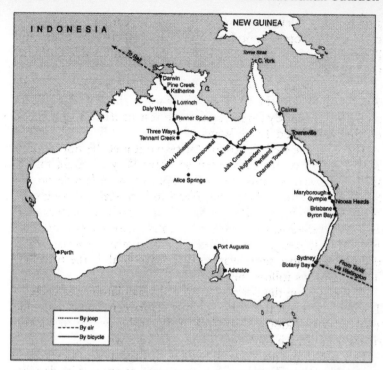

Some of them teased me. 'Be sure to zip your tent up tight at night, to keep out the snakes and scorpions, and the giant ants. And don't camp too near to water. The salties (saltwater crocodiles) get trapped upstream in the dry season. They lie in the billabongs, feeling hungry, waiting for tourists.'

By the time I neared Townsville, with 2,550 km of Pacific coast-road under my wheels, they began to think that I could probably manage it, but was mad to try. 'Rather you than me, out on your own in the wup-wup,' said the chambermaid at Proserpine.

I could see from the map that my first few days out of Townsville would be easy. Townsville – Mingela – Charters Towers – Pentland – Prairie – Hughenden. All those runs were well within my usual daily cycling-range. After Hughenden, the towns began to space out: 112 km to Richmond, 144 to Julia

Creek, 134 to Cloncurry, 118 to Mt Isa. Luckily, I was in good shape after my coastal ride and fairly confident that I could manage those distances, at a push. But I knew that the Barkly Tableland, with chunks of 199, 265 and 192 hilly kilometres between hotels, was quite beyond me. For the first time in my life, I should have to resort to a tent.

Fortunately, I had expert advice. I had met up with Margaret, a keen Australian cyclist, who had written to me after reading *A Bike Ride*. We had corresponded for a couple of years and now we were both staying with hospitable friends of hers, Jean and Wally, in Townsville. Margaret turned out to be the Queensland Camping Assessor for the Girl Guides, no less, and there was nothing she didn't know about tents. We toured the Townsville camping stores and settled on a lightweight German Salewa igloo, reduced to half-price as it had a small (repaired) rip in the fabric. Under Margaret's tuition, I practised putting it up and taking it down in Jean's living room. Then I packed my smarter clothes, mosquito net and a few books into a carton for Wally to deliver to the camping store. They had a branch in Darwin and Allan, their helpful manager, had offered to send my superfluous gear in the company's van, so as to leave me room in my panniers for food and extra water. My panniers had deep back pockets and I found that I could fit a 1½ litre plastic Pepsi bottle into each, giving me three litres of water over and above the water I always carried in my cross-bar bottle.

Margaret volunteered to cycle with me as far as Charters Towers, which was invaluable. She told me the names of birds and shrubs, and pointed out gullies where I might shelter from the heat of the day when there were no shade trees. She also took me over to inspect the windmill and tank at a bore-hole, explaining their operation so that I could see how to get water. We stayed for two nights with 'rellies' of hers, who ran a cattle station near Mingela, and after a farewell dinner in the 'eat as much as you like' buffet of the Charters Towers Chinese, Margaret turned left, taking the one road south to her home in Clermont.

I spent an extra day exploring 'The World', as the town was

called in its gold-rush days, when it used to boast 100 hotels and there were 25 pubs in the main street alone. It even had its own Stock Exchange, with three calls a day. The City Hall, modelled in pink on the Treasury of Rose-Red Petra, the Royal Arcade, the Australian Bank of Commerce, the Clock Tower and the lacy wrought-iron balconies above the stores were all from the gracious 1890s. I had my spare tyre fitted by a recent immigrant, a Bavarian from Munich with a huge handlebar moustache, and treated myself to a moisturising facial at the Clarins salon. The air was so dry that my skin felt like baked alligator and I spent a small fortune on oils and unguents designed to combat the desert. Then I was ready to follow my nose down the one road west.

The first three days took me over the Great Divide, up to Pentland and down the other side to Richmond. It was easy country, with gentle gradients and a rise of barely 550 m. The sparse eucalyptus trees, which dotted the first days of rough, open downland, gradually dwindled away until nothing was left but sere, yellow grass. Charters Towers is cattle country, but the stations are so vast and the cattle so dispersed that I saw little livestock from the road. Near Richmond, I moved into sheep country and saw the occasional flock.

What I did see in abundance was wildlife, and I saw it because I was on a bicycle. Cars are responsible for the highway massacre of thousands of kangaroos and wallabies, but the bush creatures are used to them and doze on unconcernedly as they roar past. By contrast, a slow, silent cyclist, who presents no threat at all, throws them into a panic. As I cycled along, herds of wallabies jumped up startled from the scrub and bounced away like terrified rubber balls. And trees would come alive, as great flocks of red and green parrots, grey and pink galahs or white cockatoos flew squawking into the sky. Sometimes I was followed by the sinister shadow of a bird of prey, tracking me off his territory. I saw more exotic creatures in one day in Australia than I had seen in three months up the Amazon.

I was still in rural Queensland, where I could count on finding a 'servo' for morning coffee and raisin toast. I would stop for half an hour's chat and listen to all the horror stories about the road ahead. At nights, I stayed in the one and only pub in town, where I got an old-fashioned single room, with bed, 1930s fireside chair and washbasin, and a substantial home-cooked 'counter tea'. Australia is no place for vegetarians. Steak and kidney pie, chops and king-sized steaks kept my protein level high.

I loved my evenings in the bar, listening to tall tales of deals done, gold discovered and head of cattle owned. Jan, who arrived in her little van, was a regular, a one-woman business delivering sweets and crisps to the Outback stores. Scotty was a roving signwriter, who played classical guitar. Paddy was an RAAF sergeant, marooned by a break-down. 'When I was in charge of training,' he told us, 'I wondered why they took on so many dickheads. Then I worked in recruitment and saw the dickheads we turned away. They were so thick, they needed interpreters!' An incense-trader entertained two Japanese buyers to a whisky-sozzled dinner. The landlord, Syd, had migrated from Newcastle at the age of 14 and Marlene came from Leeds. They had got their pub at a rock-bottom price, because the previous owners were splitting up and wanted to get out fast. They had built it up, doubled its value, got a purchaser and now they were looking for a homestead and a few acres to retire to. 'We could never have done so well for ourselves in the Old Country.' It was all very companionable. Strangers were embraced into the small communities and, though I was a woman in a masculine world, I was always made welcome. I even got a few proposals of marriage!

One evening, I eased myself onto a bar-stool for my well-earned meat-pie dinner. (Mother Kelly's Pies. Enough meat for a bull). 'I gather it's a public holiday tomorrow,' I said. 'What's it for?'

The landlord's eyes opened wide. 'What? You a Pom and don't know what the holiday's for! It's the Queen's Birthday.'

'You *are* lucky over here,' I said. 'We don't get a holiday for the Queen's Birthday.' I decided to stir it a bit. 'Just think what you'd miss if you went republican!'

That started them all off. The issue was debated with passion on both sides. 'Australia's future lies in this hemisphere, on the

Pacific rim. What does England do for us? We don't even have our own Commonwealth queue at Heathrow. You're either EEC or a foreigner. And what's the Queen of England got to do with all our Italians and Greeks? We're a mixed population now and an English Queen just isn't relevant any longer.'

'No. Be fair. I've got a lot of time for the Queen. She does a great job. But what's going to happen when she goes? That's the problem.'

'Well, better Charles than some self-seeking political nonentity. Fancy having a Keating for President! Just look at all the other presidents in the world. Can you tell me a single one who's any good? They're all fools or crooks. Give me a decent king or queen any day.'

Then they turned to the flag. If they went republican, should they keep the Southern Cross and get rid of the Union Jack in the corner? Or should they keep the Union Jack, as a part of Australia's history, and perhaps add the aboriginal flag in another corner? (That aroused violent feelings.) Or should they go for something completely different, perhaps in yellow and green, Australia's sporting colours?

'Yellow and green? That's a good Third World combination,' I said, to keep the pot boiling. The argument raged all evening and we had a splendid time.

The only other cyclist on the road was a Japanese. I first heard about him at the Torrens Creek 'servo' and when I arrived in Prairie, I found him camping in the pub garden. I waited for him to appear for his counter tea, so that I could have a chat with him, but he stayed in his tent. In Hughenden, I saw him from my hotel verandah. He was cycling through town in the midday heat, without a helmet or sunhat, and he didn't even stop to buy provisions. I finally caught up with him at the Maxwelton rest area, on the way to Julia Creek. It was a gravel enclosure, miles from anywhere, with a couple of tables under tin roofs, running water and a wonderfully clean lavatory block. He told me that he had been on an English course in Perth, flown to Townsville, bought a bicycle and a tent, and was on his first-ever cycling trip – to Darwin! He said that he had pitched his tent in the rest area at 2 o'clock the previous afternoon and I wondered what on earth he'd found to do since then in that desolate gravel yard. When I stopped to talk to him, he'd only just woken up and had not even begun to take down his tent. Some two hours later, I was overtaken by two skinheads in a battered van. They slowed down and cruised along beside me. 'There's another cyclist, a bloke, pedalling behind you down the road.' 'I know. He's Japanese,' I said. 'I was talking to him earlier.' Their faces were a picture of stunned respect. 'But you pulled ahead of him?' 'Yes,' I replied airily, basking in the unmerited glory. 'He was a bit too slow for me.'

I was told that lone Japanese cyclists outnumber all other nationalities on Australia's roads. They bomb along in the heat of the day, camp in their little tents and speak to no one. 'It's since they got rid of kamikaze. Cycling Australia's the next best thing. It's macho – a sort of samurai rite.'

There were stiff mountains, the Selwyn Range, and a stiff south-west wind between Cloncurry and Mt Isa. I stopped at the Burke and Mills Memorial, an obelisk to commemorate their expedition across the Australian continent in the 1860s. At a corner of the surrounding chain was a pathetic little bunch of dried flowers wrapped in cellophane 'In memory of Mark Barlow who was murdered near here. 4.3.93.' A little further on was another sad monument, to the Kalkadoon and Mitakoodi peoples. 'You who pass by are now entering the tribal lands of the Kalkadoon and Mitakoodi, dispossessed by the Europeans. Honour their name. Be brother and sister to their descendants.' It was a two-sided monument, one side for each tribe, with a poem and a picture of a broken boomerang. It was covered in graffiti and the painting of an aboriginal face was riddled with bullet-holes.

'Dorween on a bike!' said the caravanner, who stood beside me at the monument. 'You must be Hardway Harrigan.'

'Who's Hardway Harrigan?'

'You've not heard of Hardway Harrigan? When they said to Hardway Harrigan, "You've got two kids. How did you manage that?" he said, "Standing up in a rowing-boat."'

I stayed with friends of friends in Mt Isa, a zinc and copper magnet for sixty nationalities of drifting workers, where loneliness, alcoholism and domestic violence were rife. Lynn was helping to set up a Christian radio station, to try to draw the shifting, disparate population together into a community. The children had a modern, Australian alphabet poster on the wall: D for Dinosaur, K for Kangaroo, T for Television and V for Vegimite.

The next morning, I breakfasted at 6, while the family slept, filled my water bottles and crept out of the house. I was feeling apprehensive, as this was the start of the difficult bit. But I was better prepared for the Outback than for any other wilderness before or since. Queensland's RAC and the Northern Territory Government Tourist Bureau had supplied me with excellent maps showing every hotel, camp-site and filling station along the route. Rest areas were signalled with capital Rs: blue Rs for those with water and red Rs for those without. I came to rely on these maps absolutely. If they said there was water 117 km from Barkly Homestead, water there was. Sometimes the facilities had improved since the maps were printed. I found water at a red R; and an unmarked shop, newly opened to give employment to an Outback aboriginal settlement. But not once did I find the facilities less than the maps had promised. Lives depend on accurate information out there and the Australian tourist organisations are aware of their responsibilities. I also had my own personal trail-blazer. Margaret had cycled to Darwin the previous year and sent me her notes on the Red Centre, with all her camp-sites and finds of water. So, one way and another, I had a pretty good idea of what to expect, where.

Out of Mt Isa, I climbed up to the wind-swept Barkly Tableland, making for a water-tank on the edge of the Yelvertoft cattle station, where Margaret said she had camped for the night. There was not much traffic, but every driver throughout the day pulled up to ask if I had enough water. Towards evening, in a desolate stretch of bush, someone shouted, 'Ow ya going?' I looked around and saw no one. Then an apparition appeared out of the wattles. It was an old man in an Akubra bush hat with a fly-veil over his face. Near him stood a supermarket trolley full of old clothes, water bottles, cans of beer and plastic bags. 'There's water 10 kilometres up the road at Yelvertoft,' he said. 'I've just done my washing.' He pointed to a clothes-line of weatherbeaten garments hanging between two bushes. He was walking round Australia, pushing his trolley by day and sleeping in it at night. I told him I hoped he'd found a straighter trolley than the wild, careering objects I always seem to pick up in supermarkets!

The Yelvertoft homestead was out of reach, miles off the highway, but shortly after I turned up the station's dirt road, I found a Mt Isa Council depot, deserted for the weekend. I decided to hide myself away between the blocks of wooden cabins. The wind had strengthened during the afternoon and I needed all Margaret's tent-craft to fight with the flapping sheets. But it was civilised camping, for I found a white plastic table and chairs in a sheltered corner, where I could sit in comfort and write my notes. Then I dined on a tin of tuna in tomato and basil, which I made up into two rounds of wholemeal sandwich, a health food bar, nuts, raisins and dried apricots, an apple and four squares of chocolate. Who needs to fiddle with camp cooking? I even finished my excellent dinner with a mug of coffee. I'd filled a half-litre plastic bottle with black Nescafé in Lynn's kitchen and put it in the sun-side pannier. The sun had been so strong that I'd enjoyed nips of warm coffee throughout the day and it was still tepid in the evening.

At 6.30 it began to get dark, so I put on my long-sleeved silk vest and silk long johns, an extra jersey and an extra pair of socks and crawled into my tent. I was not very happy. As the site was busy all week, I hoped that cattle – and worse – had learned not to stray into it. I had visions of giant kangaroos leaping onto my little igloo by accident. I had just talked myself out of that fright, when a heavy vehicle arrived and switched off the ignition. Silence. Was it a lorry-driver pulling off the road for a rest? Or love-birds? Or someone much more sinister? I held my breath and waited. There were no footsteps. Then the engine started up again, but I didn't hear the truck move off. I lay anxiously alert to the throb of the motor in the stillness. But I was very tired and even if there was a murderer out there, there was nothing I could do about it. So eventually I pulled my sleeping-bag over my ears and fell into a fitful doze, waking with a start whenever the flysheet rustled in the wind, convinced it was wild animals or the mystery driver trying to invade my tent. The night grew colder. I put on my balaclava, wound a scarf round my feet and pulled on my cycling trousers, but there was a night frost and the ground froze under my mat. At 7.20 sunlight struck the tent and I crept stiff-limbed outside to eat a bun and drink a mug of icy coffee in the faint rays. I had got through my first night's camping.

The morning was bitterly cold, with a strong south-east wind, but luck was with me. Five minutes out of the Yelvertoft turning, a couple with a caravan pulled up and gave me a mug of hot tea. It was nectar! Later, another caravan stopped ahead of me and the man captured me on video as I battled against the wind. They'd heard about me in Cloncurry and had been looking out for me. After that, every other vehicle seemed to be towing a caravan. The retired couples of Australia were all out on the road, living the great Australian dream of 'going walkabout', of roaming the Outback in freedom. This was what they had worked for all their lives. They were amazed at my own 'walkabout', which was far more ambitious than theirs, but they understood it. They were great companions, ever ready with their offers of tea and coffee, and sometimes even lunch.

The country from Cloncurry to Yelvertoft had been surprisingly green, with abundant eucalyptus trees. After Yelvertoft, the real desert began – red, arid soil, broken only by giant termite mounds. It was a day for getting miles under the wheels. They were expecting me at the Post Office Hotel in Camooweal, as news travels quickly up the highway. I sank my frozen limbs gratefully into a hot bath, had a delicious dinner of freshly roasted chicken with Australian Chablis and retired early to my warm duvet.

Camooweal consisted of the hotel, a general store, a 'servo', a post office, a few houses and a half-finished community centre. The hotel manager gave me a good tip: he suggested I copy the tramps and use newspaper to keep out the cold. So I went to the general store for some back-copies of *Courier-Mail* and stocked up on dried fruit and biscuits. The food items in the store were selling at roughly twice city prices, which was not at all surprising, considering the distance they had to travel.

The hotel was three staff short and the manager told me it was virtually impossible to get help out there, even though he paid good wages. Everyone wanted to live on the coast. 'They'd rather be on the dole at the seaside than work for good money in Camooweal.' (I can't say I blamed them!) He'd recently recruited a living-in couple, but they'd had a major bust-up and the man had walked out on his girl friend. The girl had left three days later. Despite all their staffing problems, the manager and his wife provided me with a 6 a.m. breakfast of coffee and toast, and a good Aussie blow-out of bacon, eggs, steak and sausages for the four resident construction workers. It smelled delicious as it fried, but I resisted temptation. A heavy breakfast is a disaster for a cyclist with 130 km to cover.

That day I saw a group of wallabies poking their heads out of a patch of long grass to watch me cycle by, a huge flock of galahs, two scarlet-faced cranes, six horses, one herd of cattle and eight vehicles. There was an icy gale blowing straight from the Antarctic. Most of the time, it battered me from the side, fierce enough to unbalance me on long, slow inclines. But then the road would veer north and for a glorious stretch I would have the power of the wind behind me, propelling me forward at almost 30 kph. I reached Soudan Station in the late afternoon.

The homestead and farm buildings at Soudan stood beside the road. I made for the biggest house, where a girl who was hanging out her baby's washing told me I could pitch my tent on the lawn. I hoped to be offered a cup of tea, but none materialised. No one came out in the evening to see if I was all right, so I ate my solitary tuna sandwiches and crawled into my sleeping bag. I was disappointed with my reception, but at least the newspapers under my mat were a success. It was almost dawn before I began to feel the cold.

I was drinking my icy coffee with an Uncle Toby breakfast bar, muttering to myself about churlish, inhospitable behaviour, when an older woman emerged from a small house nearby. 'Could you manage some tea and toast?' Could I! She was the station caterer and she led me over to the restaurant cabin, apologising that she hadn't noticed me the night before, or I could have had my dinner there. She told me that the station manager was unmarried, so he took his meals with the men and let his stockman live in the big house. It was the stockman's clueless wife, Hayley, who had failed in her hostess duties, not the people in charge of the station. My belief in Australian hospitality was restored. Well fuelled with toast and marmalade, I braved the Antarctic gale, finishing the day with a stiff climb of almost 30 km up the Dalmore Downs. The normally smooth NT road had chosen that particular stretch to be uncharacteristically rough and I staggered into Barkly Homestead wind-buffeted and weary. I ignored the camp-site and treated myself to an expensive cabin in the Barkly Homestead Motel.

The next night I camped at a blue R, along with Australian caravanners and a charming young Swiss couple in a fifth-hand campervan. Monika was a qualified confectioner and Nicolas turned his hand to anything. The stars in the Outback were spectacular and Nicolas set up his camera on a tripod with a timing device, to photograph their progress through the night across a patch of the heavens. Though I'd climbed all day, the air was warm and I lay comfortably in my tent with my sleeping-bag unzipped, looking forward to my breakfast in the Swiss campervan. Perhaps life in a tent was not so bad after all!

By now, I had a good routine for the empty stretches. I cycled for 40 km in the early morning, while I was still fresh, then stopped for a chewy Uncle Toby health food bar and a good long drink. I'm not very fond of plain water and often drink less than I should. But in Australia I'd discovered powders for athletes, which restored the minerals lost through exertion, as well as having a clean citrus taste. After that longer break, I stopped regularly at 10 km intervals for a drink, a stretch and a small snack. I found that suited me better than a long lunch-break. There was always something to look forward too, just a little further down the road. Should I have chocolate next time? Or a coconut cookie? An apple? Or a few dried apricots? Loving my food as I do, the prospect of the next little treat was the spur which kept me pedalling when the wind was strong and the landscape featureless. The kilometre markers were plastic and too frail to take the weight of my loaded bicycle. I didn't want to lay it down and cover my panniers and camping gear in red dust, so I had to wait for the steel 10 km posts, which might or might not have a pool of shade nearby. An added incentive in the last days of the Barkly Tableland were the small green SH rhombi on the kilometre markers, showing the distance I still had to travel to reach the Stuart Highway. I watched the numbers diminish from three digits to two to one – and there, at last, was Three Ways with its beckoning motel and diner.

Once I reached the Stuart Highway, distances became manageable again, though the days were exhausting. Between Three Ways and Renner Springs I rode uphill for 100 of the 140 km into a gusting northeast wind. Then I sped down from the cooler Barkly Tableland into an inferno. The air was incandescent, the crackling bush so dry that I expected it to burst into flames when the wind shook the twigs. Charred stumps, the sad remains of forest fires, were the only vegetation in the red gravel wilderness. There was not a patch of shade to be found and I cursed the extra heat of my cycling-helmet, mandatory in Australia. Renner Springs – Elliott – Dunmarra – Daly Waters – Larrimah – Mataranka – Katherine – Pine Creek – each town had a pub or basic motel a day's ride from the last. Then on 17 August, I pedalled back into civilisation: there was a 'servo' between towns, where I enjoyed my first morning coffee and raisin toast for almost four weeks.

But I still couldn't pack away my tent. In Daly Waters, at the oldest pub in the Northern Territory, I ran into a 'Bush Bash', a charity rally across the Outback from Tindal to Tennant Creek. One hundred and twenty riotous contestants, all in fancy dress, had booked the pub's accommodation and the camping-ground beside it. I was swept along to the barbie of steak and barramundi, and treated liberally to jars of the amber nectar, while a folk group played their guitars and we sang late into the night. For once I enjoyed my camping. And I was happy too in my tent outside Darwin, where the rodeo season had filled the hotels. Camping in supervised camp-sites, with hospital-clean shower-blocks and decent restaurants, was a far cry from the eerie solitude of the Yelvertoft turn-off. I felt safe there and slept well, but even the comfort of balmy nights under the Southern Cross failed to make a camping convert of me!

The Australian Outback was different from any other desert. It was bigger than most, it was emptier, it was more accurately mapped, it was bright red and, although the area I covered was labelled on my maps 'semi desert', I could see little to distinguish it from the total deserts I'd crossed, either in aridity or extremes of temperature. What did distinguish it was the social life.

There was one tarmac road and everyone travelled along it. A car pulled up and a barefoot driver hopped out. 'How are you getting on with the tent?' It was Allan from the camping store in Townsville, on his way to the other branch. We arranged to meet for dinner in Darwin. Then a southbound car screeched to a halt: 'Do you remember us? We took film of you out near Mt Isa. How are you getting on? We've been up to Darwin and back since we met you. We thought we'd see you again.' They produced tea and sandwiches. Another car pulled up in the middle of nowhere. 'You're not Dervla Murphy, or Anne Mustoe, or one of those other famous cyclists, are you?' They invited me to stay with them in Adelaide. Then one morning I heard wild whoops of delight in the distance and two boys on bicycles came speeding towards me. A meeting with fellow-cyclists is always a joyful occasion, especially if they're coming from the opposite direction and can give you hard facts on the road and facilities ahead. These were two English undergraduates, doing a sponsored ride from Singapore to Sydney in aid of epilepsy research, so we spent a most useful half-hour swapping information on Indonesia for the low-down on the empty stretch between Three Ways and Mt Isa. After South America, where little English was spoken and every conversation was a struggle, it was such a joy in Australia to be talking freely to people in my own language. The road was one long party.

My spirits rose as I travelled away from the Red Centre. I felt

I'd cracked the Outback. But my success to date still didn't deter the Australian harbingers of doom.

'I'm over the worst now,' I said gaily to a caravanner over a welcome Coke from her fridge. 'The distances are getting shorter every day.'

'Yes, but it's much hotter. You'll have a terrible time towards Dorween. And wait till you meet the headwind!'

'I've had a lovely tailwind this morning.'

'That can change,' she said ominously. There was no convincing some people that Australia's climate was not the world's worst.

In fact, I decided that Australians were generally rather shy of optimism. The morning greeting was 'G'day. How yer doin'?' to which the reply was usually 'Not too bad'. No one was ever 'very well' or 'fine'. There was a strange fear of overstatement, of going over the top. It was a fiercely egalitarian society, where the gushing superlatives of upper class English would not have gone down at all well. Eloquence was mistrusted and I wondered if the roots of this went back to the very first settlers. They had come out as convicts, labourers, adventurers, people with no expectations, with no hope of ever seeing their homes again. Yet out of these dire circumstances, in this arid, inhospitable continent, they had built a prosperous and influential modern state, 'the lucky country'. They were proud to have climbed up from the bottom, succeeding against the odds. The old slums of Sydney had blossomed into the green gardens of suburbia and fortunes had been made in the mines and livestock stations. Yet grandeur was still unacceptable, 'tall poppies' were soon struck down and there was an endearing trace of self-mockery in their humour. Even their intonation was tentative. Statements were not made in a downright, positive manner; they ended on an interrogative note, as if the viewpoint being expressed was open to dissent.

All this was in startling contrast to the ethos of South America. There the *hidalgo* spirit flourished still. Everyone who could afford it dressed in style and cultivated the polished airs of a Spanish nobleman. They hoped, by their panache, to be taken for richer, grander men than they really were. In contrast,

Ross, one of my companions on a Cape York safari, had a 12-metre yacht and seven Jaguars in his garage, but wore a supermarket jumper and described his circumstances as 'comfortable'.

Admiration was allowed in only one sphere of life–sport, which in Australia is a national obsession. I've always hated organised games. Even now, I shudder when I think of the miserable hours I wasted on freezing school hockey-pitches. So it was something of a novelty to be hailed as a sporting heroine, a model of grit and athleticism, and treated to drinks in every bar in the land. I'm used to cycling through countries where the locals gape and take me for a harmless lunatic. In Australia, they understood and admired what I was doing – and it was wonderful!

7 Terrible Terrain II
The Gobi Desert

For lust of knowing what should not be known
We take the Golden Road to Samarkand.

James Elroy Flecker

There is a vast swathe of wilderness which sweeps across Central Asia from Mongolia. It starts as the Gobi Desert, turns into the Taklimakan (Tajik for 'Go in and you won't come out') and comes to a dead end, encircled by the foothills of the world's highest mountain ranges – the Himalayas, Karakorams, Pamirs and Heavenly Mountains, the Tian Shan. For much of the year, the wilderness is frozen, but in summer the Tarim Basin, at the northern end of the Taklimakan, is one of the hottest places on earth. There, the rivers of the Tian Shan dwindle into salt-flats and die in the sand and the people of the oases live in cellars to escape the burning heat. It is desolate, pitiless terrain, whipped by ferocious winds and, according to legend, haunted by demons.

In the great days of the Silk Road, it took the caravans at least five months to cross it. They began from Xi'an, the ancient capital of China, and wound their way through the Gansu Corridor, a narrow slip of relatively low land 1,200 km long, hemmed in by the Tibetan Plateau to the south and the wilds of Inner Mongolia to the north. At Jiayuguan, they left the safety of the Middle Kingdom and began their crossing of the Gobi Desert. The Silk Road forked near Anxi, because the Taklimakan is uncrossable and the caravans had to skirt it by the southern or northern route. The southern route was Marco Polo's choice, through Khotan and the Desert of Lop. The northern route continued across the Gobi to Turfan, then crept from oasis to oasis along the rim of the Tarim Basin. Both routes converged on Kashgar, the centre of the spider's web, from which roads radiated to carry the precious merchandise over the passes of the Tian Shan to the fabled Silk Road cities of Samarkand and Bokhara, or south over the Himalayas to India.

When I cycled the Silk Road in 1995, the southern route from Anxi was not really an option. Many of the ancient oases had dried up, the road was unsurfaced in stretches and it was uncomfortably close to the Chinese nuclear-testing sites in the Taklimakan. I decided to follow the northern route, which is now the Urumqi road, Highway 312, for 2,800 km, as far as the Turfan turn-off, then take what I hoped would be a tarmac B road for the remaining 1,500 km to Kashgar.

I was apprehensive about crossing China, as my Mandarin was limited and I had no idea what to expect. I had managed to find no accounts of cycling in the country and my two maps were at variance with each other. But setting out on a journey is always exciting and I cheered up considerably as I pedalled in the sunshine out of Xi'an, through a flat, verdant landscape full of spring blossoms.

The idyll ended near Lanzhou, an industrial city of three million people, where I could scarcely see the Yellow River for the pollution. Exhaust fumes and the noxious yellow and black outpourings from the factory chimneys were trapped in the narrowest part of the Gansu Corridor, and my face and clothes were soon covered in oily smudges and flecks of soot. Despite my smog-mask, I choked and gasped for breath. Sandwiched between the railway line and the spluttering trucks, I had to fight for every inch of space on the one congested road. It was a cyclist's nightmare and I learned the true meaning of 'Hell on wheels'.

Beyond Lanzhou, I stopped for the night at Hekou and had my first taste of the Central Asian wind. It started as a stiff breeze from the west and gathered strength so swiftly that within moments it was raging through its valley funnel in a tide of sand and litter. I watched with awe from my bedroom window as the poplars bent almost double and the railway line across the road disappeared completely in a cloud of flying dust. It was all over in two hours, but as a foretaste of things to come, it filled me with dismay. No one, however strong, could possibly cycle against such elemental frenzy – and it was going to be my adversary for the next 5,000 km.

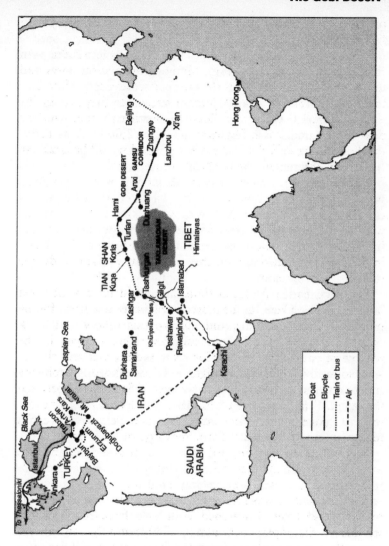

I thought my life would improve once I was clear of Gansu's Third World industry, but I hadn't reckoned on the mountains. I climbed the foothills of the Qilian Shan, through snow-sprinkled uplands where nomads in sheepskin cloaks ran to the

roadside, scattering their flocks, to get a better look at me.
Above them were serious mountain passes, not mentioned in
my maps. The wind raged and the sleet up there turned to
blizzard. I used my sunglasses as goggles to protect my eyes
from the sharp, blinding snow, and wore every garment I
possessed, even my smog-mask on top of my balaclava, yet I
still shuddered with cold. My hands were so frozen on my
handlebars that I was seriously afraid of frostbite and had to
keep stopping to stick them up the front of my anorak and
jumper, to bring them back to life. I have no idea of the altitude
of those passes. Lanzhou was already more than 1,500 m above
sea-level and since leaving the city, I had climbed steadily for
three days. I only know that I was gasping for breath; that even
the mountain streams were frozen; and April was far too early
in the year to be up on such summits on a bicycle.

Beyond Wuwei I began to see fragments of the Great Wall,
which now ran parallel with the highway as far as Jiayuguan.
They were scattered lumps of masonry and baked earth, not at
all like the restored, much-photographed section near Beijing.
Some bits had been incorporated into peasant houses and at one
petrol station in the middle of nowhere the enterprising owner
had reconstructed a Qin watch-tower as a restaurant.

I was still in the Gansu Corridor, so I was surprised to climb
up into desert, a desert of oversized shingle. The colours were
amazing. Red, blue, beige and off-white stones, worn smooth
by the elements, littered the sand. Most of them were round or
oval, ranging from pullet to ostrich eggs in size, while others
reminded me of nothing so much as bicycle saddles. It was a
spectacular landscape, completely empty, as if no one had ever
passed that way before. The only vital force was the cyclist's
enemy, the wind, which hurled clouds of sand into my face and
made every turn of the pedals an ordeal. Expressed in musical
terms, its underlying force was *ff*, with gusts of *fff* or even *ffff*.
On *ffff*, the bicycle would stand still and I had to jump off or
crash to the ground.

For the first two weeks, I struggled on, whatever the weather,
thinking the wind was constant. Then I began to understand it
better. Some days it was demonic; on others, the air was so still

that not a leaf stirred and the snows of the Qilian Shan were clearly visible, glittering in the pellucid light. It was madness to do battle with such a fickle element. So when I woke up to crashing doors, swirling sand and invisible mountains, I simply turned over and went back to sleep. There was no point in toiling for eight hours to cover 40 km, when I might well be able to cycle that distance in two hours the next day.

By Zhangye, I was over the worst of the mountains and spring had arrived. On calm days, I would cruise along in the dappled shade of the poplars, watching the players wield their cues round the roadside billiard-tables and stopping to sip cold fizzy drinks beside pavement fridges. There was little traffic. I overtook donkeys and oxcarts, their drivers enjoying a leisurely smoke on the way to the fields. And one day, on the outskirts of Jiuquan, I saw my first Silk Road camels. They were shaggy, dark brown creatures with two floppy humps, Bactrians from the steppes of Central Asia. Tough and woolly enough to withstand both the fire of the desert and the ice of China's mountain barriers, they were the patient beasts whose ancestors had made the silk trade possible. These descendants, I was pleased to see, were leading a more comfortable life, with a cheerful driver, a light load of fodder in their cart and a smooth road ahead. If camels ever enjoy anything, which I doubt, that Bactrian pair were enjoying their peaceful stroll in the morning sunshine.

But this pleasant leg of the journey came to an end on May Day, when I reached Jiayuguan, the traditional limit of Imperial China. It was the border where the civilisation of the Middle Kingdom ended and the Gobi Desert, with its howling demons and barbarian peoples began. The Fortress of Jiayuguan, 'The Greatest Pass under Heaven', stood at the end of the Great Wall, looking a little out of place among the factory chimneys on the outskirts of the modern city, but still surveying the vast sweep of the western deserts from its tall watch-towers. It was a fortress of ghosts, even on a bright May morning, the ghosts of disgraced officials and criminals, who were banished forever from China and sent out through the giant Gate of Conciliation into the wilderness. Even the Chinese merchants passed through that gate in fear and sadness, uncertain of their fate on the perilous desert-crossing. They would throw a pebble at the western wall. If it rebounded, they would return to their homes; if it dropped dead, they knew that they too would die in barbarian lands. Those redoubtable missionaries, Mildred Cable and Francesca French, passed through that gate at the turn of the century and wrote romantically: 'The scene was desolate beyond words, and if ever human sorrow has left an impress on the atmosphere of a place, it is surely at Jiayuguan. . . . The arched walls are covered with poems wrung from broken hearts.'

Despite all the gloomy literature on the subject, I felt elated as I spied out through slits in the bowmen's turrets. There was nothing before me to remind me of the present day, nothing to fetter the imagination. In my mind's eye, I could see the unending stream of camels laden with silk, spices and fine ceramics, winding out through the western gate bound for Samarkand, Palmyra and Rome. I could see the path they had trodden and I was eager to get on my two-wheeled beast of burden and follow in their hoof-prints. But first I had to make my preparations for the world's most notorious deserts.

It was not easy. Noodles are the staple food of northern China, so there was no bread to be found in the shops and I had learned to make do with packs of little sponge cakes, the only transportable carbohydrate. I ate sponge cakes for breakfast and sponge cakes at roadside stops. They were the dry, tasteless variety, which we put into trifles at home. Only hunger and plenty of water washed them down. There were apples in the market and I found some nuts and chocolate in a department store. The chocolate stuck to my tongue like wet tissue-paper, so it was the first and last bar I bought in China. There was no cheese, butter or milk, as the Chinese eat no dairy products whatsoever. All that is stuff for babies. It was a poor diet for a strenuous enterprise, so I started one of my courses of Pharmaton multi-vitamin tablets; my nails, usually so strong, were brittle for lack of calcium and I was tiring easily. As in Australia, I packed a 1 ½ litre Pepsi bottle of water into the rear pocket of each of my panniers. But in China I had to weigh down my handlebar-bag with extra water, as Cube came without a water-bottle and such exotic items were unobtainable in the shops. I couldn't even find a pump. I had to tour the pavement cycle-menders and motorcycle shops whenever I needed air. Sometimes they had a pump that fitted, sometimes they had an adaptor, and sometimes I had to cycle to the next town on flat tyres. I'm amazed that I got no punctures. In Jiayuguan I struck lucky. I spent half a day on it, but I did eventually get my tyres pumped up. Another half-day was spent groping through the mysteries of the Chinese banking system to change two traveller's cheques, and I was finally ready for the road.

Laden camels can travel between 30 and 40 km a day. In the great days of the Silk Road, they wound their way from one water source to the next and settlements grew up around the wells to service the caravans. Many of these settlements had crumbled into the sands as their water supplies had dwindled, but others had sustained their growth and become the powerful oasis cities of Central Asia. At my normal cycling distance of 80 km a day, I hoped to be able to move in double camel-legs, reaching alternate water-points for my overnight stops between cities.

When I set out through The Greatest Pass under Heaven into Cable and French's 'howling wilderness', my howling enemy, the wind, was for once on my tail. The dun battlements of the fortress gradually merged with the dun sand and I was out in the empty desert. The ride was fast and exhilarating, the landscape constantly changing. The small beige pebbles turned to shingle, then to charcoal-grey shale with tufts of camel thorn, then to red sand, then to gold, all in the space of a morning. I'd come to love the snowy peaks of the Qilian Shan and they kept me company, like watchful friends, on my left. On my right, there were lower brown hills and I passed through more small oases than I'd expected. Trains crept across the landscape, veering away from the road to rejoin it in little villages. It was a good sign when the distant carriages gained clarity and I could distinguish between goods and passenger trains. We converged on human habitations, none of them more than a few mud-brick houses and a level crossing, where a lonely man stood with his flag on an empty platform. Then desert again. The tarmac was excellent and I knew it was all too good to last. At midday, the wind began to change quarter and soon it was back in its normal direction, raging straight into my face from the north-west. The afternoon grew hot and I gave up the struggle at a *lüshe*, where my room with three beds, a television set and a mauve hat-stand with pink knobs cost me all of 35 pence.

One afternoon I passed the buried oasis city of Qiaowan and tramped over to inspect it. The ancient walls were still intact, though by now three-quarters covered in sand. I climbed the dune on the windward side and looked down on the desolation within. The size of two football-pitches, its well had dried up and its inhabitants gone. Even as I stood there, the wind was blowing fresh heaps of sand around my feet. In a few years' time, the sand would reach the battlements and trickle over the top. Qiaowan would become just another sand dune among many.

Outside Yumenchen a forlorn attempt at a desert paradise stood beside a reservoir in a bleak expanse of gravel. There was a weatherbeaten hoarding painted with trees, boats on a lake and a hilltop pagoda. Beside the hoarding stood a shuttered, tumbledown fish restaurant. Some bright entrepreneur in the New China had dreamed of success, but the trees had failed to take root and the customers had never arrived – which was hardly surprising in a society without cars. It was a puny effort, on which the Gobi had poured scorn. When the desert swallowed whole cities, how could a little fish restaurant hope to survive?

I usually enjoy deserts, but this one started to get me down. The Gobi was a sad place, even by desert standards, a place without life or hope. The sun was hot, but I rarely saw it through the flying dust, and the wind was so vicious it seemed almost malign. I grew tense and jumpy, and the hammering of my pulse kept me awake at nights.

Sometimes I had company in the evenings. Three mysterious ladies once paid me a social call. They walked in uninvited, got out their knitting and settled down in an industrious row on one of my beds. I made exhausting attempts to converse in Chinese for half an hour, and finally got rid of them by announcing that I was too tired to talk any more and needed to go to bed. They packed up their knitting with amiable smiles and left.

Another evening, at a bleak, windswept spot, where a track set off into the desert at a right angle – going heaven only knows where! – I took a room in the *lüshe* and crouched outside in the fading light trying to tighten my mudguards. Three young truck drivers, whose English consisted of 'Hello' and 'I love you' came across the yard and formed a rapt circle of spectators. They were joined by the waitress from the *lüshe* restaurant.

'May I come in?' she asked, followed by 'How should I address you?'(always a preoccupation with the correctly-behaved Chinese).

They all trooped behind me into my bedroom, followed by a fourth man, a jobbing builder who was doing some work on the *lüshe* wall. The waitress sat beside me on one bed and the four young men perched in a row on the bed opposite, like four chirpy birds on a branch. One of them wore a baseball cap and had a most engaging stammer; and they all dangled their jamjars of cold tea. I'd brought a bottle of beer over from the restaurant, but in the face of such shining innocence I didn't feel that I could decently make a start on it. When darkness fell, the proprietor arrived with a candle and a box of matches (there was no electricity) and he too joined the party. We got no further than ages, marriage, children and jobs, but we passed a merry evening together with lots of laughter, mostly at the expense of my Chinese. When we were running out of topics, I told them I was tired and they all got up immediately and disappeared, as good as gold.

I opened my bottle of beer and thought about my situation. Here I was, a woman alone in the middle of the Gobi Desert, in a locked compound surrounded by Chinese lorry drivers. Nobody knew where I was and there was no telephone. Yet I felt perfectly safe. Far from harming or robbing me, those delightful, gawky young men would have guarded me with their lives. Goodness is easy to recognise, whatever the structure and colour of its face.

It took me four days to reach Anxi, days of heat, headwinds and sparse rations. I was hungry most of the time. The *lüshes* had restaurants serving plain noodle and cabbage dinners, but they stood in isolation in the desert. There were no shops around where I could stock up on snacks, so I was soon down to black Nescafé and a handful of nuts for breakfast. I began to think longingly of sponge cakes!

I reached Anxi in one of the dust-storms for which the town is notorious. People were groping their way down the streets, wearing white face-masks against the swirling sand, and the market women were sporting white cotton hats, like the Ku Klux Klan. The once magnificent oasis city was a town of suffocating ghosts. I walked into my dormitory, the only type of accommodation in the town's one hotel, and my feet left prints in the crackling dust. Cleaning in the Gobi is a Sisyphean task; no sooner is the floor washed than the wind blows in more sand. Clothes feel gritty, hair stands stiff and skin is as dry and coarse as sandpaper. Yet the people never lose heart. The sober suits are endlessly cleaned and pressed and the dusters brandished with a will, though their use makes precious little difference.

I made a side-trip by bus to Dunhuang, to see the Mogao Caves, the Caves of a Hundred Buddhas – and to refresh myself with a couple of nights in tourist-standard hotels. Then back to the desert.

Between Anxi and the next oasis city, Hami, lay 400 km of empty terrain. My emergency life-line, the railway, ran far away from the road and there were few villages marked on the map. I'd consulted the CITS (China International Travel Service) office in Dunhuang, but the girls there had had no knowledge of the road. The men in the Workers' Travel Agency had been a bit less blank, so together we had mapped out my route. They had assured me that there would be *lüshes* along the way, but I suspected they were saying that because they knew it was what I wanted to hear. What they hadn't told me was that the road was up for at least half the distance – because I hadn't asked.

The Chinese are odd people and one of their greatest oddities is the way they answer questions. They aren't deliberately obstructive, though they often seem so, because they answer only the specific question asked and proffer no further information at all. So when I entered a town, the conversation would go something like this:

'Good afternoon. Is there a *binguan* (upmarket hotel) here?'
'No.'
'Is there a *fandian* (a more general term for a hotel)?'
'No.'
'Is there a *luguan* (a modest hotel catering for Chinese travellers)?'
'No.'
'Is there a *lüshe* (a country inn used mostly by lorry drivers)?'
'Yes.'
'Where is it?'
'You go east and it's on the north side of the road.'

When you're used to 'No. I'm afraid there isn't a hotel, but the pub in the high street has rooms – or you could try the bed and breakfast, second turning on the right,' the laborious catechism in a Chinese street at the end of a hard day's cycling could be extremely irritating.

As I hadn't asked if the road was up, I wasn't told. So when I pedalled out into the desert from the shade of Anxi's poplars, I had a nasty surprise. A new highway was being laid along a high embankment, to protect the road from flash floods, and the old road had already been torn up. Traffic was diverted across the sand, where the rare passing lorry churned up dense, choking clouds of dust. I soldiered on for 30 km. In some places, I could clamber up the embankment and cycle along a stretch of the new highway which had been levelled out, but not asphalted; sometimes I could use the tracks smoothed out by the contractors' lorries; and sometimes I had no choice but to follow the sweeping detours into the desert. It was hot, dusty work as the sun mounted the skies, but in a masochistic way, it was fun. Cube turned out to be excellent at roaring down sand dunes, builders' tips and the edges of embankments and once I'd found my nerve, these skidding swoops were tremendously exhilarating. I began to understand the excitement of real 'rough stuff' on a mountain bike. But there was not a scrap of shade and the morning heat soon became unbearable. I staggered into a workmen's camp and flopped down in the shade of a tipper-truck.

The inevitable spectators arrived, workmen glad of a diversion. 'The road's up for miles yet,' they said. 'Almost to Xingxingsia.' Xingxingsia was just about the halfway point on the map between Anxi and Hami, still 150 km away from where I was crouching in that patch of shade. 'Catch a bus!' said the workmen. 'You'll kill yourself if you try to get there on a bike.'

I knew that I shouldn't kill myself. If I cycled early and late, finding shade in the heat of the day (in my tent, failing anything darker), I should be able to cover the distance to Xingxingsia in three days. I had three litres of water and plenty of Anxi sponge cakes – and if I ran short, the labourers on the road would top me up. They might even feed and shelter me at night in their roadside camps. So I was not afraid to go on. But did I want to? It seemed rather pointless to punish myself so severely. I'd travelled once around the world, cycling every cycleable centimetre of the way. I'd done that. I'd risen to that particular challenge and had nothing left to prove, not even to myself. So why subject myself to three days' unnecessary hardship in the burning desert? I should just be squandering three days of my life. I ate a sponge cake, then pushed my bicycle across the sand to the detour. It amused me to think of my carefully planned route. The men in the Workers' Travel Agency had solemnly helped me to work it out, when they must have known quite well that the distances we planned were a physical impossibility, given the state of the road.

The first vehicle that came my way was a minibus. It was crammed to bursting. The driver got out and opened the back door to show me just how full it was, and three passengers fell out onto the road! Even a mouse would have had difficulty in finding a space in there. They were all apologetic and the driver checked anxiously on my water supply. As they drove off, leaving me standing alone in the desert, I could see their astonished faces peering at me through the rear window.

Nothing suitable came along for the next hour, but then I was in luck. A wheezing lorry with a cargo of glass for Hami came bumping over the rocks. The nice young driver and his mate roped Cube on top of the glass, found corners for my panniers and helped me into the cab. They had already picked up another passenger, so the poor mate had to crouch between the window-panes over 150 km of agonising bumps. I offered to take a turn in the back, but they wouldn't hear of it. We drove over the mountainous dunes of the Bei Shan, a tortured landscape, where the rocks were white, brown, red and grey in undulating strata no more than a metre thick. The perfect new highway began a short distance before Xingxingsia, but I rode on. I had made up my mind to go all the way to Hami in the truck. But when we pulled in at Xingxingsia, the driver's mate was vomiting from the heat and had cramp so badly that he had to be helped across the yard. He didn't complain, but I couldn't possibly subject him to more of the same torture. A room was free at the *lüshe* and I announced that I would spend the night there, to everyone's evident relief. The morning ended with a noodle lunch. The driver had refused my offer of money for the lift, so I slipped discreetly over to the cash-desk to pay for lunch, only to find that the driver had settled everyone's bill in advance, including mine. It was a matter of pride for him and though I knew that I was rich beyond the dreams of avarice, compared with a young Chinese lorry-driver, there was nothing I could do but accept his generosity. He wouldn't even take a Marlboro cigarette, the favourite brand and a rare imported treat in China.

Xingxingsia marks the border between Gansu Province and Xinjiang, an area which is three times the size of France and occupies one-sixth of all Chinese territory. Xinjiang has been fought over for millennia by Chinese, Turks, Huns, Mongols and Tibetans, all of whom have left their descendants there. Its thirteen nationalities are now held together in an uneasy alliance by their resentment of their Chinese overlords. Traditionally, the region has been a buffer-zone between the Han Chinese and the turbulent peoples of Central Asia. It is rich in minerals, including oil, and far enough away from the Chinese heartland to make it a convenient testing-ground for nuclear weapons. It is desolate country, China's Siberia, feared and hated by the Chinese who are posted there. But it obviously has its uses.

The *lüshe* at Xingxingsia stood alone in a barren gorge. There was no running water and the toilet facilities were the desert, which I much preferred to a stinking trench with planks across it. Electricity was provided by a generator. The notices were in Uigur as well as Chinese, the elegant Persian script curving sinuously under the chunky Mandarin ideograms; and every room had a picture of a forest glade, with emerald green grass beneath the summer leaves. They must dream of trees and shade out in that wilderness.

After a broken, rat-infested night, I was ready for an early start. I was outside in the yard attaching my panniers, when a lorry-driver came over. He was in charge of a convoy of six trucks on its way to Hami and one of them was empty, so he could easily take me there. His team came up and reinforced the invitation. I thanked them all, but said that I wanted to cycle to Hami. The great iron gates were locked and it was some time before the proprietor's wife emerged. She was immediately surrounded by six worried lorry-drivers. I asked her to open the gate for me and she refused.

'The drivers will take you to Hami,' she beamed. 'I've arranged it all. Come and have some breakfast.'

'I want to go on my bicycle.'

Like everyone else in China, she failed to understand how I could choose to cycle when a lift was available. Then she had what she thought was a flash of illumination.

'It's quite safe to go with them, you know. They're lovely boys. They've been coming here every week for months now. They're like my own sons. You don't need to worry at all. You can trust them one hundred per cent.' The drivers smiled encouragingly.

'I'm sure they're good boys and I'm very grateful to them for their kind offer. But I still want to ride my bicycle.'

The woman called her husband, who came to add weight to her argument, along with the chef and the waitress. The ten of them surrounded me, all shouting and gesticulating. It was so like a scene from a comic opera that I should have laughed aloud, had I not felt so frustrated. At last, they agreed to open the gates and at 7.30 I pedalled away from Xingxingsia, leaving a disconsolate group waving me down the road.

I was so glad to have persevered, as it turned out to be a perfect morning for cycling, overcast, with a furious tail-wind. I sped along the newly laid road, sometimes reaching 40 kph, even on the flat. The jagged black fangs of the Bei Shan were soon succeeded by level desert with the occasional dune to climb. It was at the bottom of one of these dunes that the convoy caught up with me. They must have had a leisurely breakfast, because I was already 70 km down the road. All six of them got out of their cabs and again urged me to ride with them to Hami. I made the only Chinese joke I ever managed. I told them that they had their *Dong Feng* (East Wind), the most common make of lorry, and I had mine, pointing to the heavens and the wind billowing in my anorak sleeves. They watched me in puzzlement as I sped off down the road, then waited craftily until I was halfway up the next long climb. 'Now do you want a lift?' they crowed, confident that the hill would have changed my mind. But I waved them off and the convoy steamed ahead.

I was feeling in good form myself, but by mid-afternoon Cube was less happy. Both wheels were catching badly. Tightening the nuts on the mudguards did nothing to help and I decided that the problem lay with the spokes or the brakes, a repair which needed a mechanic. The wind had swung round to the north-west and the one *lüshe* I passed looked as if it might well be another rat-house, so I thumbed a lift into Hami. I had completed most of that leg under my own steam and honour was satisfied.

Hami was a delight, though it was too early in the year to savour the melons which are famous throughout Asia. It was a green oasis with vine-covered porches and the scent of roses in the air. Sentries and traffic police did duty under striped parasols, shopkeepers played *mah jong* or chess outside in the sun and there was colour everywhere. The people were mostly Uigurs with Caucasian features, a Turkic language and a passion for fancy clothes. I sipped iced drinks at the pavement cafés and watched them all go by. A portly woman in a silver lamé robe and purple georgette headscarf rode in a donkey-cart behind her husband in his brightly embroidered Muslim cap. A young mother in a lilac suit and shocking pink headscarf rode past on her bicycle, with her little daughter in pink flounces and lilac socks perched on the rear carrier. Gaudily dressed families rattled by under coloured awnings, drawn by brightly caparisoned horses. One woman carried the first pet dog I had seen in China, a small Pekinese, and even he had his hair dyed pink! I saw women's legs for the first time in weeks; the Hans in their drab trouser-suits were now in the minority. Middle Eastern pop music, flat bread, kebabs, arrays of sticky sweets and cakes and a thoroughly relaxed life style transported me nearer home. It was like being in the Turkey that I knew and loved.

One day out of Hami and I had my first difference of opinion with the Public Security Bureau. I cycled into San Dao Ling, which was not to be seen on the map, in torrential rain and a wild wind, and left ignominiously the next morning, bundled off on the Turfan bus by the local police. The storm was over, but a weird sand-mist veiled the landscape and the road was full of potholes. I watched from the window as the Gobi became the Taklimakan and was secretly rather glad of my easy passage to Turfan.

Turfan was a city of grapes, where even the pavements and cycle-paths were shaded by overarching trellises of vines (fine for picking the grapes: 15 yuan). It was all so green, yet in the height of summer, it's said to be the hottest place on earth. It lies 100 m below sea-level and its temperature can rise to 50°C. The oasis flourishes, not on rain, but on an ingenious system of underground water channels, called *karez*, which are fed by distant glaciers. I stayed in the Tulufan Binguan, my best hotel for a long time, and spent my evenings at the Uigur dancing displays in the beer-garden. After these spirited, colourful performances, it was the turn of the sober-suited Chinese. I escaped to my bedroom when the ballroom music began, in case I was asked to join in, and looked down in fascination on the silent, unsmiling, straight-backed couples, executing their perfect foxtrots and cha-cha-chas. Western ballroom dancing was much in vogue.

I did a tour of the Bezeklik Caves and the foothills of the Flaming Mountains, sharing a taxi with a Basque television producer and a tall, scholarly Parisian. There was so much dust in the air that we could scarcely see the landscape and the driver ran out of petrol half-way down a gorge. We had to go on foot to the Buddhist Caves, while he walked back into town with his petrol-can. In a restaurant that night, I bumped into a group of Americans, who had heard my talk on the Silk Road at the British Embassy in Beijing. Turfan was a cosmopolitan town, full of foreign tourists, where it had once been full of foreign traders. I felt cosmopolitan too, in my Japanese trainers, New York socks, Indian trousers, Peruvian shirt, Russian watch and Abu Dhabi necklace – all picked up on my travels.

Although I was unaware of it at the time, I had only four days' cycling left in China. I rode through the green Turfan oasis to Toksan, where I dined on the local speciality, noodles soaked in reed water. They were browner and more glutinous than usual, but they tasted as dull as ever. I washed them down with plenty of beer, served by a cook with a bottle of spirits in her apron pocket, from which she took regular swigs. The Uigurs may be Muslims, but they are certainly not orthodox!

After Toksan, the road turned south towards the Taklimakan Desert. I climbed a long, slow gradient out of the oasis up to a wide plain. The ground looked like grey gravel, but when I examined it more closely, I saw it was a mingling of red, white, grey and black grit. Clouds of flying dust veiled the mountains, so I was almost on the Kuruktag before I saw them. They seemed an impregnable range. The road wound into a gulley beside a sliver of stream, which it followed uphill to the source. Beyond was bare rock, with mountain peaks towering above me. It was hot and too steep to cycle. As the day wore on, I lost the shade and got really ratty at the truck drivers, who persisted in tooting their horns at me – as if I couldn't hear their overloaded, ill-maintained leviathans grunting up the mountain behind me! I plodded past a road-worker sitting on the edge of a precipice. A minibus had hurtled over the edge and lay shattered in the chasm below, with a neat row of bodies beside it. The road-worker asked me to take his photograph, posing on the edge with the mangled minibus and corpses in the background. He smiled hugely.

I was almost at the top of the climb before I realised that I must be in the notorious Dry Ditch Gulley, the mountain pass most feared by lorry drivers. They climb it in convoy, with tow-ropes, spare parts and extra mechanics. Needless to say, the tourist office in Turfan hadn't warned me of it – because I hadn't asked if it was there!

The summit was 60 km from Toksan. As I hadn't known that I was heading for Dry Ditch Gulley, I was carrying only half a litre of water and there was none to be found up the mountain. I reached the top, parched and footsore, and a lorry-driver revived me with *kaishue*, the hot water that every Chinaman carries. I wheeled down into Kümüx just after sunset and drank three Jianlibau soft drinks straight off in the first shop I came to.

Kümüx was a poor town, little more than a row of primitive noodle-stalls along the highway. The *lüshe* behind the shop was a row of brick-floored kennels, but the bed was clean (how do they manage it in that grimy landscape?) and the owner kept coming in with bowls of hot water until I was reasonably dust-free. There was no running water; the lavatory for the town's men lay behind one sand dune, while the ladies disappeared behind another. I was too tired to eat a normal meal, so they brought me a bowl of soup with noodles in it, and I managed to talk them into a fried egg to follow. I drank a bottle of beer and basked in the admiration of the lorry-drivers. 'You got through Dry Ditch Gulley on a bicycle?!' They couldn't believe it.

Despite my vitamin pills, the poor diet and gruelling cycling were beginning to get me down. I woke the next morning with a headache, a strained leg, a blistered heel, a painful stye and the prickling start of a lip-sore – none of them serious ailments in themselves, but in combination they were enough to make me feel thoroughly miserable. I needed a couple of days' rest out of the sun, but two more days in my dog-kennel at Kümüx were not to be contemplated. I had to move on. Then I discovered the slow puncture in my back tyre. That was the last straw and I caved in. I accepted a lift in a hot, noisy lorry (which didn't help my headache) into Yanqi, the next town with a proper hotel.

When I was over my stye, I cycled to Korla along the edge of the Bositeng Lake, where men in straw hats were fishing and there were even a few gulls and hoopoes. It was a lake of reeds, where people lived in reed houses, cut and stacked the reeds into roadside bundles and wove them into screens. For once, it was a morning without wind, overcast and perfect for cycling. It was one of the rare mornings in China when the weasel voices weren't whispering: 'What are you doing this for? Why are you punishing yourself like this? You could be sitting comfortably at home.' But my pleasure was short-lived. That was the day I was detained by the Korla PSB and forbidden to cycle again within China.

Korla – Kuqa – Aksu – Kashgar. Three long, excruciating days on crowded buses, with Cube roped upright to the roof-rack to give him a better view. Outside Korla we ran into roadworks on the new raised highway and took a hair-raising cross-country detour over ditches and ramps, culminating in a sharp right-angled turn at the top of a steep ramp down to a narrow stone bridge without sides. The bus reversed twice to take the corner, then teetered unsteadily on the edge before diving down to the canal below. The Uigurs were crying '*Allah! Allah!*' and had I been a Catholic, I would certainly have been crossing myself. But we made it over the bridge.

At first, the Tarim Basin looked to be an improvement on the Gobi. It was flat as a pancake, with marshland, shrubs and even patches of green pasture. I knew we were travelling just south of the Heavenly Mountains, the Tian Shan, but I couldn't see them for the fog of desert sand. I was crammed in over a wheel, clutching three bags, while my two panniers obstructed the gangway. The young Uigur beside me chain-smoked and spat regularly on the floor, so that his feet were in a pool of spittle by lunch-time. I was glad of the wheel, which kept my own feet above spit-level. Between cigarettes, he slept, leaning heavily on my shoulder. The windows were opaque with dust and many were broken, yet the Uigur women were happy in their finery – red nylon tutus, gold-embossed brocade gowns, gaudy taffeta skirts and red nylon tights with fancy clocking, all worn incongruously over heavy winter long johns. They teased the bus conductor, who responded in kind and kept the women in fits of laughter. The men were more sombre in their dreary suits, though their fur hats and silver embroidered skullcaps gave a bit of variety. Little boys were miniature men in drab suits and oversized flat caps, worn at a jaunty angle, but little girls were as frilled and tinselled as Christmas Tree fairies. I was taken for a Russian.

The worst stretch was the fourteen hours from Aksu to Kashgar. The desert was horrendous, so arid that even the camel thorn refused to grow, and there were great stretches of roadworks, which sent us bumping over the sand. Despite my pleas that there were fragile things inside it, a card-player sat in the aisle on one of my panniers throughout the journey. (He burst a large plastic bottle of sun lotion, ruining maps and books and giving me a terrible time with laundry in Kashgar.) Babies and young children wore split knickers and were held out over the floor, so the bus was soon awash with urine, spit and nutshells. Everyone stared at me. The Uigurs are kind people and very picturesque, but at close quarters their manners are far from polished. I began to look longingly at the bare red rocks and the clouds of driving sand. Anything, even cycling in the Taklimakan, would be better than fourteen hours on that bus!

Kashgar was the end of the desert, its lovely oasis and good hotels the reward for discomfort. I nursed a cold there and contemplated the Gobi and the Taklimakan. Deserts are always a challenge. Some, like the Nevada Desert, are breathtakingly beautiful; others, like the Australian Red Centre, are sociable. I would cycle those deserts again tomorrow. But you would have to pay me a fortune to get me back to the deserts of China.

First of all, there was the wind. Wind is the cyclist's chief enemy. It usually blows against – and even if it starts out as a tail-wind, it soon realises that there's a cyclist out there on the road and changes quarter. This phenomenon has been described in an Australian cycling magazine as BDOH (bi-directional opposing headwind): a 15-knot gale, for example, which blows in the face both on the ride out and on the ride home. Wind is always somehow unfair. Mountains appear on maps. Their marked contours predict the difficulty of the ride and the cyclist knows in advance that a hard day's work lies ahead and prepares for it mentally. But winds are sneaky. They brew up on smooth, flat roads and what should have been a gentle afternoon cruise turns into a battle of Titans.

On long hauls, I always seem to choose the wrong direction. I cycled north up the coast of Brazil, when the prevailing wind was blowing south from the Equator; in Peru I cycled south, into the north-bound Pacific wind; then I followed the Silk Road out of China, when the Gobi gales blow into China from Central Asia. I thought my life would be easier once I'd turned the corner into the Taklimakan and started to cycle south-west, instead of north-west, but the wind turned the corner too, and it still flung the sand in my teeth. The Gobi wind was relentless and my nerves were worn to shreds. Add to the violence of the wind the bitter cold, the blizzards, the burning heat and the sudden rain-storms, and you have the worst climate that human beings choose to inhabit. Siberia might be marginally worse, but its residents are usually selected!

I found two maps of China in Stanfords. One was the usually reliable Nelles Verlag, but it covered only the Gansu Corridor. The other was a Hildebrand, which tried to map the whole of China, with inevitable inaccuracies. I had plenty of nasty surprises – high mountain passes, and in one case a whole mountain range, which appeared on neither map. Towns were marked which no longer existed, or were no more than tiny shopless villages when I got there. On the bonus side, the odd town loomed out of the dust when the map showed a blank stretch of road.

It was no use applying to the tourist offices for help. They were invariably managed by the son or nephew of a local *cadre*, who had landed the job through influence, not because he knew anything about tourism or could speak any foreign language. He was usually assisted by a bevy of jolly girls, who spoke English. But in a country without cars, few of them had any knowledge of the roads outside their own town. The offices were dingy and empty of tourists. In Kuqa, the staff were all so under-employed that I found the girls in mud-packs, with slices of cucumber over their eyes! 'To keep us beautiful,' they explained. The one thing these offices could do, which was a great help, was write in the names of the next few towns and villages on my map in Chinese ideograms, beside the names in Latin script. I could then show the map to people in the street, if I needed to ask the way, and point to the place I was aiming for. Outside Beijing and Xi'an, there were no roadsigns in Pinyin, so I had to try to memorise the Chinese characters. I would cycle up to an intersection looking for a sign like a house without a roof beside a fancy bar-stool with splayed legs. It was all very hit and miss and the terrain ahead was often a mystery. How I longed for the clear English, the accurate maps and the shiny red patrol-cars of the Queensland RAC.

Traffic on the one road across the desert consisted of Dong Feng trucks, with the occasional bus, jeep or official car. No one rode bicycles outside town centres. The British Embassy had warned me that northwest China was still 'pirate country', outside the control of Beijing, and it was clear that the historic Silk Road was today's Contraband Road, running heroin into China from Central Asia in return for Chinese liquor (bound for the Muslim states where it was banned) and cheap electronic goods. But far from being bloodthirsty pirates themselves, the lorry-drivers were unfailingly kind and I never felt in any personal danger. Communication was my real problem and I grew weary of the effort of making myself understood and even more weary of being an object of amusement. For once in my life, I felt very, very lonely – and that was a greater burden than the wind.

Two days after I arrived in Kashgar, I cycled along to the Kashgar International Hotel to book my ticket to Tashkurgan. In the car park was a heavy 4WD truck full of camping gear and bicycles, which a young American in neatly pressed jeans was unloading. I pushed my bicycle across.

'You look as if you've been on a really serious expedition,' I said.

'You can say that again! Ten of us have just cycled across the desert from Ürümqi. This is our support vehicle. Mr Wong here was our interpreter. He travelled with us.' He introduced an English-speaker from CITS.

'I've just done that.'

'What?'

'Cycled across the desert. From Xi'an.'

'Not on your own?'

'Yes.'

There was a long pause.

'I'm impressed,' said the awestruck American.

I strolled nonchalantly out of the car park, as if I cycled the Gobi Desert every day of my life. It was one of those rare occasions when a little conceit seemed justified.

Setting out from home

The Via Domitia crosses the Orb at Béziers

Silk Road transport

The Fortress of Jiayuguan looks out across the Gobi desert

Left My kind Tajik
hosts in Dabdar

Below The
Khunjerab Pass, at
4,733 metres
(15,518 feet), the
highest paved road
in the world

Left Putting up my tent in the Outback

Below Road signs in Australia are different!

Left I arrive in Darwin

Below Puncture repair in Java

Above Condor
being carried off a
ferry boat in
Sergipe

Right The statue
of Pizarro, the
conqueror of the
Incas, in Lima

Above Mummies in the Chauchilla desert outside Nazca

Left Me and a moai, Easter Island

Left and above Karakoram land-slide notices

Below The Palace of Ishak Pasa at Doğubayazit guards the Silk Road as it crosses from Iran into Turkey

8 Terrible Terrain III
The Khūnjerāb Pass

An excursion for the ladies.

Sir Aurel Stein

When I set out from St Paul's Cathedral on my first journey round the world, I was so bad at hills that I even had to push my bicycle up Cannon Street to get to London Bridge! On the roller-coaster hills of the Pas de Calais I almost abandoned the trip in exhaustion and despair; and I walked all the way up the Alps. A year later, I was such an energetic and experienced cyclist that I sailed over the Rockies, all 3,132 m of the Cameron Pass, without once having to get off and push.

Since then, I've cycled over many mountain ranges – the Pyrenees and the Spanish Sierras, the watershed of the Andes, the Western Ghats and some fearsome passes in China's Qilian and Tien Shan. But my greatest vertical challenge has been the Khūnjerāb Pass across the Roof of the World, between China and Pakistan. Rising to 4,733 m (15,528 feet), almost the altitude of the summit of Mont Blanc, it is the highest point of the highest paved road in the world. Even to have climbed it in a bus is a feat to be crowed over in the travel columns of Saturday's *Times*.

Khūnjerāb means 'Blood Valley' in the language of the Tajik nomads. It may have got that name because so many Silk Road caravans were ambushed and massacred up there; or it may simply be that nose-bleeds are common in the rarefied air and pack-animals were traditionally spiked in the muzzle until the blood flowed, to help them breathe more easily. The road is no longer spattered with blood, though four hundred Chinese and Pakistani lives were lost in the construction of the Karakoram Highway. It crosses a turbulent zone, where the young mountains are still in motion, and the traveller has to contend with rockfalls, mudslides and avalanches as well as climatic extremes.

In Kashgar, as I was preparing to climb the Pass, I caught a cold. It was a bad one, which streamed for four days, then turned to catarrh. I knew that I should never be able to cycle at 4,733 m with a cold. It was going to be difficult to get enough oxygen up there, without the extra handicap of a blocked nose, so I had to kick my heels in Kashgar for a fortnight, waiting for my breathing to clear.

The delay was in fact providential, as Kashgar was already 1,340 m above sea-level and my cold gave me time to get really comfortable at that altitude before I had to climb higher. And there are worse places to kick your heels in than Kashgar, the legendary 'listening post' of Central Asia. In the days of the Great Game, the British Consul-General, Sir George Macartney, spied on Russia from one end of the town, while his rival, Nikolai Petrovsky, spied on Britain from the other. In the end, neither of them won, as it was the Chinese who tightened their grip on Xinjiang while the European powers were occupied with the First World War and the Russian Revolution. Now the Chini Bagh, the Macartneys' old home, is in the grounds of the Kashgar International Hotel and Lady Macartney's famous garden has been uprooted to make room for this gleaming monstrosity. I stayed in the Seman Hotel, which incorporates Petrovsky's old Consulate.

Kashgar is still a 'listening post', but not for political power games. Travellers gather under the striped umbrellas at John's Café and swap information over ice-cold beers – how to evade the PSB and get into off-limits Tibet; how to fool the border-guards on the road to Samarkand; where to buy horses for an expedition to Lake Karakul; how to bribe your way out of prison in Tashkent. John's was a serious adventurers' club, to which my arrest by the Chinese Police in Korla gave me undisputed entry.

As the Korla Police had banned me from cycling until I reached the Chinese border at Tashkurgan, Cube was roped to the rack on top of the daily bus for Pakistani traders. It joined their amazing quantities of Chinese tea-sets, electric toasters, irons and thermos flasks, those cheap domestic items for which there seemed to be an insatiable demand in the bazaars of Hunza and Gilgit.

I boarded the bus with Jim, an American history professor from the University of Savannah, who had travelled by train across Russia to reach Kashgar and was now bound for Rawalpindi. He was a quietly colourful character, who had been on a year's exchange at a Chinese university at the time of the Tiananmen Square riots and had spent 48 hours in an Uzbek prison for nothing more serious than a visa irregularity. We managed somehow to squeeze ourselves in between a consignment of ironing-boards and a pile of Chinese carpets, and the overloaded 11 a.m. coach finally coughed its way out of the Customs yard at 1.30.

'The Chinese are crazy,' said the Pakistanis. 'Too many employees. They talk all day instead of getting on with the job.'

They beamed at us, full of fellow-feeling: we were all Indo-Europeans struggling together against the inefficiencies of outlandish foreigners. They passed round nuts and sunflower seeds and dropped all the shells on the floor. But at least they didn't spit on our feet, which was a welcome relief after my other bus journeys in China.

We drove through the Kashgar oasis, luxuriant with rice paddies, olive groves, apricot orchards and fields of ripening wheat. Then a stretch of desert, a small oasis and finally a perilous climb up the gorge of the Ghez River. The road had been washed away in places by flash floods and we had to get out and walk, while the driver inched the bus precariously across streams and boulders. At sunset, we came through a jumble of red, cream, black and grey rocks to a lake shimmering beneath a white powder mountain. With cries of 'Allah! Allah!' the Pakistanis rushed down to wash in the lake and say their evening prayers. I sat in the bus with mixed feelings. My bicycle would have felt much steadier on the road, but it was an eerie, desolate moonscape and I was secretly rather glad that I didn't have to cycle it.

We continued climbing to 3,350 m, then emerged from a narrow gorge onto the vast, windswept plateau of the Pamir (Tajik for pastureland). It seemed to stretch to infinity under a wild sky. Streams which wandered aimlessly before losing their way and subsiding into marshland, provided rich green summer pasture for greater flocks of sheep and goats than I had ever seen in my life before. Their shepherds were Kirghiz nomads in fur hats, mounted on horses and camels.

Our overnight stop was Tashkurgan. There was a dormitory at the bus station, but Jim and I set off into town to look for greater comfort. We found it in a new hotel, which had beautiful bathrooms with gleaming showers, washbasins and lavatories, but no running water. The menu at dinner began with: 'Drinks. Travelling to Pakistan? Enjoy now!' We did. We enjoyed three large bottles of beer between us, which was probably a mistake at that altitude, because I woke in the night with a headache and Jim started the next day feeling distinctly queasy.

Tashkurgan (Tajik for Stone Tower) was mentioned by Ptolemy in the second century AD as the westernmost trading-post of the Land of the Seres (Silk People). At Tashkurgan, the Chinese traders on the Silk Road sold their wares to the Indian and Central Asian merchants who would carry them over the Karakorams into India or across Afghanistan into Persia, before trading them on to Syrians and Greeks for the final leg to the Mediterranean. Except for the brief period of the Pax Mongolica (AD 1260–1368), when Marco Polo could travel across the whole of Asia under the protection of a single power, it was never politically possible for the same merchants to carry their wares from one end of the Silk Road to the other. The Tashkurgan where we spent the night might or might not have been Ptolemy's Tashkurgan, but it was certainly the final trading-post in modern China. The Pakistanis were up at first light, rushing round doing last-minute deals. They had seen the driver unloading Cube and that left room on the top for a few more tea-sets!

I got to the Customs-post early, anxious to be on my way, only to find that it didn't open until 10.30. I joined the queue of fuming Pakistani jeep-drivers. 'This is China!' said a portly young trader from Gilgit, his lips curled in disgust under his neat little moustache. 'What a country! Hopeless!' When the Customs officials finally arrived, they took their time over emptying their briefcases, arranging their files and changing the dates on their rubber stamps – the power ploys of petty officials the world over. The trader from Gilgit was evidently a regular, as he pulled me to the front of the queue and introduced me to the Chinese officials as his friend. We were dealt with first. My passport was handed back after a cursory glance and I was free to cycle away.

I had wasted the best three hours of the morning hanging around in the Customs-shed, and I was worried. There was nothing marked on my maps after Tashkurgan, not even the tiniest dot of a village. The thin yellow road wriggled up beside the Tashkurgan River through the Pamir, across the dotted line of the Pakistan border at the Khūnjerāb Pass, then fell down the Karakorams in a frenzied corkscrew to Sust, the Pakistani village round their Customs-post. The entire area was coloured in palest grey, with a concatenation of white stripes for ridges and a few marked peaks. Even during the brief summer, when the Tajiks grazed their flocks on the high pastures, they were sometimes buried in snow. It was going to be a hard, cold ride, which would probably take me three days – and I was late starting.

I tried to pedal fast, to make up time, but at that altitude I got so out of breath that I had to settle for a steady 12 km an hour. My friend from Gilgit shouted, 'See you in Gulmit, at the Marco Polo!' as he roared past in a cloud of dust. He was followed in convoy by the other Pakistani traders in jeeps and last of all by my bus, two hours later. Everyone waved to me out of the windows, all of them grinning hugely except Jim, who looked profoundly anxious. After that, there was nothing and nobody.

I wondered where I should spend my nights. I hate camping, even in a warm climate, and I'm never happy for long outside a town. My idea of a good day's cycling is a quick ride across country to the next habitation, where I can find a comfortable hotel with a hot bath and a warm bed. As for camp cooking, crouching under a tent-flap over a Primus stove and a mess of dehydrated chilli con carne, I'd rather exist on bread and water! I was carrying my small tent and a supply of Chinese sponge cakes, nuts and dried fruit, in case of emergency, but I was hoping against hope that I wouldn't have to subsist out there under canvas in sub-zero temperatures. There must be some alternative.

For the first night, my hopes centred on Dabdar. It was described on the sketch-map in my *Lonely Planet* guide as 'the largest permanent Tajik settlement along the highway'. With any luck, I might find a basic inn there, one of the *lüshes* I'd used throughout the Gobi.

The Pamir rose gently, dominated by the snowy flank of Muztagh Ata, 'Father of Ice Mountains'. There was just one steep climb, so I managed to reach the settlement in the late afternoon. I had passed only two people all day, an old man in a tall fur hat, belted greatcoat and high boots and a boy in a Chairman Mao cap and crumpled grey suit, with a goat on a string. They were standing in the road in the middle of nowhere, deep in conversation. '*Wasalaam aleikum,*' I said, as I wheeled past. '*Aleikum salaam! Wasalaam aleikum! Aleikum salaam! Wheeeeeee!*' Their delighted cries followed me out of sight down the road, the old man waving his shepherd's crook in the air until he was no more than a speck on the horizon. It was good to be back among Muslims.

But Dabdar was a disaster. There was no *lüshe*, not even a roadside noodle stand or village shop. There was nothing at all for the traveller – or for the residents either. Where on earth did they go for provisions? A row of adobe huts and a few brick buildings with courtyards lined one side of the road. The rest was marshland with a mangy camel, a couple of donkeys and one horse. The only building of any significance was the Road Works Depot, standing in a compound with a high brick wall. There was not a soul in sight.

It took me just one minute to cycle through the village and out the other end. I was tempted to go on, to try my luck at the Chinese border-post at Pirali, but I met a man on a donkey who told me that Pirali was far away and I should never reach it before dark, so I turned back to Dabdar.

This time there was life in the village, in the shape of one young man, who was leaning against the gate-post at the depot, smoking a cigarette. I asked if I could pitch my tent and sleep inside the compound. I should be safe in there, once the iron gates were locked for the night, and the ground looked drier than the marshes outside.

The young man, who seemed to be the caretaker, followed me round at a wary distance while I selected my site, a sheltered spot under a tree in the gap between two buildings. Then he offered me tea. I could think of nothing more wonderful. Cycling at 3,650 m was an exhausting business and after 65 km of it I was buckling at the knees. I would drink his tea, then pitch my tent and crawl inside for a nap.

To my surprise, he didn't take me into the depot. He took my bicycle and wheeled it through the compound to his home, a tiny two-roomed stone cottage, where he lived with his wife and two children, his sister and his wife's sister. He was a skinny young man with bad teeth and a shabby suit, but at home he was treated like a rajah by his three adoring women. I was taken through to the main room. It had a brick floor and a raised platform covered with rugs. There were rich red Afghan rugs on the walls and pictures of the Great Mosques at Mecca and Damascus, cut out from calendars. A pile of quilts, a tin trunk, three suitcases and a wooden water-barrel completed the furnishings. It was a timeless Central Asian scene – except for the lurid poster of 'Rambo. First Blood' which had pride of place on the door.

The young man, whose name I could never grasp, kept me company on the edge of the platform, while the women busied themselves serving us tea and flat dry bread. We all smiled a great deal. Conversation was limited. They were Tajiks and Wakhi-speakers, so their Chinese was little better than mine. But 18-month-old Ibrahim (Billy) lightened the occasion. Someone would say '*Wasalaam aleikum*' and he would give me a toothy grin and a military salute. After an hour of this entertainment and my fourth cup of tea, the wife, whose name was also a mystery, got up and quietly laid out a quilt and blankets on the platform. She mimed a rest.

'I'd love to take a rest,' I said. 'I'm very tired. But first I think I'd better go out and put up my tent. I'd like to unpack my bags and make my bed before it gets dark.'

'This is your bed,' she said simply. Whatever the test was, I'd obviously passed it.

I slept gratefully for about two hours, but then I became conscious of people creeping in and out to get at the water-barrel and I felt I was in the way. It was time to get up, particularly as I had drunk rather too much tea. The man's sister, a beautiful girl appropriately named Pamirgül (Rose of the Pamir), was deputed to escort me. We went round to the end of the compound, where there was an open shed with a pit and a plank across it. Privacy is unknown and unwanted in the East. Pamirgül came into the shed with me and watched with undisguised curiosity as I unzipped my trousers and displayed my underwear. Then I asked to wash and the wife's sister, Bagh (Garden), poured water over my hands, while Pamirgül knelt beside me in the yard with a towel at the ready.

There was no electricity in Dabdar and the man brought a candle into my room. He was joined by the children and Pamirgül. It was the start of a very heavy evening. I produced my guide-book, which had a few Wakhi phrases, and read them out, to howls of laughter. They corrected my pronunciation and I did my best to improve. Then I read out all the phrases in English and it was their turn to repeat and be corrected. They were quick learners and were soon counting up to ten. When I got out my notebook and started to write up my day, they all sat on the platform behind me, peering over my shoulder at the notes. To distract them, I handed them the guide-book, open at a page of photographs. What happened next took me by surprise. The young man and Pamirgül began to study the chapter on the Karakoram Highway with great concentration. They could obviously make out some of the Roman script, because they suddenly shouted 'Aga Khan' and pointed excitedly to his name in the text. The Tajiks are Ismailis, followers of the Aga Khan, and Pamirgül asked me to tell them what it said about him in the book. I did my best, in pidgin Chinese, to summarise the article on the Aga Khan Foundation and the Aga Khan Rural Support Programme. They were interested in the schools and hospitals and the schemes for helping farmers; but most of all, they were proud that their spiritual leader featured in a western guide-book and was praised for his good works there.

A call from next door took us into the kitchen. It was the same size as the other room, with the same platform, though this one was only thinly carpeted. A cauldron of water was boiling on a coal-fired stove with a long flue. On the wall hung a small, cracked mirror and a plastic bag of tobacco, from which my host rolled his scented cigarettes. Pamirgül started to make the inevitable noodles, tugging, twisting, whirling and twirling the lump of dough into a flying cat's cradle. The skill was dazzling, but the noodles which finally reached the bowls were the usual slimy, overcooked mess. Mine was topped with morsels of mutton fat and mixed vegetables, but the family managed on a few scraps of cabbage with theirs. They started a game of guessing ages. I knew it was because they were dying to know mine, but were unusually shy of asking. My host teased his wife and sisters. He told me his wife was 59 and the girls were 10.

That caused great merriment and I could see why his family loved him. He was so kind and good-humoured. He was even kind to his little daughter, Seurat, who was sorely neglected by all the women in favour of little Billy, the highly prized son. 'Take no notice of her. She's always grizzling!' they told me, when I tried to amuse her.

After the meal, time hung heavy. I got out the photographs I always carry for such occasions and showed them my family, my flat and some views of London. As their contribution to the evening's fun, they produced a tape of a prayer-meeting addressed by the Aga Khan. They said it had some English in it, but it didn't. It was an hour of incomprehensible mullahs droning. Then three neighbours came calling and I made the excuse to retire to my quilts next-door. I tried to slip out unnoticed to the compound shed, but Pamirgül spotted me and came in pursuit. We walked up and down for a while under the frosty stars and she told me how much she hated those neighbours, who were a bad influence on her brother. 'He's a good man, but weak,' she said. I thought that was probably a fair assessment and was impressed by the poise and maturity of this seventeen-year-old. She was beautiful, intelligent and discriminating, with a good command of Chinese. What a waste of talent in a dump like Dabdar!

I had been wondering for some time what the sleeping arrangements would be. At 9 o'clock I found out. Pamirgül followed me into the main room and laid out her quilts beside mine. Then the others arrived. First Bagh with Seurat and little Billy, then the wife and finally the husband, who established himself in the far corner. It was a very cosy arrangement on a cold night. My only problem was my length. I was far taller than the rest of them and my feet stuck out over the end of the platform, but I couldn't curl up on my side to cover them unless everyone else did. We slept in a line, elbow to elbow, like sardines in a tin, and my feet froze. But anything was better than the tent!

The next day started with bowls of 'Pakistani tea', a treat in my honour. I'm not at all keen on dairy products and can just about cope with cow's milk in tea. But this milk was so strong and sharp that my gorge rose. Was it goat? Or yak? Or camel? I didn't have the vocabulary to ask and it was perhaps as well that I didn't know. Whichever it was, the tea was tepid, sour and quite disgusting. I plied my chopsticks valiantly, dunking pieces of bread and trying hard to swallow them. But the stuff just wouldn't go down. In the end, I had to apologise and tell them I was allergic to milk. 'Allergies' are universally understood and accepted, whereas plain dislikes can often offend. I was given a mug of hot water instead.

Paying for hospitality is always a problem. My Tajiks were poor people, scratching along on the bare necessities, their one luxury in life a tape-recorder with two religious tapes. Yet they had entertained me with great kindness, giving me the best they had to offer. Money would have been an insult. Fortunately, I had the perfect gift. I was carrying a Polaroid camera for just such a situation. The previous afternoon I had taken a snap of little Billy and watched their delight when the picture gained definition, as if by magic. Now I offered to photograph them all. The trunk and suitcases were raided for finery. My host put on a new shirt; his wife a red brocade skirt with gold appliqué work and a white silk mantilla over her hat; Pamirgül produced a glittering red and gold shawl; Ibrahim was dressed in a white and green silk bomber-jacket with a pink woolly hat; and even poor miserable little Seurat was dressed in a new grey track-suit. Bagh seemed to be the maid-of-all-work, perhaps because she was younger than Pamirgül, or maybe she had less status in the family as the wife's sister. Whatever the reason, she had the job of helping all the others to dress up. Then she put on a new scarlet jacket and a new version of the round cake-tin hat which she and her sister wore all the time, indoors and out. They had never been photographed in their lives before and they stood stiff-backed, staring into the camera. When they saw the prints, they clamoured for more. They rushed to change their clothes and we had more sessions, indoors and out in the yard. Finally, Bagh was told to take a photo with me in the group. I stood there in my dusty cycling-gear and trainers, at least a head taller than the tallest of them and considerably fatter. I felt clumsy, gawky and unkempt in the middle of all those slender little people in their best clothes. I don't care to think about it too often, but I expect I'm being displayed, with a mixture of pride and hilarity, to all comers in the village of Dabdar!

They packed me off with two unleavened loaves the size and shape of giants' shields and a jamjar of tea on a string. The hoar frost had melted and I wheeled my bicycle out into the sunshine, feeling quite pleased with myself. I had got through the first of my three nights in the mountains and managed it all in amazing style – seven-in-a-bed with Tajiks!

My next objective was the Chinese border-post at Pirali. The ribbon of road rose steadily. It was weary work and I was soon down to 8 km an hour. When I was half-way there, I passed a jeep track running off to my right towards a distant gap in the mountains. This was once a major branch of the Silk Road along the Mintaka Valley to Hunza and Kashmir. The Karakoram Highway had robbed it of most of its legitimate traffic, but it was still a smuggling route leading to Afghanistan's Wakhan Corridor.

I climbed above the flocks of sheep and passed into camel and yak country. A Tajik family approached with the frame and felts for their yurt on one camel and their pots and pans clanking along the flank of another. Later, I overtook two traders in Mao caps and ill-fitting grey suits, their wares for market piled up on a mother camel, while her baby walked beside, learning his road-drill. I must have been his first cyclist, because he jumped in the air like a jerked puppet, then skidded across the road crab-wise on wild, uncoordinated legs. His owners laughed indulgently. A kilometre further on, I sat on a roadside stone for a snack and a rest. By that time, the little camel was used to the idea of me and my bicycle, and bold enough to leave his mother to investigate. He trotted across the road and stood right in front of me, his nose almost touching mine as he watched me eat my apricots. But his courage failed him when I held out my hand to offer him one. He backed off and fled.

Those were my only encounters until I arrived at Pirali in the early afternoon. Although I'd covered less than 40 km, I'd been climbing steadily in the thin air and was feeling quite shaky. The border-post consisted of a shabby brick barracks with dirty windows, some of them broken, opposite a walled yard of heavy trucks. A few dilapidated buildings in the vicinity were clearly the boarded-up ruins of the bank, noodle-stall and simple guest-house mentioned in one of my guide-books. Once more, my hopes of overnight accommodation were dashed, and I had neither the time nor the strength to attempt the Khūnjerāb Pass that day. I had somehow to get myself invited to spend the night with the Chinese military.

The sergeant on duty inspected my passport and stamped me out of China.

'May I sit down here beside the road and rest for a little while? I'm very tired.'

At this, the Commanding Officer appeared. 'Bring a chair for the lady,' he said. 'She's tired.'

A chair was fetched at the double by one of the privates and they all looked on with approval as I produced my jamjar of Tajik tea. A jamjar of tea on a string, to be topped up with hot water at frequent intervals, is carried by every working

Chinaman, and the soldiers were obviously pleased that a foreigner had adopted their practice. The Officer sent for a flask of hot water. I asked how far it was to the Khūnjerāb Pass, although I knew the answer only too well.

'33 kilometres? Oh dear! I'm so tired. I shall never manage that today!'

I pointed to my tent and asked if I could pitch it in their yard. The Officer nodded.

There was no traffic on the road, so we sat in the weak sunshine and I told them about my journey from Xi'an. They said nothing, but little by little I felt the tension ease. Then the Officer led me into the barracks and pointed to a green dralon couch in the soldiers' recreation room. The dralon couch with eight dralon armchairs, two large tables with stools, an empty bookcase and a TV set with video were the only furnishings in the bleak, cold room with its unscrubbed composition floor. But for me, out in the emptiness of the Pamir, it was more luxurious than a Sheraton.

I was beginning to appreciate the value of my little tent. The Tajiks and the Chinese border-guards were very wary of me when I first arrived. Had I rushed in and asked either group outright for accommodation, they would almost certainly have refused. But they could hardly refuse me tent-space. And when we had spent a little time together and they had got used to me and my halting efforts at Chinese, their kindness had overcome their circumspection and they had cheerfully offered me a bed. I decided that a tent was a useful thing to travel with, even if I preferred not to sleep in it!

I'd just begun to unpack my panniers, when the Officer returned and with great ceremony escorted me to the Mess and seated me at his right hand. The men remained standing for some shouted oath of allegiance, or similar, then we all tucked into the most delicious meal I'd eaten since Beijing – fresh fish from Lake Karakul, pork, beef with a delicate hint of ginger, and six vegetables. The Officer kept selecting choice morsels from each of the dishes and transferring them deftly with his chopsticks into my bowl. I ate ravenously after my scant rations of the last two days, reflecting that the provision of such appetising food was probably deliberate, a consolation for what must surely be the worst posting in the Chinese People's Republic.

The border-post complement was one Officer, two NCOs and eight men, none of them much above 20 years old. They were all serious boys, who settled down in the evening over English text-books and Chinese calligraphy. The afternoon's duty-sergeant approached shyly.

'I noticed when I stamped your passport that you had pages and pages of visas. It was so interesting. May I look at it again?'

We sat down together on the dralon couch and I went through my passport with him.

'How wonderful to be able to travel to all those countries! Is Brazil nice? Did you like Turkey? What food did you eat there? Were the people kind to you?'

We were joined by the others, all except the Officer who held himself slightly aloof. The dralon couch overflowed, as they crowded round me, like children in a kindergarten at storytime. They came from Xi'an and Lanzhou, at least a week away by bus and train, so that most of their home-leave was spent travelling. They looked wistfully at my photographs and told me how much they missed their families.

Then we settled down to the video. First, we watched a government documentary about the construction of a river barrage. Then, the highlight of the evening, two instalments from a Chinese soap about four twelve-year-old girls at a military academy. They wore soldiers' uniform and performed modern ballet in khaki tutus and high boots, between getting into all sorts of scrapes with their officers. It was amazingly naïve entertainment, but the soldiers were riveted. In the middle of one naughty incident, a midnight feast in the dormitory, our duty-sergeant appeared to say that he was having trouble with the passengers in a coach from Pakistan. The Officer put on his cap and strode out authoritatively. Five minutes later, he rushed back into the room with 1,200 contraband cigarettes under his arm. 'What's happened? Have I missed anything? Did the girls get into trouble?'

The generator was switched off and I dressed myself up for

the night by candlelight – two pairs of silk long johns, two pairs of socks, a thermal vest, a silk polo neck, a shirt and a jersey. Inside my sleeping-bag, with my anorak on top, I was just about warm enough. Like the previous night's platform, the couch was a foot too short and it had high wooden arms, so that I couldn't stretch out. But I lay and listened to the howling wind and was grateful to be under cover. The men slept in a dormitory, heated by the cooking stove. The Officer had his own quarters, a combined bedroom and office, with the station's only telephone and a two-way radio.

I awoke the next morning to shouted commands. One of the sergeants had the men out on the road for their early morning drill, watched from a distance by the Officer and the station's trainee guard-dog, an exuberant labrador puppy. We breakfasted on rice, served in its glutinous boiling water, spicy stuffed chapattis and pickled chillis. The cook gave me hot water for a mug of coffee and topped up my jamjar of tea for the journey. I packed up my gear while the men swept, mopped and washed up, paraded again, had a stirring talk from their Officer, and finally came into the recreation room with notebooks for a lecture.

I was full of admiration for the young Officer in his first command. He and his men were Han Chinese, strangers in a land of Wakhi-speaking, Indo-European Tajiks who resented them. Yet out in that desolate stretch of moorland, he somehow contrived to keep his men busy and maintain their morale. He was courteous and dignified, keeping his distance, as an Officer should. He must have been the loneliest boy in China.

Loading up my panniers proved surprisingly difficult, as I gasped for breath at the slightest exertion. But at least I had no altitude sickness. Bus-travellers over the Khûnjeráb Pass are prone to headaches, nausea, nose-bleeds, dizziness and sometimes total disorientation, but I was fortunately free of all those ills. Cycling up a mountain slowly has its compensations. I felt fit and quietly confident.

The first 15 km were easy cycling over the gently rolling Pamir, but the gleaming ice-peaks of the Himalayas and the Tian Shan were gradually closing in. The sentinels of the ginger

Himalayan marmots whistled at my approach and sent all their neighbours scampering down their burrows. Their whistles always startled me; they were so piercing in the stillness, as loud as the whistles of football referees. I came to my first patches of snow on the ground and ran into a headwind.

The plain finished at a Chinese Road Transport Depot, where I stopped to replenish my jamjar. The road ahead climbed steeply in a series of hairpin bends. At that altitude, cycling up a steep hill with all my baggage was quite beyond me, so I started to plod. There were regular kilometre-stones and, between them, red spots in the middle of the road marked every 100 m. I fell into a snail's routine which kept me going. I counted 120 paces and that took me to the next red spot. There I flopped over my handlebars, fighting for breath to a count of 60. Then on to the next red spot. At each kilometre-stone, I allowed myself 10 minutes' rest. When my breathing became less painful, I took a mouthful of tea and perhaps half a biscuit or a couple of dried apricots, a tiny snack to keep up my strength. Each kilometre took me at least half an hour, but I made steady progress without exhausting myself.

At the top of the hill, I expected to see the Khūnjerāb Pass, but was dismayed to find another plateau round the last Chinese check-point, followed by another steep 3 km climb. I braced myself. The wind strengthened, funnelled down through the Pass, and it was so icy that I had to put on my balaclava. Just before I reached the top, a coach pulled up and the passengers took photos of me drinking tea out of my jamjar on a kilometre-stone.

Finally, I reached the summit and did a little dance on the top. 4,733 m and I'd made it! I was jubilant.

The last 14 km had taken me seven hours and it was already late afternoon. The frontier was deserted. I'd seen some old photographs of the Pass and expected a few buildings, where I might find a bed for the night. But the flat stretch of road at the summit was empty now, except for two stone markers. Once again, there was nowhere to stay, so I paused to stuff a copy of *Tough Puzzles* down the front of my anorak for extra protection from wind-chill and started the long descent.

The Khūnjerāb Pass is not only the border between China and Pakistan; it also marks the end of the gentle, green rounded Pamir and the start of the jagged, precipitous Karakorams. The transition was swift. I passed three men, huddled in blankets and scarves, watching a herd of dhu on the last patch of grazing. Then the road took off, like the start of a helter-skelter, and I hurtled down a gorge in the mountains. Karakoram means 'black crumbling rock'. It was angry, unstable terrain and I had some bad moments as I negotiated rockfalls and screeched on my brakes round gaps where the road had simply dropped into a chasm. The peaks were covered in snow, but the flanks of the mountains looked like collapsing slag-heaps, which the slightest noise or gust of wind might bring crashing down to bury me. In places, where the road had been blasted out of the sheer cliff-face by workmen suspended on ropes, there was no more than a narrow ledge over a vertiginous drop. Where the mountains were even more menacing than usual, the Pakistanis had put up 'WARNING. SLIDE AREA STARTS. BE CAREFUL' signs. A little further on, their nice sense of humour would assert itself in another sign: 'RELAX'. But there was grandeur as well as fright. I started off above the snow-line and watched the Khūnjerāb River emerge as a thin trickle from a snow-field, then gradually take on volume and speed to become a swift, turbulent little stream, cutting its way through a gorge. And I had the amazing experience of looking down from my great height and seeing eagles gliding below me.

The sun went down behind the mountains and the evening gloom made the road seem even more threatening. It was a race against the night. The bad patches were hard to negotiate in the dusk and I was afraid of taking a tumble or getting a puncture, far away from help. I passed the first Pakistani Police Post, where the duty-officer assured me that there was a rest-house 30 km further on, 'all downside, no uphill'. A group of road-workers waved to me from a hole in the ground, where they were huddled for warmth under canvas sheeting. In the nick of time, just a few moments before total blackness descended, I came to the barrier in the road which marked the end of No Man's Land. Three members of the Karakoram

Security Force leapt out of their sentry-box, two Tajiks and a Hunzakut in his distinctive flat white cap.

'Good evening, madam. How are you? Welcome to Pakistan!'

They beamed and shook hands. After months of struggling with the enigmatic Chinese and their difficult language, I was home.

The frontier-post at Dih, was straight out of Aldershot. Whitewashed stones picked out the edges of the paths between mown grass and neatly trimmed rose-beds. Fresh paint gleamed in the lamplight and flags flew. It was a world away from the broken windows and dusty floors of Pirali. I sat on the step with Ismud, the Commanding Officer, to sign the register.

'I shall need my spectacles for this,' I said.

'And your pen,' he added gravely.

It was a small exchange, but we were on the same wavelength and I felt immensely cheered.

I enquired about the rest-house. 'If you don't have a special permit, you'll never get in there,' said Ismud. 'There are only four rooms and they're always full of big-wigs from Islamabad. They like it up here.'

'I'm carrying a small tent,' I said. 'If they're full up, perhaps they'll let me pitch it in their garden.'

Ismud bristled with indignation. 'You will not be sleeping in tent, madam. You will be sleeping in station!'

With that, he seized my bicycle and marched ahead of me up the path. He had the clipped English of authority in Pakistan and was clearly brooking no argument. He took me into his office, where there were two beds, and sat me down while he busied himself over a paraffin stove, brewing up a most welcome mug of tea. I'd missed dinner, but I was carrying a slab of solid Kashgar apricot and walnut loaf and I dined on that.

'You will sleep here, in this bed. I will sleep in another room. As soon as I leave, you lock the door and bolt it, then you turn off the paraffin lamp. Tomorrow, 7 a.m. sharp, I come to radio HQ Gilgit.'

His commands were barked, but his eyes twinkled. He was a

tall, spare man with sandy hair, a sandy moustache and hazel eyes, who reminded me of my Scottish grandfather. According to the maps, I was in Pakistan, but I was still among the same peoples I had met in Western China, on the borders of Russia and Afghanistan. Fair-skinned men and confident women without veils, they spoke their Turkic, Persian and Tibetan languages across frontiers and felt they had more in common with the western backpackers than they had with the plump, dark Punjabis, who were officially their fellow-countrymen.

It was my first night in a proper bed since Tashkurgan. I'd dropped over 1,200 m in my hair-raising descent from the summit of the Pass and my breathing was already easier. I zipped myself into my sleeping-bag and slept the sleep of angels.

Ismud duly arrived at 7 a.m. sharp to radio Gilgit, bringing me a cup of 'bed tea'. That was followed by breakfast and more tea. We showed each other family photographs and he told me about his clever daughter at college in Gilgit and his two sons at an English-medium school in Gulmit. I read him a passage about his station from my guide-book: 'If you're coming from China you'll get a warm welcome which may bring tears to your eyes.' He liked that and produced more tea. Then I cruised the 30 km, down to Immigration in Sust, to be welcomed officially into Pakistan with another pot of tea. I went next-door to Customs', where the Customs Chief served me custard creams and yet more tea in one of the ubiquitous Chinese tea-sets. After my third cup, he escorted me out of the yard. 'You have cleared Customs', he said, without so much as a glance at my baggage. Old ladies on bicycles could obviously make a killing smuggling heroin! Out on the road, my trader friend from Gilgit popped up as if by magic and insisted on treating me to tea. And finally, when I checked into my Sust hotel, the manager said, 'You must be ready for a nice cup of tea after all that cycling'.

The weeks which followed were idyllic. The Karakoram Highway was not all downhill, but the magnificent mountain scenery and the cheerful company made up for the effort. From my bedroom window in Sust, I looked out over the same Khûnjeráb River I'd followed down from the snow-field, though by now it had taken in tributaries and changed its name to the Hunza. Brightly dressed women went back and forth across it on a swaying rope suspension bridge and the snowy summit of Mt Kirilgoz, as sharply pointed as a child's drawing of a mountain, towered above it. Dinner in the hotel was a communal affair, a set meal of lentils, potatoes and vegetables followed by Hunza apricots and custard. The food in the mountains was blander than the curries of the plains and the influence of the British Raj was much in evidence. Egg and chips, porridge and custard were favourites with the locals as well as the visitors. Seven nationalities sat round the table – English, Australian, Spanish, German, Dutch, Japanese and Pakistani – all trekkers, cyclists or serious travellers on their way to and from China.

The Khūnjerāb had knocked the stuffing out of me. Once I'd got over the top and started to relax, lethargy descended. I left Sust late, looking forward to a downhill run, but there seemed to be as much up as down. I gave up in Passu, a green village wedged between glaciers, where I stayed for three days, resting and catching up on my letter-writing under the apricot trees in the hotel garden. The owner brought me a bowl of freshly picked cherries and strawberries, then knelt in the grass to gaze lovingly at eighteen tiny chickens, acquired as future egg-producers for his kitchen. He was so enchanted with them that he went out in the evening and came back with another dozen cheeping in a cardboard box on the back of his bicycle. He was a Tajik and he told me proudly that even the Chinese trusted the Tajiks and gave them jobs in government service – unlike the Uigurs, who were greedy people and cared about nothing but money. Interestingly enough, Marco Polo made the same comment about the Uigurs almost eight centuries ago!

My shower-room was unusually spacious, with a concrete floor, so I 'took a shower with a friend'. I wheeled my bicycle in there and splashed the dust of China off the pair of us. Afterwards, a Dutch doctor practising in Karachi spent a happy hour tightening Cube's brakes and adjusting the mudguards and carrier. 'You've made his day,' said his wife. 'He likes nothing better than playing with bicycles.'

It was a lovely hotel in a spectacular situation, with delightful staff and fellow-guests. Its only drawback was the bedbugs. I've stayed in some fairly basic places on my travels round the world, but never before had I had an infestation of any sort in my bed, nor have I had one since. At first, I thought they were mosquito bites, but I was surprised to find them on the plumper parts of my body. Mosquitos usually go for easy access to veins. Then I saw them. They looked like black ladybirds, without the red blobs, and they scuttled inside the quilt when I put the light on. They gave me fiendishly itchy spots, which I scratched for a whole week, all the way down to Gilgit.

The hotel had been recommended to me by Patrick and Dixie, two well-informed travellers from Oregon who had helped me while away my cold-ridden days in Kashgar. They were both born in Pakistan and loved the country; and the hotel in Passu was one of their favourites. I could see why. And when the owner and staff were so warmly hospitable, I hated the idea of complaining about the bedbugs. But something had to be said. When I checked out, I took the son of the hotel to one side and had a tactful word in his ear. He registered shock, which may or may not have been genuine, and thanked me for letting him know. We parted friends and I went on my way scratching.

The road from Passu went round three extraordinary fingers of rock, pointing out over the Hunza River from the Passu Glacier. Further along, the Ghulkin Glacier came right down to the edge of the road. It didn't look like my idea of a glacier. It was a grey mountain with brown stones at its foot and a stream rushing down its flank. There was no ice to be seen, but the temperature dropped about 15°C where the glacier met the tarmac. I stood there for a while and enjoyed the cool air.

I was still among fierce, dark rocks, where jagged peaks yawned over chasms and the collision of the mountains had been so violent that the rock-strata stood absolutely vertical. It was country where road-mending was a permanent occupation, involving the engineering skills of thousands of Pakistani troops as well as hordes of civilians. There were teams round every corner, shoring up edges, clearing rockfalls and filling up gaps. The carving out of the Karakoram Highway was financed chiefly by China, presumably as a political gesture of solidarity with Pakistan in the face of Russia's support of India. It was certainly not built for commercial traffic. Two buses a day and a few jeeps loaded with tea-sets, for six months of the year, hardly justify the expenditure of so many millions. It must be the world's most gigantic white elephant. And it's the Pakistanis who now have to bear most of the burden of maintenance. The Karakorams resent the road and come crashing angrily down to destroy it, whereas the Pamirs, on the Chinese side, are relatively gentle. I was glad that I'd chosen to cross the Khūnjerāb from China instead of trying to toil up the precipitous Pakistani approach.

Amazingly, there were trees and tiny patches of wheat wherever soil could cling. Sophisticated irrigation schemes, financed by the Aga Khan's Rural Support Programme and other overseas aid agencies, have channelled the glacial melt-waters to make agriculture and afforestation possible, and the Northern Areas are renowned for their 'vertical agriculture'. They even export fruit. As I travelled down the highway, the green valleys widened until I came to the breathtakingly beautiful Hunza Valley, the original Shangri-la.

But first, I had to spend a night in Gulmit. I tried to enter the town secretly, to avoid the trader from Gilgit who was keen to meet me in the Marco Polo Hotel. I'd arranged to join some Dutch travellers from Sust in another hotel by the polo ground and I was just creeping up the hill past the Marco Polo when the trader jumped out like a jack-in-the-box.

'You're here at last! Come in. Come in. I've been waiting for you,' he cried.

'How nice to see you again! But I don't really want to stay in this hotel. It's too expensive,' I said.

'No, it isn't. The manager's a friend of mine. He'll give you special price.'

The manager came out beaming and, between them, they hijacked me and Cube and bundled us into the garden. I protested that I was only a poor cyclist – and the price immediately came down by half, 'because you are friend. But don't tell anyone else.' I gave in reluctantly. Apart from the trader from Gilgit, I was the only guest in the hotel.

I ate my 'full dinner' that evening in solitary splendour, in a vast dining room under the gaze of a portrait of the Mir of Hunza. There was enough food for a regiment, and that one meal cost as much as my three sociable dinners in Passu. There was a whole tureen of soup, a plate of steak and chips, rice, dahl, mutton stew, potatoes, spinach and salad, followed by apricots in custard and green tea. The trader from Gilgit came in just after the second course and sat uninvited at my table, helping himself to chips from my plate. Then came the evening's great embarrassment. An eighty-year-old musician hobbled in, decked out in his embroidered white Hunzakut cloak and woollen cap. He pulled up a chair beside mine and for the next half-hour sang me a tuneless serenade to the twanging of his sitar. He was such a poor old thing and his music was so awful that I gave him a huge tip to get rid of him.

A thunderstorm broke over breakfast, with raging winds and torrential rain. Had I been in any other hotel, I should have stayed put, but another day of gargantuan meals, squawking serenades and the trader from Gilgit was not to be borne. I waited for the storm to die down, then set out for Karimabad in the drizzle. After three rainless months, it was bliss to be cycling through the cool, moist air. I teetered along ledges, over dizzying drops down to the Hunza Gorge, feeling much more secure on my bicycle than I would have done on a speeding bus. On the final descent to the bridge at Ganesh, the heavens opened again and I sped down the exposed mountainside with rain like needles driving into my face. Karimabad, the capital of Hunza, nestles in its valley high above the main road. I couldn't face the steep approach, which had turned into a river of churning mud and stones, so I made a 'special booking' of a passenger van to carry me with all my belongings up to the town.

The bazaar at Karimabad flows down the slope from the polo ground and the Mir's Baltit Fort. For the first time for months, I saw crowds of western tourists and Pakistani holidaymakers escaping the heat of the plains. The hotels were buzzing with trade and it was quite a relief to walk or cycle out into the quiet of the valley. The views were breathtaking. What was once arid land with few flat surfaces had been transformed by human ingenuity into an amazing profusion of crops and fruit trees. There were peaches, apples, plums, cherries, walnuts, grape vines and, above all, the apricots for which Hunza is famous. Snakes of green along the encircling mountains showed the intricate paths of the water-channels which travelled great distances to feed them. And above them all towered the majestic snow-capped bulk of Mt Rakaposhi.

I paid a visit to the Northern Territories' educational show-piece, the Aga Khan Academy for Girls. I went without an appointment and had to wait for some time as a suppliant at the security gates, but status eventually triumphed. I'd been careful to arrive in a taxi, wearing my best silk suit. Then I sent in my card to the headmistress, with the information that I'd been President of the Girls' Schools Association. That piece of rank-pulling opened the door immediately and I was given a full tour of inspection by Mrs Sultan.

It was an elegant boarding school, set in rose-gardens on a terraced site, with facilities which would be the envy of many schools in the western world. The Aga Khan Foundation had decided, quite rightly, that a nation's progress depended on the education of its women and was investing heavily. Teams of staff toured the Northern Territories to administer entrance tests, as it was difficult and expensive for small children to be brought to Karimabad. The successful applicants who could afford it paid about £2 a month for tuition and £16 a month for board, but there were subsidised places for poorer girls. Fifteen places for further education in Karachi were reserved by the Foundation for the brightest students. Mrs Sultan explained that so many Hunzakuts have migrated to Karachi that most of the students have relations there, who will put them up while they study. There was only one problem. 'My girls are hard-working, sincere and very ambitious,' said Mrs Sultan, 'and they don't want the silly boys who are available round here.' Perhaps the Foundation should start up a boys' academy too, to provide suitable husbands for all these clever, articulate girls!

I spent a few days in Karimabad, mostly holding court. I was modestly surprised to find that my fame had gone before me down the Highway. Two young Australians even went so far as to tell me that I was 'legendary'. Once I was established and my whereabouts known, I had a steady stream of cyclists and trekkers who wanted first-hand advice on crossing the Khūnjerāb and I was pleased to be able to give it. I could tell them from my log book exactly how many kilometres there were between points, what the terrain and temperature were like and where I'd spent the nights. They were all younger and fitter than I was, and would obviously find the going easier, even though they were attempting the more gruelling Karakoram approach. My only worry was that none of them spoke any Chinese, and I don't know how I should have managed up there without my smattering of Mandarin.

Between the counselling sessions, I caught up on world events, thanks to the satellite television in the cafés. The local men were avid followers of the BBC. One tea-time I sat with a crowd of them in The Shaq, watching a programme on European integration. What they made of it I don't know, but there was one moment of enlightenment. A Danish chef was asked his views on the single currency as he was working in his kitchen. 'Cutting vegetables!' cried a delighted Hunzakut. This programme was followed by a documentary about seals off the west coast of Scotland. None of the locals had ever seen the sea, let alone a close-up of a basking seal. They gazed in astonishment. 'Is it one fish?' asked one of them. 'No. It's a mammal,' snapped a backpacking girl, who was obviously destined to be a schoolmistress. Silence. I thought I'd better explain to the bewildered Hunzakuts. 'It's not a fish. It doesn't lay eggs. It has babies and feeds them with milk.' 'Babies!' they said, in hushed, awestruck voices.

The cosy bonhomie of the Hunzakuts and the westerners in the cafés was sometimes disturbed by the arrival of Pakistanis from the south. They turned up in their four-wheel drives, draped in camcorders, Walkmen and Rolex watches, with their gaggles of plump, covered women and sons in designer casuals. The spare, frugal Hunzakuts would lapse into silence. One proprietor came crab-like across to my table. 'Stay here,' he whispered. 'When this rubbish has gone, I make you Hunzakut speciality with walnuts – but not for them!' And what a speciality it was! Incredibly light puff pastry, stuffed with walnuts, cheese, onions and garlic in a strongly flavoured walnut oil. It was specially prepared for me and offered as a gift, and it was utterly delicious.

My longest cycling day took me 108 km down the Hunza River from Karimabad bazaar to Gilgit. I followed the Aliabad linkroad, which is now fully paved, from Karimabad through leafy orchards and terraced gardens down to the river. It was a pleasant downhill ride, but then the slog began. I toiled up a long, shadeless ascent to a dizzy ledge overlooking the fields of Sikanderabad, then the river turned south and I ran into rain and a headwind. Another enormous climb through Lower Rahimabad took me up the the ridge of Upper Rahimabad, where I stopped to look at the memorial to the workers who lost their lives in the construction of the Karakoram Highway. A simple monument, crowned with an old pneumatic drill, it quotes in Urdu some lines by the Pakistani poet Iqbal and, most touching for an English visitor, a couplet from Rupert Brooke: 'And there shall be in this rich earth, A richer dust concealed.' I've since been told that Gray's *Elegy* is quoted at the top of the Khūnjerāb Pass, but I was too cold and preoccupied the evening I was up there to notice it. In Pakistan, as in India, the English literary tradition lives on. Poetry has forged a stronger bond between our peoples than politicians could ever manage.

Two young men drew up in a jeep and gave me a branch of delicious little red and yellow plums, and an old man in a white Hunzakut cap ran out into the road to present me with three ripe peaches. I wish the children in those parts were as pleasant. Three little goatherds with long poles chased me, trying to poke them through my spokes (fortunately, I was going downhill at the time, so it was easy to escape); gangs of schoolboys chased me down empty roads screaming 'One pen! One pen!'; junior hustlers tried to sell me apricots and single cigarettes at extortionate prices; and even little girls in this more open society chased me down the street in mobs. I was plagued by little boys wherever I went, but I found I could scatter them in all directions simply by getting off my bicycle and glaring. Gangs of big boys would have been more difficult to deal with, but the problem never arose. By some miracle, those threatening little Pakistani beasts change into prince charmings at fourteen or fifteen.

Gilgit, the communications hub of the region, was just that – a dusty, traffic-ridden bazaar with no charm and few women. Islam kept a tighter hold on them there than in the mountains further north. The women of the mountain valleys went out to the shops and fields in their colourful *shalwar kameezes* and embroidered pillbox hats, stopping to chat to their friends and looking strangers straight in the eye. In Gilgit, they stayed at home.

I was looking forward to the next leg down from Gilgit. I'd followed the Hunza River from its first snow-melt trickle to the point where it joined the Gilgit and took on its name. But its most dramatic moment was still to come, the moment when it poured into the mighty Indus some 30 km south. At just about that same point, the two highest mountains in the region, Rakaposhi and Nanga Parbat (at 8126 m, the eighth highest mountain in the world), would be visible simultaneously. In fact, that stretch of road offered the best views of the greatest number of snow-capped peaks along the Karakoram Highway.

Unfortunately, it also offered the wildest, most dangerous tribesmen. My guide-book detailed attacks on tourists. Cyclists, who carried all their worldly goods on the back of sophisticated and highly desirable machines, were said to be particularly at risk, and women travellers had been raped. The waiter in my Gilgit hotel was horrified when I told him that I was planning to cycle through Kohistan, and so was the famous Mr Beg in his bookshop. I'm not a coward, but there's a limit to the risks I'm willing to take. I opted for the bus down to Beshan.

It was a dark journey. The Indus veered west to skirt the flank of Nanga Parbat and cut a gorge so deep that there was sunlight for only an hour or two around noon. Our bus crawled along a black ledge, high above the crashing tawny river. It was a landscape of giants, where traffic was dwarfed to the size of Dinkytoys and the great highway was no more than a fragile thread winding its way under towering, treeless cliffs. From time to time, when there was a slope up the otherwise sheer rock-face, a dirt track would zigzag upwards to some village hidden in the crags. Apart from the soldiers manning road-blocks, the landscape was empty. We were often stopped and the bus searched, more for arms than drugs. The breakdown of law and order in Russia and Eastern Europe has provided an easier route to western markets, and Pakistan has consequently lost much of its drug trade. At each check-point, the foreigners had to queue to sign a register. Then there were prayer-stops, when the foreigners stretched their legs, while the locals prostrated themselves to Mecca. Night fell early and I dozed for a while in the dark and woke with a start in Beshan. It was just the sort of arrival I try to avoid – midnight in a filthy, crowded bazaar, where I had to fight to get my bicycle down from the bus roof while keeping a close watch on my panniers, then a search in the blackness for a decent hotel. It was one of those times when I longed for a friend, someone to guard the bags while I organised the bikes, or vice versa.

From Beshan I made a detour from the Karakoram Highway, riding in a minibus through the magnificent Shangla Pass. I was getting quite blasé by this time about precipitous, broken roads over chasms, so my nerves were steady enough to enjoy the lushness of the trees and ferns and the rich emerald green of the rice paddies in the hollows. Through to the main Mardan road, we joined the crystal-clear Swat River and cruised beside it down the beautiful Swat Valley. Thanks to my Kashgar friends, Patrick and Dixie, I even had an introduction to the legendary Akond of Swat ('Who, or why, or which, or what, Is the Akond of SWAT?' to quote Edward Lear), but his address was Islamabad, so I had to content myself with a modest hotel in Mingora.

The Swat Valley was Alexander the Great's route into India and I spent a happy morning in the museum at Saidu Sharif, where the exhibits were beautifully arranged in a splendid new building funded by the Japanese Government. There were putti with garlands, figurines in Phrygian caps, Buddhas in Greek tunics with straight Greek noses, Corinthian capitals with lotus flowers among the acanthus leaves – all elegant examples of the Gandhara Culture, the fertile blending of Greek with north-west Indian art, and proof that Alexander and his troops really did pass that way.

There was terrorist activity in Malakand, along the road I had hoped to cycle, and the police were advising tourists not to pass that way. Once again, I was forced into the bus and it was not until I reached Peshawar that I was able to take to my own two wheels again. But I enjoyed watching the local cyclists as we passed through the villages. Their 'cykels' were their prized possessions and what they lacked in gears and oil they made up for in the splendour of their ornamentation. If there were prizes for invention, mine would have gone to a bicycle totally wrapped in tin foil, with an epergne of paper flowers sticking up from the handlebars, tinsel streamers threaded through the spokes, a Davy Crocket wolf-tail flapping on an aerial over the rear carrier and, the final master-stroke, two yellow plastic hands which waved at passers-by from the rear hub.

It was the first time I'd been in that part of the world in the summer and I couldn't believe the ferocity of the heat. No wonder the British in the days of the Raj, and the wealthier Pakistanis today, escaped to the coolness of the mountains! Even with air conditioning, my bed was hot to the touch, as the thermometer climbed to 49°C. I set out at dawn along the Grand Trunk Road towards Rawalpindi, but reeled into a hotel in Nowshera just 44 km, later. There I lay all day in a stifling bedroom under a ceiling fan, emerging in the evening for a 'chest piece' of chicken in the restaurant opposite, then collapsing in a sweating heap onto my bed again.

The next morning, I set out even earlier. The little sweeper boy was already on his knees, washing the entrance hall. He said 'Good morning, sir' and gave me the sweetest smile. Then he helped me down the hotel steps with my bicycle and passed me the bags for loading, but when I offered him a 5-rupee tip, he rejected it with indignation. If anyone needed and deserved a tip, it was that ragged little eight-year-old cleaner, but I couldn't persuade him to take it. In the end, he settled for three ginger biscuits.

I had to stop at a village stall for my first cold drink of Sprite within half an hour. An elegant silver-haired gentleman came up and pressed me to join him for tea. His English was good and I was faced with a dilemma. Should I refuse and rush off on my bicycle while the morning was still cool, looking at nothing and talking to no one (in which case I might as well not be in Pakistan), or should I stop and socialise, losing the only bearable part of the day? I compromised with a very quick break for a Pepsi. followed by a cup of tea in the village tea-house.

By the time I reached Jehangira, just 23 km on from Nowshera, I was feeling dizzy with the heat, so I went into the chemist's shop to buy some salt tablets against dehydration. The shop was staffed by two extremely pleasant young men and was as well stocked as any pharmacy in the West.

'Why do you want salt tablets?' asked the chemist.

'I think I'm getting dehydrated.'

'Well, just sit down and drink some water, and then we'll discuss tablets.'

There was a plastic tank of cooled mineral water in the shop. I gulped down three glasses, one after the other. Then the assistant went out and got me a large tumbler of fresh mango juice from the corner stall, 'to top up the vitamin C'.

'Our people don't take salt tablets any more. They can have side-effects. We all chew vitamin C. It works just as well against dehydration – and it's good for you too.'

He sold me a box of tablets and stood over me while I crunched my first dose. It was a very nice shop and I was happy to sit there and chat for a while. We discussed the Pakistani passion, cricket, then they told me that their hobby was wild pig shooting, which they did in the cool of the evening.

'The wild pigs are a pest. They root up the vegetables.'

'What do you do with them when you've shot them?'

'We don't touch them,' the chemist said, horror-stricken. 'It's against our religion.'

'So you just leave them there to rot?' He quickly changed the subject.

'I don't think you realise how near to the edge you were when you came into the shop. You wouldn't have lasted another five minutes out there in the heat of the road. You'd have collapsed and ended up in hospital. None of us would dream of cycling in this temperature, and we're used to the heat. You must be out of your mind to try it. We're going to put you on the bus to Rawalpindi – and no argument!'

With that, they locked up the shop, wheeled my bicycle to the bus-stand and organised everything for me. Within moments, a woman had been ejected from her seat near the open door and I was installed in her place. Cube was lashed to the roof and off we sped down the road to Rawalpindi. It was the ignominious end to my cycling that summer in Pakistan. I'd cleared the Khūnjerāb in style, but fallen on the flat.

9 Transports of Less Delight

The Liner she's a lady, an' she never looks nor 'eeds –
The Man-o'-War's 'er 'usband, an' 'e gives 'er all she needs;
But, oh, the little cargo-boats, that sail the wet sea roun',
They're just the same as you an' me a-plyin' up an' down!
Rudyard Kipling

One of the great joys of cycling is its lack of complications. I get up in the morning, pack my panniers, check my route and start pedalling. No timetables, no deadlines, no dawn starts or midnight arrivals, no chaotic, teeming bus stations to fight in, no awkward officials to placate. I go as I please, when I please and stop when I'm ready. Life is simplicity itself. But as soon as I have to get myself and my bicycle onto some other form of transport, my problems begin. In some parts of the world, even the most straightforward arrangements can be struggles of Byzantine complexity.

Take China, for instance. I was in Beijing with my new bicycle and I wanted to take it by train to Xi'an, to start my ride along the Silk Road. In England, we go to the station, buy a ticket and get on the train. In Beijing, I knew that I had to have an advance booking, so I cycled to the railway station, found my way across the vast, crowded concourse and presented myself at the special window for tourist tickets, open until 23.30 hours, according to its notice. It was 4.30 on Friday afternoon.

'Come tomorrow,' barked the surly woman in her navy blue serge trouser-suit. I returned the next afternoon. 'Come tomorrow,' she barked again. This time I had the wit to enquire about the time. 'Before four.' The painted notice evidently bore no relation to the actual opening hours. The next afternoon, I finally succeeded in buying my ticket to Xi'an.

But worse was to come. I still had to despatch my bicycle, so I went for help to the laughingly labelled 'Service Desk'. Two women in navy suits were carrying on a conversation behind the counter, while a third was reading. When I eventually caught the eye of one of them, she didn't understand my Chinese, she didn't speak English and she wasn't even prepared to look at the request I was pointing to in my phrase book. I wandered through one giant hall after another, growing more despairing by the minute, until I finally sighted the baggage office at the far end of the car park, beyond a Hampton Court maze of barricades, each with its band of ticket-checkers.

There was a guard on duty at the door. He told me that I was not allowed to take my bicycle into the office and, in any case, it was impossible to send a bicycle by train. My Chinese was not up to an argument, so I went away and lurked. An hour later, he was replaced by another guard. This one smiled, escorted me into the baggage office and pointed to a window which was actually labelled 'Bicycle Despatch' in English.

A man in the regulation navy blue suit sat with his back to the window, reading a newspaper. When I tapped on the glass, he turned round, took one look at me and immediately returned to his newspaper. The side-door to his cubicle was ajar so, undaunted, I pushed it open and stood directly in front of him. 'I want to send my bicycle to Xi'an,' I said, in Chinese. The effect was magical. As soon as he heard those few words in his own language, the clerk beamed and mobilised the whole department. Forms were filled in for me, labels tied on, queues jumped, the bicycle weighed and a ticket issued, all in a whirl of good-humoured activity.

'Face' is all-important in China. The baggage-clerk was a kind man, but his only language was Chinese. When he saw a 'big nose' at his window, he simply ignored me; he would rather appear rude than show his lack of education. But as soon as I began to speak my appalling Chinese, *I* became the one who was ignorant, the fool who couldn't speak the celestial language or fill in the celestial forms (in triplicate). Speaking a few words of the language is always an ice-breaker, but nowhere more so than in China, where the people have a horror of looking foolish. They laughed at my pronunciation and repeated my mistakes with unconcealed glee, but I was cared for wherever I went. The blank stares were reserved for the foreigners without Chinese.

This may seem a trivial incident, unworthy of such lengthy treatment, but it is typical of the problems of coping with China and many places in the East. The simplest journey, purchase or enquiry becomes a major undertaking and whole days have to be set aside for tasks which, at home, would be the work of moments. Package tours may have their hiccoughs, but those who wrestle with eastern bureaucracy single-handed need an iron-clad immunity from headaches. No wonder the Chinese prefer to travel by bicycle, as I do!

Boats are much less stressful. There's something infinitely calming about water – the slap of sails or the steady chug-chug of the engine. If I can't cycle, a journey in a slow boat is the next best thing.

Katherine and I had cycled north up the coast of Brazil, from Salvador to Belém, at the mouth of the Amazon, and there the roads ran out. Some maps optimistically drew a dotted line through the Amazon Basin and over the Andes, linking the Atlantic with the Pacific. But this Trans-Amazonian Highway was no more than a planner's dream, doomed to failure by the vastness and density of the jungle, with its reptiles, insects, diseases and tribes of uncertain temper. The Amazon River was still the only road deep into the interior and taking a series of boats upstream was my only practicable course. I planned to start from Belém and sail over 4,000 km from the Atlantic up to Yurimaguas, the last port below the rapids, where I could join the Peruvian dirt road over the Andes. After the long, hot ride up the coast, I was looking forward to my cruise.

Katherine was travelling with me as far as Manaus and together we toured the Belém docks, comparing vessels, prices and sailing schedules. There was a bewildering choice and we got no help from the travel agents. Anyone who is anyone in Brazil flies from city to city, so no one we spoke to had actually sailed up the Amazon. Of course, that in no way deterred them from holding forth on the dangers of the journey. 'Well, if you want to get robbed and raped, that's your business! We don't arrange such trips,' said the haughty assistant at American Express. The receptionist at our hotel went even further, advising us to divide the nights into watches, so that one of us slept, while the other stayed awake to guard our possessions and our virtue. (The reality turned out to be quite different. We not only slept simultaneously, but even left our cabin door open to enjoy the night breezes!)

The luxurious air-conditioned tourist liners, which plied between Belém and Manaus, had such a deep draught that they had to keep well away from the banks, so we looked for a clean and comfortable local boat, which would travel closer in and give us a better view of riverside villages and wildlife. We settled on the *Cisne Branco*, (the White Swan) which sailed in six days' time. The first class fare was 52,000 cruzeiros each (about $110) for the five-day voyage, including all meals.

After five weeks on the move, it was good to have those days at leisure in one place; and after five weeks of unbroken sunshine, we even enjoyed the rain. Belém is one of the world's most rained-upon cities and February was in the depths of its rainy season. How it poured! Surprisingly, as it lay so near to the Equator, it was not at all steamy. The mornings dawned clear and sunny. Then the heat built up, the sky clouded over and at 2 p.m. the rain burst down in tropical torrents. Two hours later, it was all over. The sun came out again and the evenings and nights were pleasantly cool. It was an agreeable climate and easy to cope with, as the daily downpours arrived like clockwork just at siesta-time.

We had been told to take plenty of fruit and mineral water, plus a few tins of sardines and bars of chocolate to supplement the basic diet on board ship. We did our serious shopping in the supermarkets, but it was fun to wander round *Ver-o-Peso* (Watch the Weight), the huge dockside market, looking at the strange Amazon fish, the hundreds of thousands of shrimps spread out on tarpaulins to dry in the sun, and all the dried snakes, alligators' teeth, herbs and roots of which traditional Amazonian medicines are compounded. We tried all the fruits: biriba, which looked like a bunch of tiny plastic bananas, bacaba, maracaju, pupunha, inga, pitanga, tabereba, all exotic fruits with surprising flavours – but we stuck to bananas, pineapples and mangos for our voyage.

Thanks to the good offices of the British Consul in Belém, Katherine had managed to ship her bicycle by cargo boat to Harwich. So on Friday afternoon, she was free to take our luggage in a taxi to the docks, while I cycled there. The *Cisne Branco* was the smartest, whitest ship at the quay. She had three decks and our cabin was on the middle one, next to the bridge. With its two bunks and washbasin, it was about the size of an overnight sleeper to Scotland. The wardrobe was only three nails on the wall, but the electric light was bright and there was a socket for our kettle. We were given a key to the first class showers and lavatories.

There were thirty of us in first class (fifteen identical cabins). The rest of the passengers, over three hundred of them, brought their hammocks and slept on the two lower decks, sometimes whole families to a hammock! They were allocated just enough space on the ceiling bars to tie their hammocks securely and the result was a seething mass of humanity. My bicycle had to travel down in the hold, which was so damp that it emerged in Manaus with dripping handlebar-grips and white mould on the saddle.

The ship sailed at 6 p.m., just as the sun was setting. We went up to the top deck, ordered a couple of beers and settled down to watch the lights of Belém fade into the distance. There was music on board and Edson and Dirce, a couple we got to know well on the voyage, danced the *pagode* with tremendous style and verve. As the stars came out and we caught the breeze from the Atlantic, I had a sudden flash of awareness. It was one of those rare moments when I was supremely happy and knew it. There was nothing on earth I would rather be doing and nowhere I would rather be than on that ship, at that particular moment, slipping out of the shelter of Belém harbour into the black velvet of the Amazon night.

The Amazon is a deceptive river, which conceals its vast size in a multiplicity of channels and islands. It never looks particularly wide, yet it contains one-fifth of the world's fresh water in its 1,100 known tributaries and its delta is a staggering 320 km across, a navigational nightmare of narrow waterways, mangrove swamps and shifting banks of silt. The Portuguese never managed to work their way upstream. Even when they found a passage through the intricacies of the delta, their ships were swept aground by the fierce current or damaged by floating tree-trunks, and their crews perished through disease, hunger and the hostility of the natives. Food in the rainforest was scarce and the local Indians fought hard to keep out the competition. As there were no precious spices and no gold to reward them for their hardships, the Portuguese soon gave up the struggle and concentrated on the easier coastal trade. It was left to the Spanish under the Conquistador Francisco de Orellana to sail the entire length of the river in 1541, but from the Peruvian Andes downstream to the Atlantic. The voyage was a nine-month nightmare of hunger, hardship and skirmishes, in which Orellana lost an eye, while many of his crew were killed by '*Amazonas*', the women captains who commanded troops of Indian bowmen. It was after these female warriors that the river was named. To those of us accustomed to travelling light, the most extraordinary feature of this expedition was that the Spanish climbed the Andes and fought their way through steaming jungle, clad in full suits of armour and steel helmets!

We soon got into the ship's routine. Meals were served at one long table on the middle deck and it was amazing how briskly and efficiently the crew managed to feed everyone – a feat which was possible only because the Brazilians are, after the British, the world's most disciplined queuers. They all waited obediently while the children were served at a special first sitting, then they took the places allocated to them and no one ever pushed. The two main meals were substantial. Huge lumps of plain beef or chicken were accompanied by bowls of rice, mashed potato, *farofa* (ground manioc), spaghetti and, just in case anyone was still feeling low on carbohydrates, haricot beans. Not a shred of salad or vegetable passed our lips. We were glad of the pineapples and mangos in our cabin. Breakfast was good strong coffee and cream crackers (a Brazilian passion), which we used to scoop margarine out of large communal tubs.

Between meals, I read *Don Quixote*, Katherine embroidered and everyone watched the river go by. It was an indolent life. We sailed near enough to the banks to see the thatched huts on stilts and watch the Indians fishing. Children as young as four or five paddled their own dug-out canoes on the fast-flowing river with tremendous skill and confidence, and toddlers dived fearlessly into the water while their mothers did the laundry on the banks. The river was their road, their livelihood and their playground.

On Sunday, whole families went on outings, dressed in their Sunday best, the father paddling at the back of the canoe, the mother in white under a parasol and the children kneeling in a neat line in front. One evening a young man sped by with a bright new Honda outboard motor attached to his canoe. With his slicked-back hair, black shirt, black trousers and huge gold-coloured wristwatch, he was decked out like Elvis Presley and I wondered where on earth he could be heading so purposefully in the moonless night. There was no sign of human habitation and he melted into the distance as mysteriously as he had appeared.

Occasionally, entire villages of Indians would paddle out to the ship. They were coming for the cast-off clothes which the richer passengers threw overboard for them.

Our fellow-passengers were mostly Brazilian, kind, simple people with no English. They smiled at us, patted us, stroked our hair – anything to establish contact and show us that we were welcome. There were a few young western backpackers in hammocks, a German travel-writer who found it all too much for him and jumped ship in Santarém, and a Swiss official from Amnesty International. I talked to him most evenings and was cheered by his optimism. He told me that South America was making remarkable progress in human rights. The people had woken up and realised their own power. They had ousted dictators, set up branches of Amnesty and were pursuing justice with an energy and confidence which would have been unimaginable even ten years ago. They were transforming their continent.

Of wildlife we saw disappointingly little. We heard the birds and crickets, and occasionally saw a hawk wheeling, but otherwise it was pigs, horses and cows with egrets on their backs. One day, a school of grey freshwater dolphins followed the ship, arching and diving in its wake, but we never saw the pink dolphins which are peculiar to the Amazon. Nor did we see any crocodiles. The landscape was rural and domestic, not the thick, impenetrable jungle we had imagined.

It was the Amazon itself and its dramatic weather which provided the greatest excitement. The water was brown and opaque, in colour and texture a cross between oxtail soup and butterscotch sauce. The main stream and its tributaries which rise in the Andes are rich in silt and nutrients, and consequently in fish, while those which rise in the Brazilian highlands and the Guyanas are so poor that they are known as 'rivers of hunger'. When those rivers joined the main stream, they were clear and black, and their sinister waters flowed alongside for a mile or more before merging into the turgid brown. There were storms on the river, which tossed the boat like a ship at sea. Sometimes we would see the storm coming downstream to meet us. It was as solid as a shower-curtain. One moment we were in sunshine and the next, with no transition, we were under the deluge in an eerie darkness. Tarpaulins were swiftly fastened round the deck rails to keep the hammocks dry, until the ship had lurched its way through the storm and come out into the sunshine at the other end. On cloudy days with black stormclouds, the intensity of the hidden tropical sun turned the brown water into burnished copper, and on clear nights with brilliant stars, lightning would flash at all points of the compass simultaneously. There was always some spectacle to watch.

We had expected clouds of mosquitoes and had come fully equipped, but mosquitoes dislike wind and never settle on moving ships. I was well protected by Atlantic and Amazon breezes wherever I went in Brazil, and used my mosquito net only twice, in small riverside towns. Of course, a trek into the heart of the rainforest would have been a different matter.

Cargo was the main business of the Amazon ships and we stopped at every port to unload consignments of shampoo, refrigerators, stacks of foam mattresses like sliced bread, lavatory paper and the inevitable cream crackers. Everything the communities needed came by river and all the shops in a town were either overflowing with Nescafé and chocolate, or right out of them, depending on the cargo of the last ship. When we docked at the larger ports, the crew changed from their shorts and flip-flops into superbly tailored white uniforms and spotless white shoes, which would have done credit to the grandest fleet in the world. It was somehow rather touching, this effort to maintain professional standards on a modest little tub trading in isolated dirt-road villages, hundreds of miles up the Amazon. It reminded me of Somerset Maugham's colonial officers in god-forsaken postings, who kept the flag flying by dressing for dinner, even on their own in the jungles of Sarawak.

We ran aground on a sandbank and reached Manaus a day late, giving Katherine just enough time to take a quick look at the opera house before flying off to Rio.

For years I had longed to see Manaus, the fabled product of the 1890s rubber boom, hacked out of the jungle 1,500 km upstream. In its heyday, it was so wealthy that its citizens sent their linen to London to be laundered and competed with the capitals of Europe in the magnificence of their buildings and fashions. The famous opera house, an exuberant mixture of Italian Renaissance and French *fin de siècle*, was crowned with a glistening dome of blue, green and yellow tiles, the colours of the Brazilian flag; and the great M. Eiffel himself was commissioned to design the market-hall, modelled on his Paris market, Les Halles, and ship out its cast-iron parts for local assembly. But the city's real wonder was more prosaic – the floating dock, designed by a Scot in 1902 to cope with the seasonal 12-metre rise and fall of the river. This ingenious structure, still in use today, made possible the city's development as the major port of the Amazon.

The bubble burst when rubber seeds were smuggled out of Brazil by an Englishman named Henry Wickham, nurtured at Kew and planted in Malaysia. The rubber tapped from random trees in the Amazonian rainforest could not compete with the efficient product of the newly planted South-East Asian estates and the jungle once again enfolded Manaus in silence and obscurity.

Today the city has fresh vigour as a free port and the capital of the mineral-rich Brazilian interior. Skyscrapers are springing up between the red-tiled roofs and the shops are bursting with electronic equipment, French perfumes and Scotch whisky. Businessmen shelter their Armani suits under English golf umbrellas, but the air is so warm that everyone else strolls around in vests and suntops, oblivious to the downpours.

Perhaps because I was nursing a cold in the head and no longer had Katherine to cheer me up, I was low spirited in the rain. I bought the only type of Brazilian sandal available that week – in pink and mauve plastic of hideous design – because shoes rotted in the perpetual wetness and the tasteful imported alternatives, by Ferragamo and Bally, would have been a waste of money. The trees dripped, the shopping streets were awash with puddles, weeds sprang luxuriantly from every crack in the masonry and I started to see mildew everywhere. I even mistook a display of faded mauve and green plastic flowers on the hotel stairs for a patch of mould! At one time, I'd planned to take a trip deep into the rainforest, but the longer I stayed on the Amazon, the less attractive became the idea of camping out in the pouring rain on the off-chance of seeing a few snakes or parrots. I decided to move up-river as fast as I could. The rain was getting on my nerves and I longed for the clear skies of the Andes and the whirr of my bicycle wheels.

But ships on the next stretch, from Manaus to Tabatinga, were not so frequent and I had a week to wait. It was a week in limbo. No country seems quite so cut off from the rest of the world as Brazil. The media were obsessed with the antics of the President, a previously decorous man, who had arrived at the Rio Carnival entwined with a model in a T-shirt and no knickers! The scandal was rocking the nation and there was no room in the papers for anything so unimportant as international news. And we were even, in our little rainforest world, out of synchronisation with the rest of Brazil, as the locals refused to change their clocks to summer time and were sticking doggedly to what they called 'God's time', causing havoc with airline schedules and bank hours.

It was raining when I crossed the famous floating dock to board *Voyager*. I'd chosen her in preference to her main rival, *Jesus*, because she looked marginally cleaner and more stable. Another possibility, *The Lady Lourdes*, I'd also rejected because she had 'If God is for us, who will be against us?' painted on her bridge and 'Watch over me, O God, for You are my only refuge' all round her prow. I felt distinctly nervous of any ship which needed so much protection from the Almighty.

Voyager was similar to the *Cisne Branco*, but there were fewer first-class passengers, as the top deck cabins had been converted into a floating palace with blue satin curtains for the owner. He'd generously given me a double cabin for the single fare of $87 and this time I had a private shower with my own private pair of cockroaches. When the ship finally sailed, a day late, I realised that I was the only foreigner on board and, apart from the owner and his PA, the only pale-face. The passengers were poor. They fell on the food like vultures, clawing it out of the bowls with their fingers. And all day they swung in their hammocks or sat beside me, watching. If I read out on deck, they peered over my shoulder. If I did a crossword puzzle, they wanted to know what it was and how I did it. If I went to my cabin, they followed me and stood in a silent circle, gazing through the open door. My only rivals for attention were two boys redecorating a cabin, who drew rapt crowds throughout the day. But fascination has its advantages. The plump little Indian steward was my devoted attendant, bringing morning coffee to my cabin and saving me the choicest bits of chicken. He rejoiced in the name of David Jennings da Silva (after a Welsh seafaring grandfather) and he liked nothing better than to perch in my cabin, discussing Queen Elizabeth, Tower Bridge and other topics of interest to those with British ancestry.

As we sailed further upstream, the ship began to empty and the towns became poorer and poorer. Even the ports marked on the map were no more than a row of wooden shacks on a dirt road. The children who came on board to sell fruit were grimy and unkempt, and by the time we reached Tonantins, they had dwindled in number to two little tots who scurried down the river-bank with a coconut each. Yet the villagers still wore baseball caps and dreamed of North American fortunes in their Michigan Wolverines T-shirts. Sail Club, Move It, Excite your Body, A Human with Sporting Ilusions (sic), Fighting Irish – all wore their logos with pride, though nobody understood them. One old Indian woman sat outside her hut, gazing into space, her ragged T-shirt emblazoned with 'Fasten your Flies'. We had come to the end of the line, to Brazil's backyard, neglected by the bureaucrats of Brasilia and untouched by the new prosperity of the coastal cities.

At São Paulo de Olivença, an Indian family came on board. The wife carried their meagre possessions on her back and their baby son in a scarf at the front. Her husband struggled up the gang-plank, weighed down by a bulging hammock. Later in the day, I saw that it held his invalid mother, a little wraith of a woman with a wizened simian face. At mealtimes, while his wife fed and cleaned the baby, he patiently did the same for his mother, feeding her porridge with a spoon. When they sat down afterwards to their own meals, I noticed their quiet courtesy, how they passed the dishes to each other before helping themselves, in contrast to the others, who just grabbed. And yet they kept their eyes down on their plates, because they felt inferior to their shouting, guzzling table-mates. I wanted so much to talk to them, to give them some encouragement. But they were shy, they couldn't speak Portuguese and they didn't understand. I last saw them heaving their bundles up the dirt road in a downpour at Benjamin Constant, presumably looking for a doctor.

In Benjamin Constant I disembarked myself, at the dockside shack which advertised 'Eggiesburgers'. There I feasted on fried eggs with delicious fresh bread – a vast improvement on my usual breakfast of broken cream crackers and marge. Travellers need such treats to keep them going.

The voyage ended at Tabatinga, a despairing town of half-empty shops, fetid open drains and rat-infested rubbish-tips. Hopelessness hung over the people as tangibly as their tattered shorts. 'Don't go to Peru,' was David Jennings Da Silva's parting plea. 'They take cocaine there and they're murderers. Stay here with us – or go to Argentina. We're civilised people.'

By this time, I was bored with river travel and delighted to learn that the stretch to Iquitos could be covered in a day by motor-launch. The ticket-agency had its own wretched hovel of a hotel, where passengers spent the night before the 4.30 a.m. departure. The fat young manager showed me to my room, then lay down uninvited on my bed for a chat. He complimented me on my splendid athletic form, considering my age. I was annoyed.

'You should get a bicycle yourself,' I said sharply, 'and get rid of some of that weight!'

He patted his huge belly with satisfaction. 'I'm fine as I am. I can still pull in the *chicas*. They fancy big men.'

Needless to say, neither he nor the idle night porter gave me the promised 4 a.m. call. I woke with a start at 4.40, dressed in a panic and rushed down to the docks in the dark, past scavenging dogs. But I needn't have hurried. Fat Boy turned up at 5.20 and the launch finally appeared at 5.35. Then terror struck. Everyone shouted and screamed. I stood bewildered for a moment, before jumping up myself to join them on top of a table. A giant boa constrictor had swum up and was slithering onto the jetty. Two of the crew seized paddles and beat it on the head. It hesitated a moment, then decided to slide back into the safety of the dark Amazon waters. It was my closest encounter with a reptile in South America.

After weeks of slow boats, it was an exhilarating experience to skim across the surface with spume flying. By 6 a.m. we were at Santa Rosa in Peru, where I got my tourist card from a yawning official and the crew picked up our breakfasts of garlic sausage sandwiches and coffee. A high ranking Army Officer, all shiny belts and gold braid, came on board and crossed himself repeatedly as the launch set off. He wasn't the only nervous passenger. Most of my companions travelled through the heat of the day buckled up in their life-jackets! The engine kept overheating and had to be doused with buckets of Amazon water. And every time we stalled, the powerful current swept us back downstream and we had to overheat the engine again in the rush to recover lost time. I read my guide-book on Peru, while everyone else slept throughout the day, or gazed unblinking at the passing jungle. South Americans have a real gift for doing nothing.

At 7 p.m. we arrived in Iquitos. We were now 3,700 km upstream, but great ocean-going vessels were still moored at the quay. Of all unnerving experiences, arriving in the dark in a strange port is just about the worst. Dock areas are generally unsalubrious, far away from the town centre and crowded with shifty-looking characters waiting to prey on nervous arrivals.

Iquitos was worse than usual, as the quay was at the bottom of a long flight of stone steps, which vanished like Jack's beanstalk into the night sky. Without a word, a man pushed me out of the way, seized my bicycle and began to run up the steps with it. A boy grabbed my panniers and followed. I panted up in pursuit, convinced that I'd seen the last of my possessions. But at the top of the steps I found a pleasant, well-lit square and my two smiling porters. I had no Peruvian soles, so I gave them all my Brazilian cruzeiros and Colombian pesos. They zipped gleefully into a café to get them changed.

Iquitos must be the world's most remote state capital. The Andes and the jungle form such impenetrable barriers that manufactured goods from the rest of Peru have to travel by sea up the Pacific Coast, through the Panama Canal and the Caribbean, then up the Amazon from the Atlantic, a voyage of 11,000 km – yet the distance from Lima, as the condor flies, is a mere 1,000 km. But Iquitos, unlike Brazil, was avid for world news. When I walked into my hotel, Peruvian television was showing the ordination of the first Anglican women priests in Bristol Cathedral; there was news on Bosnia, and informed comment on Iraq and the North American political scene. *El Comercio*, the quality newspaper, even had a front-page photograph of the Queen Mother posing with the Irish Guards on St Patrick's Day.

My Spanish is far from brilliant, but it's better than my Portuguese, so I was able to talk to the boy who came along to tidy my room. He asked me where I came from.

'England? Is that where Paris is?'

'No. Paris is the capital of France. The capital of England is London.'

'Oh yes. Big Ben! Tower Bridge! Who's your president in England?'

'We don't have a president. We're a monarchy. We have a queen instead. Queen Elizabeth.'

'A queen!' His face lit up. 'How wonderful! I wish we had a queen. What's your money?'

'The pound sterling'

'That's the best money in the world. A pound is worth even more than a dollar.'

And so it went on. 'How did you learn to speak Castillian? (The Peruvians never call it Spanish.) Did you learn it at school? What languages did you learn there? How many years do children have to go to school in England?' All the time he made my bed, he fired questions at me in his thirst for information, for education. I was to find this eagerness throughout Peru. Education was revered, not simply as the way out of poverty, but in some spiritual sense, as the path to truth and light. The Maoist guerrilla movement, 'The Shining Path' (a cleverly chosen name) had exploited these deep aspirations. From its inception at the University of Ayacucho, it had shown its leader, Guzman, as a bespectacled teacher with a book in his hand, and had justified terrorism and mass murder with specious morality. Fortunately for tourists, the Peruvian *campesinos* had at last lost faith in The Shining Path and the Army was winning its war.

I loved Iquitos, despite the rain. The three-wheeled taxis puttered along on their little moped engines, bursting with civic pride, 'Iquitos in my heart' and 'Iquitos I love you truly' splashed all over their hoods. The evenings were particularly cheerful, with well-lit shops, families strolling along licking ice-creams, bands playing in the parks and giggly girls eyeing the local boys. It was a Spanish town, where the evening *paseo* was alive and well. The Peruvians had inherited the Spanish love of elegance, of cutting a dash in true *hidalgo* style. They dressed up in their finery on every possible occasion, in startling contrast to the Brazilians in their eternal T-shirts and flip-flops.

As the Tourist Police had banned the boat journey to Yurimaguas, I booked my flight out and spent my last hours by the mighty waterway which had dominated my life for the past six weeks. If the coasts of South America are Baroque, the Amazon is *fin de siècle* and *art deco*. I searched in vain for M. Eiffel's iron building, without which no self-respecting river town was complete, and admired the hand-painted ceramic tiles, the *azulejos* shipped in from Portugal to embellish the Malecon's grand houses. Then I treated myself to a final dinner in the best restaurant overlooking the Amazon. Lights twinkled on its black waters, the air was filled with the din of frogs and crickets, and the waiter, with a gloom matching his empty tables, said, 'Don't go up into the mountains. We're nice people here in Iquitos. Up there, they've got drugs and there's the Shining Path. It's dangerous. Stay here.' But people the world over are suspicious of their neighbours. I took no notice and was just as safe in the Andes as I'd been on the peaceful Amazon.

If slow boats are top of my list after bicycles, planes are way down at the bottom, not because I'm afraid of them, but because they're the most boring means of transport. I've had only one exciting flight, the flight across the Andes from Iquitos – and that was far too exciting for comfort.

I was aiming for Cajamarca, near the watershed of the Cordillera Central, the point at which the Police had told me it would be safe to start cycling again. But there were no flights direct from Iquitos to Cajamarca. I had to fly right over the Andes to Trujillo, on the Pacific Coast, then back-track up the mountains in a smaller plane or by bus. It was a demanding journey, as I had to cope with three completely different climates in a little over twelve hours. At noon I was still on the steaming Amazon; by 4 p.m. I was cycling through burning desert from Trujillo Airport to the city centre; and at 3 a.m. I arrived in frosty Cajamarca, under Andean stars as big and bright as street-lamps.

To catch my plane, I cycled out to Iquitos Airport and deflated my tyres as usual, in preparation for what I assumed would be a normal flight in a jet with an unpressurised baggage hold. I checked in and strolled calmly out onto the tarmac. Then I saw my aircraft. My heart leapt into my mouth. I'd never seen such a contraption. It was an ancient Russian military transport plane with twin propellers and battered sides. There was no passenger door, so we had to board by scrambling up the cargo-ramp in the tail. There were thirty-six makeshift seats inside the grey steel shell and six tiny windows, high above our heads. My bicycle lay on the suitcases behind the passenger-seats and we had to clamber over it to find our places. We were given boiled sweets to suck, just like the old days, and I must have looked quite worried, because the young cabin steward came over and made solicitous enquiries about my comfort – which was non-existent!

It was a hideously bumpy flight and I was soon surrounded by vomiting Peruvians. The steward came round halfway to Tarapoto with plastic cups of luminous yellow Inca Kola, but there was so much jolting and tossing that half the contents flew over the passengers before they could be served from the tray. It was the last plane I should have chosen for a crossing of the Andes. I had the irrational feeling that any movement I made might cause the machine to keel over, but I braced myself once or twice to stand on tip-toe for a glimpse of the landscape out of the high porthole ahead. I saw the Amazon and its rainforest give way to the Eastern slopes of the Andes, which are drenched in torrential rain from October to April. The result is spectacular cloud-forest, where rivers crash down through canyons of tropical vegetation as much as 1,500 m deep.

We landed with a terrible jolt at Tarapoto, where a few passengers got off and on. Then we took off straight into the mountains. As we climbed higher, the tree-tops swam in and out of view through the drifting mist until, with a final heart-stopping lurch, our plane burst through the clouds and we began to glide serenely across the blue immensity. More Inca Kola was served, to keep our minds off the mountains which pierced the clouds beneath us with their jagged black and white peaks. I looked at my fellow-passengers and wondered who would be eating whom if we crashed up there in the snows. But we arrived safely in Trujillo on the Pacific Coast.

If the plane I'd just flown in was transcontinental, I dreaded to think what the 'small local aircraft' to Cajamarca would be like, so I opted for *terra firma*. The bus was bound to be safer. It would also give me a preview of the road I had to cycle and, more importantly, it would do the climb from sea-level to 2,750 m more slowly, giving me time to adjust.

Buses rank only one higher than planes on my transport-list and this bus was a particularly ramshackle specimen. With Condor roped to the roof, it ground its gears through the night, groaning like a grampus on the climbs. When I finally mounted my bicycle in Cajamarca bus station, two wheels and a good pair of brakes had never felt safer!

10 Men and Other Animals

L'homme est, je vous l'avoue, un méchant animal.

Molière, *Tartuffe*

When I give talks on my solo travels, I'm always asked two questions. Men ask 'Aren't you lonely?' and women ask 'Aren't you scared?' Their thoughts go immediately to rape and bodily harm.

The day before I set out along the Silk Road, I gave a talk at the British Embassy to the Beijing International Society. It seemed a bit of a cheek, because I didn't know China nearly as well as my audience did. They all lived there, but they were still horrified at the idea that I was going to cycle alone through what the Vice-Consul called 'pirate country', the provinces of Gansu and Xinjiang. I was talking gaily about my preparations for the journey, when an American woman in the audience came up with a new twist to the old question: 'Do you think it's because you're matoor that you're so unafraid?'

I gave it some thought. 'Probably,' I replied. 'Maturity is a help. If I were a twenty-year-old blonde, I should expect a lot more problems – and I should be less good at dealing with them. But at my stage in life, I'm a pretty wise old fox. I'm careful not to let myself be drawn into situations I can't get out of.'

Looking back over my travels, I've made a few mistakes with men, and all of them have been funny rather than serious. Like the incident in a Turkish hotel. Every time I went to reception, there was a man in a smart suit sitting nearby, fiddling with a string of worry beads. I took him for the proprietor and smiled. The third time I did that, he rushed after me into the lift, flung his arms round me and invited me to his bedroom for whisky! He was not the proprietor and I'd given the poor man quite the wrong impression. I rose to my full height, which was much greater than his, and fixed him with an icy stare, enough to send him crestfallen back to the lobby.

Age brings worldly wisdom and it also brings respect, sometimes a little too much. I was waiting for a ferry boat in India, when a class of small school-children joined the queue. 'Good morning, auntie,' they chorused, most politely. The schoolmaster corrected them. 'You shouldn't call the lady auntie. That's rude. You should say, "Good morning, grandmother."' He meant it as a compliment to my years, but for westerners striving to be youthful, remarks of that sort are more depressing than eastern people realise.

Another great advantage I have when cycling is my unisex appearance. I'm quite tall and in my cotton trousers, baggy shirt and cycling cap, I'm taken for a man at a distance. Even close up, villagers often gaze at me in bewilderment and ask, 'Are you a man or a woman?' In many parts of the world, it's only the men who cycle and the locals can't believe their eyes. I must be a man! The only areas where I make a real effort to look like a woman, by wearing brightly coloured, tighter-fitting clothes, are areas of terrorist activity. There, an unknown man might be shot at, especially if he's wearing khaki, fawn or olive green, the colours of combat. A woman is never suspected of fighting or spying.

It's often assumed that travelling in Muslim countries must be particularly difficult for a woman. When their own women are veiled or have their heads covered and rarely go out unescorted, how do the men treat a foreign woman, alone and unveiled on a bicycle? The answer is that I'm treated very well indeed – so well, in fact, that Muslim countries are a pleasure to cycle through.

First, there's the Muslim law of hospitality towards the travelling stranger. It's the duty of a Muslim to help, feed and entertain any strangers who come along, even if it means giving them the last scrap of food in the house. Then, as a travelling woman, I get extra help. Muslim men are protective towards women (too much so in western eyes, if they keep them in purdah) and they always go out of their way to look after me.

Islamic countries vary, of course. Turkey is a secular state, where women have the vote and considerable freedom. Malaysia is an easy-going society and the Indonesian women

I've met seem to move about quite freely. It's in the Arab countries, and in North Africa and Pakistan, that the laws of Islam are applied most strictly. There, women travellers have a real advantage. Except in the most sophisticated families, a travelling man can't be invited home, in case he sets eyes on the women of the house, but a travelling woman can be asked in to meet mothers, wives and daughters, and is often given a bed for the night. I've stayed in a number of orthodox Muslim households and enjoyed the experience. I've spent my days in mixed family company or sitting with the women. Then in the evenings, I've been transformed into an honorary man and gone out for a restaurant dinner with the head of the house and his male friends.

'We do enjoy talking to western women,' they say. 'They're so well-informed and full of life.' I don't pull my punches.

'Perhaps your wives would be better-informed and more lively if you took them out occasionally. Why aren't they with us tonight?' They have the grace to look embarrassed.

'This is not the West. In our society, that would never do.' And they switch to the safer topic of cricket.

In freer societies, where men are used to the idea of women as friends, I meet no more problems than I do in England. But in Pakistan, where I've cycled twice, most men never talk to a woman outside their own limited family-circle and they can't work out how they're supposed to deal with me. When they're being respectful, they address me as 'sister' or 'mother'. But when I check into a small-town hotel, where they've never seen a woman travelling alone before, I become a provocation. Their hopes rise. A diet of western films has given them the idea that all western women are wanton hussies and they can't believe their luck when one of these abandoned creatures turns up on her own in their hotel.

In Peshawar, I arrived rather late in the day and found that the three most reputable hotels in the city were full. I asked a shopkeeper the way to the fourth on my list and he kindly pushed my bicycle there, haggled till he got me a discount, then helped to carry my luggage upstairs. He sat down uninvited on my bed. 'I am your helper. You are very tired. I give you massage.' I managed to get rid of him with a warm expression of thanks, a formal handshake and a promise, which I had no intention of keeping, to visit his shop the next day. No sooner had he left the room than the manager burst in. He put his arm round me and he too offered me a massage. I moved nimbly out of his grasp.

'How old do you think I am?' he asked. I guessed that he was about fifty, so I said 'Sixty-five', to take the wind out of his sails. He was most affronted.

'I'm thirty-six,' he said, 'and a most active man! How old are you?'

I smiled sweetly and told him I was eighty-nine. He knew then that I was having him on and made a dignified retreat. But he was not too proud to have another try the next morning. He came up himself with my 'bed tea', dreaming no doubt of the nice massage he would give me, and was disappointed to find me already up and dressed. I drank my tea in stony silence while he tried one engaging topic of conversation after another. He left with the empty cup and dashed hopes.

That was just one example out of many. I usually find I can ward off the approaches of hotel staff with a touch of humour or a frosty glare, without antagonising or shaming them. The funny thing is that age plays no part in these games. I was startled one night to be seized and kissed most passionately by a hotel porter who must have been all of twelve years old!

'What do you think you're doing?' I asked, in my sternest headmistress voice. He scuttled out of the bedroom and went into hiding when I appeared at breakfast next morning.

In the next block to my Peshawar hotel, there was an Afghan shop. Pakistan supports about two million Afghan refugees (an act of humanity which burdens the country and receives too little recognition in the world). Many Afghans have fled their homeland with their family heirlooms and these treasures eventually find their way into the shops of the North West Frontier. Oriental rugs are one of my weaknesses and I was drooling outside the Afghan shop when the proprietor invited me in to look at his stock over a cup of tea. He showed me beautiful embroidered waistcoats, hand-beaten brass trays, hand-carved stools and tooled leather saddles. They all looked wonderful in the shop, but I knew from experience what a disaster they would be in my London flat, so I resisted the temptation to buy. In any case, I didn't have room in my panniers.

The old Afghan talked with great longing of his country. He knew he would never go back there and was fated to die in Pakistan. 'This terrible war!' he said. 'This shitty, shitty war!' And a tear fell into his tea-cup.

I think his grief was genuine, but it also turned out to be part of the softening-up process. Having worked me into a sympathetic frame of mind, he turned the conversation round to me, my husband and why I was travelling alone when I was married. Was it because my marriage was unhappy? (I never confess to being a widow, as it sends out the wrong signals.) This was a far more subtle approach, one wise old fox weighing up the possibilities with another. We both enjoyed the fencing over our second pot of tea, but there was no sale and no afternoon of passion for the melancholy Afghan.

A less subtle old man approached me in the street in Rawalpindi. He was walking along with his son, who looked about thirty. 'My son is in love with you. Do you like him?' 'No,' I said, at which the father bundled his son into a taxi and they sped off. In Mingora, a chauffeur was the go-between. He came up as I was buying fruit in the market. 'Come and talk to my master. Have a good time,' he said, pointing to a Mercedes with black windows. All the men from Beshan onwards – porters, electricians who came unsummoned to my bedroom to check my lights, Afghan dealers, tycoons in limos – all were alive to the potential of an unescorted foreign woman. I was obviously worth a try. How different they were from the Tajiks and Hunzakuts of the mountains, who seemed at ease with women and talked to me as a friend. How different too from the Chinese, who must be the least threatening men in the world to lone western women.

To begin my cycle-ride along the Silk Road, I took the train from Beijing to Xi'an. It was an eighteen-hour journey, so I treated myself to 'soft sleeper', a place in a four-berth compartment straight out of the great days of steam. There was a deep plum-coloured carpet with a gold pattern on it, yellow velvet curtains with flounced white nets, and lace antimacassars on the luxuriously soft seats. Later, when the beds were made up, they had spotless white sheets, duvets and feather pillows. Towels were provided and, as everywhere in China, thermos flasks of boiling water for tea. The only links with the late twentieth century were the muzak and the television set in every compartment.

When we drew out of Beijing Station at 2 p.m., two men sat opposite me, one aged 67 and the other 20. I knew their ages within moments. 'What is your country? Where are you going? How old are you? Are you married? Where is your husband? How many children have you got? What is your profession? How much did your bicycle cost?' This is the question-and-answer routine which haunts every traveller in the East. At the first stop we were joined by a third man, who climbed into the bunk above me and immediately fell asleep. By 3 p.m., I was sharing a compartment with three sleeping men.

Travel in China has many problems, but sexual harassment is not one of them. It must be the only country in the world where those twenty-year-old blondes I mentioned in my Beijing talk can walk about alone in comfort. The main reason is that the Chinese find other races unattractive. They call westerners 'big noses' and are said to find our skins corpse-like, our bodies hairy and our smell revolting. They take an even dimmer view of races with darker skins. The result of all this, happily for women tourists, is that even Chinese rapists give them a wide berth.

But quite apart from personal feelings, there are official restrictions. One of the duties of the Public Security Bureau is to prevent sexual relationships between Chinese nationals and non-Chinese. Couples may be challenged by the PSB in hotels and clubs, and even when innocently sharing a taxi. The foreign partner usually gets off with a reprimand, or the temporary loss of his passport, but the Chinese can be arrested and punished. Because men have more freedom in China – as they do elsewhere – a Chinese man will be excused a foreign liaison more readily than a Chinese woman. So western men must be careful not to 'insult' a Chinese woman (the official term) by becoming too friendly. It's ironic that China was a stern critic of apartheid in South Africa.

Fortunately for me, I was respected for my age as well, so I was totally free of unwanted attentions in China – a blissful change on my lone travels.

Men find legs peculiarly fascinating. 'Word of her horsewoman's legs had spread across the 600 km of that wild province,' wrote the South American novelist, Isabel Allende, in one of her stories – and the South Americans certainly went in for cyclists' legs! Not in Brazil, where the city centres are full of shorts and bikinis and all but a few stuffy businessmen are Children of Nature, splendidly at ease with their bodies. But in Peru I had queues of men wanting to feel the strength of my thighs. And 'you must be in fine fettle!' was a common greeting in Australian pubs, as the men at the bar looked admiringly at my legs. Shorts drive them crazy, which is why I stick to my baggy, unisex trousers. A woman alone in shiny black cycling knickers is asking for trouble.

Until I cycled the Silk Road across Turkey with Shirley, I thought it was only solo women who got themselves into scrapes. But our night on Kop Gecidi (Kop Pass) changed my views on that. We had left Aşkale early in the morning and were hoping to reach Bayburt by evening. For a few kilometres we cycled through a pleasant river valley with poplars for shade. Then we started to climb. We soon left the villages behind and the hills became bleaker and steeper. Soon we were plodding up one of those depressing roads which climb in a long series of hairpin bends, every one of them visible from the foot of the mountain. It was so exposed up there that the only shade we could find for our lunch was the shadow behind a parked steam-roller. We flopped down with our water, nuts and fruit. Then, to our amazement, we saw two boys on bicycles racing down the mountain we were climbing. As always on the road, we greeted fellow-cyclists with delight and the boys joined us behind the steam-roller. They turned out to be English cyclists on their way to Nepal. We said we were on our way to

Trabzon, and Shirley told them that I'd just cycled across China and Pakistan. 'I know who you are now,' cried one of the boys. 'You're that schoolteacher!' They'd read *A Bike Ride* when they were planning to set out on their travels and it was the book which had inspired them to go on their bicycles. I basked in glory.

We had a wealth of practical information to exchange, as each pair of us had just cycled from the other's destination and knew all about the road-surfaces and hotels. We sat in the shadow of the steam-roller longer than we'd intended, so it was early evening when Shirley and I reached the 2,400-metre summit of the pass, too late for us to make Bayburt in the daylight. We had to get ourselves invited to stay in the roadworks depot at the top.

We found the caretaker standing in the doorway, looking anxiously down the road. He should have been relieved at 2 p.m., but the relief was already more than three hours overdue and he was getting agitated. He had no food left, as the caretakers do four-day stints and he'd eaten everything he'd brought up the mountain with him. He showed us into a spacious dormitory with seven pine beds and clean white duvets, accommodation for the workers who have to stay up there in the winter snows to keep the pass open. A gang of road-menders arrived for tea, and Shirley and I joined them – Shirley, to their amazement, arguing with them about Turkish politics, in Turkish. Shirley was born in England, went out to Turkey to dance with the Turkish National Ballet and married a Turkish tenor. She still dresses like the westerner she is and rides a bicycle, so Turks are always surprised to find that she's a Turkish citizen and speaks Turkish almost as well as they do.

The relief custodian finally arrived. He was a plump, comfortable, fatherly man, who was pleased to find he had company in his isolation. He'd brought up pasta and tomatoes from home and was hoping to buy some sheep cheese and milk the next morning from the nomads in their tents. We contributed our tins of tuna and beans and he volunteered to cook dinner, while Shirley and I walked up to see the obelisk on the highest peak. It commemorated the soldiers who had died of hunger and exposure up there in the War of Independence. We stood on the bleak, windswept hill looking out over the empty steppes and thought what a cold, desolate posting it would be, even in midsummer.

After dinner, we sat and chatted – or rather Shirley and the custodian chatted, while I did my best to follow what was being said, with a bit of interpreting from Shirley. They discussed politics, always a fascination to the Turks, and the old chap blamed the rise in the cost of living on the Americans. He told us that he'd sold two fields in the valley below to buy a Tempra, but he couldn't run it, as he couldn't afford the petrol. It was all very pleasant and companionable, but suddenly Shirley froze. I knew there was something amiss, but my Turkish wasn't good enough to understand. She bade the caretaker an icy goodnight and swept me off to our dormitory. It seems that he had invited the two of us to his bed together for a fun-packed night. Turkish villagers are terrified of catching AIDS from licentious foreigners, but he told Shirley that her friend looked quite clean, so he was sure he would be safe! Anyway, he was prepared to take the risk – which is more than I am these days, even with more tempting propositions than an old Turkish caretaker.

When we reached Bayburt the following afternoon, we couldn't find the hotel we'd chosen from our guide-book, so Shirley stopped a young boy on his bicycle to ask the way. He was horrified. 'You can't stay in a hotel!' he said. 'Not ladies like you. Hotels aren't safe. They're full of old donkeys.' 'Old donkeys' is the Turkish term for old lechers. We never discovered the name of the Kop Gecidi caretaker and he remains our 'old donkey' to this day.

Drunken men can be as tiresome as amorous men (sometimes they're both together), but they're often more amusing. My favourite drunk is the one who accosted us in a Brazilian hotel on New Year's Eve. Katherine and I were sitting in the bar, tucking into our delicious *crab moqueca*, a spicy crab stew which is the speciality of the Bahia coast. A reveller came lurching over.

'Do you know Aristotle?' he asked.

Given the Brazilian habit of naming children Leonidas, Amilcar, Leander or Arquimedes, he could easily have been referring to his next-door neighbour.

'Do you mean Aristotle the philosopher?' I asked with caution.

'Yes. The tutor of Alexander the Great.'

He couldn't have chosen a better conversational opening for a Classicist who had once specialised in philosophy!

'I know him well,' I said.

'He didn't go with Alexander to the wars, you know.'

'I know he didn't. He was too old to go – even if he'd wanted to, which is doubtful. He retired to Athens.'

I decided to dazzle him with learning, so I added, 'But Alexander always remembered him. Wherever he went in the world he collected botanical specimens and sent them to him in Athens.'

'You *do* know a lot about Aristotle. Aren't I lucky to meet you! My name is Alexander too, but I'm not gay like Alexander the Great, or Cyrus, the black man. He was gay too.'

I didn't think Cyrus the Great of Persia would like to be called 'the black man' or labelled a gay, but I let it pass. Alexander sat down uninvited at our table and rattled on about Aristotle while we concentrated on our *crab moquecas*. Then he got up to fetch himself another drink. At this, the proprietor (another Alexander, who modestly described himself as Alexander the Small), seized his opportunity and nipped smartly across to occupy the empty seat at our table, tactfully relieving us of Alexander the Great and his admirer, Alexander the Drunk. Our conversation had verged on the surreal. It marked that New Year's Eve – along with the fireworks, the beat of the samba and the chambermaid's hut where we slept with her extended family of seventeen – as a truly memorable occasion.

Violence from men has never been a problem. I've been robbed three times on my travels, twice in Europe and once in Brazil, but most thieves are sneaks and opportunists, who avoid confrontation. I've never had to deal with a robber face-to-face. On the whole, cyclists are lucky. They're regarded as poor people, unable to afford a car, so they're not worth robbing. And when I'm not on my bicycle, I walk in a confident, purposeful manner. If you're nervous and look like a victim, you soon become one.

Sometimes my lack of fear has astonished even me, in retrospect. One morning in Brazil, Katherine and I were cycling along a lonely road between fields of tall sugar-cane, when a gang of cane-cutters emerged with machetes over their shoulders. They were rough men, who could easily have overpowered us, raped us, killed us, and walked off with our bicycles and all our possessions. But they smiled and gave us a polite '*Bom dia*' – and it never occurred to either of us that they would do anything else. I've stayed alone in hostels for lorry-drivers in the Gobi Desert and *muzzafir khanas* in the deserts of Sind, where I've been the only foreigner, and the only woman, for hundreds of kilometres in all directions, and yet I've felt perfectly safe. Despite what the newspapers tell us, most ordinary people throughout the world are remarkably good and I'm no more likely to meet robbers and rapists in Jakarta or Guadalupe than I am in the Marylebone Road. As for China, where robbing a tourist is said to carry the death penalty and westerners are physically repellent, a woman would have to be very ingenious to come to any harm!

The only times I thought I might be attacked were the times when Shirley challenged the Muslim fundamentalists in the wilds of eastern Turkey. Shirley, who divides her time between Ankara and the Mediterranean coast and moves in cosmopolitan circles, was horrified when we arrived in Erzurum and she saw women dressed in long black cloaks and *shadars*. At first, she refused to believe they were Turkish. They must be Iranian tourists. Then she started to tackle their husbands.

'How can you men bear to walk about with these black boxes? If your wife's pretty, aren't you proud to be seen out with her? You're wearing nice, cool, comfortable shirts and trousers and you make your poor wife dress up in all these hot, black garments. Even black gloves! Ataturk must be turning in his grave. It's not what he wanted for Turkish women. You're betraying his ideals.'

She carried on so indignantly that I thought we should be stoned any minute. But Shirley has the charm to argue without antagonising, and the fundamentalists were so astonished to be harangued by a cycling woman in a spotted jockey cap, who spoke fluent Turkish, that they melted completely. We discussed the Koran and the Bible. They praised the simplicity of Islam compared with the complications of the Trinity and tried very hard to convert us, but all with remarkable good humour. Even when she told two zealots that she worked in the ballet (a sinful profession, where women display their legs on stage!), their reply was, 'Paradise is large. There is room in it for everyone.' But I was always alarmed by these confrontations. The fundamentalists could so easily have turned nasty and it was a relief when I managed to drag Shirley away.

Guerrillas and political dissidents are no trouble to foreigners who keep their noses clean. British Embassy advice is usually to avoid getting mixed up with excited crowds, to keep out of political arguments and to stay in at night if there are disturbances.

Fear of The Shining Path has kept tourists away from Peru, to the great sorrow and economic distress of the Peruvians. I cycled through their country and found the guerrillas were doing far less damage than the Peruvian man in the street. The Peruvians were gentle people, but they were talking-up violence. Everyone accused his neighbour. In Iquitos they said, 'Stay here with us. We're good people here on the Amazon, not like those guerrillas up in the mountains.' In the mountains, they told me horror stories about the people on the coast. 'Up here, we're all one family. You can trust us. But they're crooks down there, so you'd better be careful.' On the coast, they warned me against the villains in Lima. And in Lima, they worried because I was cycling through the lawless south. The Shining Path seems to be a spent force now and if the Peruvians would only shut up about crime, they could take the share of the tourist trade which their fascinating culture deserves.

The Kurdish separatist movement, the PKK, was more of a force to be reckoned with, but I cycled freely in eastern Turkey too. The British Consul in Ankara kept an up-to-date list of

PKK strongholds and I was careful to skirt them. Kidnap is the greatest danger for a western traveller, as hostage-taking is the surest way to bring a cause to the attention of the West. But if I had to be kidnapped by anyone, I would rather be kidnapped by the Kurds of eastern Turkey than by most organised gangs. They and the Turks may be up to their elbows in each others' blood, but I'm sure that to an innocent stranger (whom Allah commands them to entertain) they would be apologetic, and so hospitable that I should be more in danger of death through overeating than political execution. I know of no western hostages who have come to grief with them.

If anything, I felt more nervous of the little National Service boys who were sent out to deal with these seasoned fighters. Shirley and I met one of them on the train, when we were travelling east from Ankara to begin our Silk Road ride. He was a twenty-year-old country boy from a village near Bitlis, who was stationed in the mountains near Erzurum to contain the advancing PKK. He was terrified at the prospect of going back there after his leave. He had other problems too. He'd been married by his family at the age of sixteen and had two children. Then last year he'd fallen in love, for the first time, with one of his cousins. He wanted to take her as his second wife, but his first wife wouldn't hear of it. (Turkish men can have only one official wife under Turkish law, but the Koran allows them to have four, so the Imams in the mosques will perform extra 'religious marriages'.) The boy was very worried about the situation and told us that he brooded over it, especially when he was patrolling through the long watches of the night in the Erzurum mountains. His father had four wives, eighteen sons and twelve daughters, but he had the money to support them, while the boy found it difficult to provide for his one wife and their two small daughters. Shirley told him he should spend his nights learning English and French, instead of thinking about wives all the time. Another passenger joined in. 'It says in the Koran that every language is the equivalent of a person,' he said. 'If you could speak three languages, you would be worth three men – and then you would qualify for three wives! Why limit yourself to two?' The boy looked at him wide-eyed. He was innocent, nervous and stupid, just the sort of boy to run berserk on a dark night with a machine-gun. He was a tremulous rabbit, more to be feared than a whole division of experienced PKK fighters.

In China, political dissidents were not organised into movements. If they stuck their heads above the parapet, they were soon despatched to the labour-camps of desolate Qinghai (part of Tibet in all but name) and the Taklimakan Desert. Dissidence in China took the form of impotent, seething resentment. It was particularly strong among the Muslim peoples of western China, the thirteen or so races of Xinjiang, who were ethnically part of Central Asia, but were ruled by the Han Chinese.

These peoples have been contained by turning them into minorities in their own lands. Forty years ago, Xinjiang was reckoned to have a population of about 5 million, of which over two-thirds were Uigurs. Since then, the Chinese have steadily drafted more Hans out to this so-called 'Uigur Autonomous Region', until the Uigurs constitute only about half the population of 13 million and the Han Chinese are definitely in charge. They run the factories and quarries, man the desks in the post offices and generally keep the place under control with their intrusive military presence. Chinese is the official language and the only medium of tertiary education. Violence is quick to erupt. A Han Chinese woman cycling through Kashgar rode into a little Uigur boy and knocked him down in the street. He was unhurt, but a crowd of Uigurs soon gathered. I watched from a safe distance as they screamed and spat at the Chinese woman. Fortunately, the police arrived and escorted her away from the scene before it turned really nasty. That same evening I saw a Chinese civilian stoned by a group of Uigur youths, who disappeared swiftly down a maze of alleys. The Chinese were clearly apprehensive. Soldiers manned the road junctions and the body language of solitary Chinese betrayed their unease in the streets. Since my visit, rumours have emerged from China of riots in Xinjiang, but the news has fizzled out after the first announcement and I don't know why. Xinjiang is a remote area, but news-gathering these days is efficient. When we can get news from outer space, I don't see why we can't get news from Xinjiang – unless western governments have decided to put a blanket on it, so as not to offend the Chinese.

Anyway, I managed quite well when I was in Xinjiang. If I asked a Han Chinese about the next town on my route, he would say, 'You'll be all right there. There are three new factories on the outskirts and lots of Chinese.' But a Uigur would say, 'Don't stay in that place. It's full of Chinese. Cycle straight through to the next village. That's where our people live and they'll look after you.' I smiled at them all – Hans, Uigurs, Tajiks, Kazakhs and the rest – and came to no harm.

Other creatures frighten me more than men. With a fellow human being, there's always the chance that a smile, a few well-chosen words or a bit of downright Machiavellian cunning may avert the danger. As long as there's rational communication, there's hope.

Animals are more difficult to deal with. Some species are always dangerous, while others are unpredictable. In Java, my route took me through the Baluran Game Park, an 80 km stretch of dense forest. The only tourist facilities were a few wooden observation platforms with thatched roofs, where scooter-riders were sleeping through the heat of the day. The park had the only tarmac road across that corner of the island, but there was little traffic on it and I was alone on my bicycle in the midst of hordes of beige monkeys. They sat in troops in the middle of the road and swung on the branches of roadside trees, with a large male as sentinel. They were obviously unused to cyclists. When I approached, the females and babies fled chattering into the depths of the forest, but the large males stood their ground, dominating my route. They had white moustaches which they twitched at me and they bared their teeth. I knew it could be dangerous to show fear, so I cycled steadily towards them, displaying a confidence I didn't feel. I had no idea how they would react. A large angry male could quite easily have leapt up and knocked me off my bicycle. And if he bit me, there was the very real danger of rabies. I'd been immunised against the disease, but as far as I could understand, the immunisation didn't give me full protection; it simply gave me a few days' grace to get to a hospital for treatment. I was really afraid in that forest. On each occasion, the sentinel monkey stared menacingly at me until I was almost on top of him. Then he moved out of the way and strolled nonchalantly into the trees. As each confrontation came to nothing, I began to relax a little, but I never really trusted the monkeys. I didn't know enough about them to be able to predict their behaviour and it would take only one rogue to inflict serious injuries. I don't cycle alone through forests if I can avoid it, and I would certainly not have chosen a Javanese jungle if there had been any alternative. I didn't like the monkeys, but at least I could see them. And if I concentrated on the monkeys I could see, I had less time to think of the animals I couldn't see, who no doubt saw me as I cycled past! Situbondo and civilisation were very sweet when I reached them unscathed.

Apart from the boa constrictor which came too close for comfort on the Amazon, I've met no ferocious wild animals. There are said to be snow leopards high in the Karakorams, but I saw neither them nor the rare Marco Polo sheep with their exaggerated curly horns. My worst animal encounter was with domestic dogs run wild.

I had reached Tacna, the most southerly town in Peru, and was planning to cross into Chile. Tacna lies on the edge of the Atacama, the driest desert on earth. In some parts of the desert, it hasn't rained for a hundred years; in others, rain has never been known to fall, ever. Because of the extreme heat and aridity, I set out from Tacna before dawn to cycle to Arica on the Chilean border.

I cleared the outskirts of Tacna and the sun rose to reveal an absolutely empty stretch of desert – not a shack, not a human being, not even a clump of scrubby grass. It was still too early for cross-border traffic and I had the thin ribbon of tarmac to myself, 40 km of peaceful cycling to the Chilean frontier.

I was bowling contentedly along, when my ears began to pick up the sound of barking. It was a long way off, but it seemed to be growing louder and more frenzied. I peered across the sand and saw a dust-cloud, which soon took shape as a pack of dogs. There were six of them tearing across the desert in my direction. Four were yappy little creatures, but the two leaders of the pack were huge beasts, like overgrown Alsatians.

My usual technique for dealing with an angry dog is to get off my bicycle and put it between us. It's the bicycle which most dogs find upsetting, and once the dog sees my two legs and smells my human smell, he generally trots away, especially if I speak softly to him. But that technique only works with one dog, not a pack, whose instinct is to surround. The only way to deal with six aggressive dogs is to get away from them as fast as possible.

Fortunately, the road surface was excellent, there was no head-wind and I had spotted the dogs in good time. As they rushed towards me across the sand, I accelerated furiously, and by the time they had bounded up to the tarmac, I was already doing 30 kph. The little dogs soon fell back, but the two Alsatians positioned themselves one on either side of my rear wheel and flew along behind me, snapping at my heels and snarling. The fury of the chase was on then, and I knew that if they once got a jaw-hold, they would pull me off the bicycle and savage me. I pedalled with the strength of desperation – 31, 32, 33, 34 kph. I kept on accelerating for what seemed an eternity, but was probably only three or four minutes. It was a battle of wills as much as speed. Fangs grazed my ankles and tore my socks. Frantic, I squeezed out one more burst of speed. 40 kph and I knew I'd reached my limit. I couldn't go on.

The dogs lost heart just a moment before I did. They began to lose ground. At first, it was almost imperceptible. Where their jaws had been level the whole time, they started to vanish from sight for a split second between lunges. That was the push I needed. My pedals flew round and the Alsatians gradually fell back.

Not trusting my luck, I kept up the desperate pace. It was only ten minutes later, when I felt it was safe to stop and catch my breath, that the full danger hit me. I had had a close encounter with death, out there on my own in the desert. My legs turned to jelly at the thought of it and I flopped down in the sand by the roadside, shaking uncontrollably. My hands trembled as I pulled off my socks to examine my ankles. No blood, no rabies. Was I glad of my hot, sweet coffee at the border café!

Dogs are no problem in China, because there aren't any. Nor are there any cats. To be more accurate, in my three months in China I saw five guard dogs (three in desert *lüshes*, one at the Pirali frontier post and one in a Kashgar garage, one pink-dyed poodle in Hami and one thin tabby cat without a tail in San Dao Ling. When Chairman Mao was in control, an edict went out from Beijing that dogs and cats were consuming food needed for humans and must be consigned to the wok.

There were no birds either. The well-tended fields in Chinese oases could have belonged to any country which cared about its land, except that the trees and hedgerows were eerily silent. The Great Helmsman had decided that the birds were eating seed and must be destroyed. The Italian journalist, Tiziano Terzani, in *Behind the Forbidden Door*, gives a chilling account of the day when the populace was ordered to go out into the fields with drums, tin cans, dustbin lids and rattles. They made such a din that the terrified birds flew up into the air and were too frightened to come down again to rest. As the day progressed and the racket continued, the birds fell one by one out of the sky, dead from exhaustion. The campaign was a success, but Chairman Mao's satisfaction was short-lived. He had not foreseen that such gross interference with the balance of nature would break the food-chain, allowing the pests which fed on the crops to multiply unchecked. More seed was devoured after the onslaught than before and China had lost its birds. By the time I cycled through, they had been allowed to drift back, but sighting one was a rare event, worthy of a diary entry: 'Saw two sparrows . . . Saw a swallow today . . . Saw a lovely hoopoe on a sand dune.'

For a cyclist, the lack of sheep dogs in the high pastures came as a relief, but I was curious to know how the shepherds managed without them. When I passed a couple of nomads tending their flock near the road, I got off my bicycle to watch. The shepherds were nomads on a spur of the Qilian Shan, Tibetan or Mongolian to judge from their rosy cheeks and high cheek-bones. Their sheepskin cloaks flapped round their legs as they rushed to the roadside to stare. I greeted them in Chinese and they waved their crooks in reply, but they were too nervous to smile. I was probably the first foreigner they'd ever seen.

A ewe began to stray from the flock and one of the shepherds took a catapult out of his pocket and aimed a stone, with wonderful accuracy, to bounce from the ground just in front of her nose. The ewe was startled and rushed back to the security of her sisters. The flock was shaggy and gold in colour, like the soil, though the lambs were white. The shepherds drove them to the roadside ahead of me and I watched in wonder as they all waited with remarkable good sense until their shepherds gave them permission to cross, when they poured over in one unbroken yellow wave. Perhaps sheep, like people, behave more responsibly when they're not hounded and chivvied?

For the traveller away from the main tourist centres, the destruction of the dogs and cats has produced a chilling problem – a plague of rats. Without their natural predators, the rodent population has expanded to ten times the norm for a country of China's size. That's the official estimate; no doubt the reality is worse. There are rats in the barns eating the grain, rats scuttling across the darkened streets and rats in the hotels.

The first time they came to my bedroom, my blood froze. It was 4 a.m. and I woke with a start to the rustle of plastic, as they tried to get at the dried fruit in my open panniers. The hotel generator was off, so there was no electric light. I coughed loudly and rattled my torch on the bedside table before I flashed its beam round the room. I wanted to scare the rats away without having to see them. I succeeded. There was a scamper and a scuffle, but not a rat in sight. When I was sure the coast was clear, I stamped loudly across the concrete floor, wearing my shoes in case a panicky rat rushed over my feet, and fastened the straps on my panniers. They came back an hour or so later, but this time I felt more relaxed, as I knew they had no hope of gnawing through the tough canvas by dawn. My bad moment came when I had to undo the panniers to pack my overnight gear. Would a trapped rat jump out at me? But all was well, except the very thought that rats had been in my bags, rooting about among my things, made me shudder with disgust. I would have to empty them as soon as I reached my next hotel and give everything a thorough scrub.

Chinese country hotels are sparsely furnished, with no storage, apart from the ubiquitous plastic hat-stands. So I had got into the habit of dumping my panniers down on the floor, leaving them undone for easy access. As distances between shops were great, I had to carry emergency supplies, usually dried fruit, nuts and sponge cakes, and these were packed in the rear pockets. It was all too convenient for the rats. After my first experience with them, I was more cautious. I fastened all the buckles and hung the panniers on the hat-stand – more difficult than it sounds, as the stands were frail objects, while the panniers were heavy. It was a delicate balancing act. Occasionally, in grander hotels, I would have a real wardrobe, but the lower reaches were suspect and I never stowed my panniers inside unless there were high hooks to hang them on. Despite all my precautions, the rats still invaded my room, drawn by the smell of my food. Cheaper hotels had rat-holes; in more expensive ones, they got in through the central heating ducts.

The revulsion never left me, but I slept more easily when I'd dealt with my worst fear, the fear that the rats would run over my face as I lay in bed. Except in desert *lüshes*, I always had a private bathroom and I would put an apple core or the remains of a Chinese sponge cake in the bathroom wastepaper basket. Then, when I woke in the night to the dreaded rustle, it would be coming from the bathroom, not from my bedroom, and I could turn over and ignore it. I suppose it amounted to feeding the rats, but it was the only way I could cope with them.

As I cycled through the silent landscape, reflecting on the slaughter of the dogs, cats and birds, I began to see it all as part of a pattern. The Cultural Revolution had always puzzled me. How could such kind, sensible people, with millennia of civilised living behind them, suddenly go on the rampage and at a word firom Chairman Mao set fire to their cultural heritage, destroy their temples, libraries and museums, and banish their intellectuals to pig farms? Many must have joined the movement out of fear of the Red Guards; it was better to burn than to be burnt. But however strong the regime, the Red Guards could surely not have flourished without the acquiescence of the majority. The bizarre destruction of the animals provided me with the key.

The Chinese are obedient people, polite and deferential to authority. If the Great Helmsman orders them to consign their pets to the frying-pan, they comply without a murmur. They add the onion and ginger, pour in the corn oil, then take their chopsticks to poor little Fido, no doubt smiling and remarking politely on his tastiness. And there lies the cultural difference. No British government which threatened the nation's pets could hope to survive. And any leader who called for the torching of St Paul's or the National Gallery would be escorted from Westminster by men in white coats. Western individualism and mistrust of authority may be tiresome at times, but at least it can be relied upon to curb government excesses. The Chinese are simply too respectful for their own good.

They are also very practical. They approve of useful animals – the horses, camels and donkeys, which still provide much of the rural transport. I almost acquired a donkey myself. In Turfan, three of us hired a car and guide for the day to see the local sights. We passed a donkey and his cart tied up in the shady courtyard of a farmhouse and I asked, out of idle curiosity, how much a donkey cost. I knew that the standard heavy-duty bicycle cost between 750 and 850 yuan (£60-£70), and I was interested to compare prices. The guide told me that a donkey sold for anything between 800 and 1,200 yuan, depending on age, strength and breeding potential. When I stepped out of my hotel that evening, on my way to dinner, I was astonished to find the morning's guide outside the main gate with a row of men leading donkeys. There were donkeys of all ages and colours and both sexes, and the prices were very competitive. The guide was sure I could find exactly the donkey I needed!

The last word on men and other animals must come from Brazil. Katherine and I were in Indiaroba, a dreary little inland town, light years away from the smart beach resorts we had stayed in on previous nights. We were eating our suppers in the only café there, when a *gaucho* came clattering over the cobbles on his horse. He tied it to the rail outside and strode in for a Coca Cola. The café's tiny white kitten had caught a cricket almost as large as itself and was chasing it round the table legs. The cricket was clattering like a pair of brilliant green castanets. The *gaucho*'s formidable moustache and swaggering gait concealed a tender heart. He walked softly over to the cricket, picked it up in big, gentle hands and laid it on his shoulder to rest for a few moments before he released it outside.

I often think of that fierce-looking *gaucho*. For me, he stands as a symbol of the safety which lurks behind seeming danger. He provides my answer to that perennial question, 'Aren't you scared?'

11 Magic and Romance

Journeys are magic caskets, full of dreamlike promises.
                                                        Claude Lévi-Strauss

As an anthropologist, Claude Lévi-Strauss had ample time to meditate on travel during his lonely years of fieldwork among the Amazonian Indians. For him, a journey was not just a trip in space; it was also a trip in time and social standing.

On the Trojan Plain I've watched grain being threshed and winnowed in exactly the way that Homer described it and been transported back two thousand years to the days of Hector and Achilles. In Beijing I've wandered through the 9,000 rooms of the Forbidden City, through the Gate of Heavenly Peace, over the Golden Stream and into the Hall of Supreme Harmony, where the Son of Heaven once sat on the Dragon Throne, and have been transported five centuries to the China of the Mings. And in developing countries I've lived in many centuries at the same time. Men plough the fields with oxen, as they have since agriculture began; then they go to the tea-house in the evening and look at the latest panoramic photographs from Mars on the colour TV. Country women are up before dawn, drawing water from the well, grinding their own corn and building a fire to bake the bread for breakfast, while their sisters in the neighbouring town gobble a bowl of supermarket cornflakes before rushing off to their computerised offices. The cross-country cyclist changes century a dozen times a day. As for changing social standing, you have only to watch a group of tourists in a luxury hotel to see what Lévi-Strauss meant. For two weeks in the year, people who live in modest houses and do all their own chores, are transported to fairy palaces, where minions hover to gratify their every whim. Bowing waiters bring their iced drinks to the poolside in Thailand and they feel like the King of Siam.

But journeys are not just escapes from present-day realities. They are avenues of promise, leading to unimaginable delights.

Sometimes the 'magic casket' is a disappointment. We open it, full of anticipation, but like Shakespeare's suitors, we find in its precious casing only a death's head or the portrait of a blinking idiot. At other times, a leaden casket, of which we entertained little hope, turns out to hold our heart's desire – in life, as in journeys.

Like Lévi-Strauss, I'm a romantic traveller. I choose historical roads, and cycling for me is not so much a matter of gears and sprockets as an attempt to get into the lives of the millions of people throughout the centuries who have trodden those roads. Roads are resonant with history, with the struggles, the faith and the aspirations of those who built them, and to travel them slowly in the old ways, on foot, on a horse or its modern equivalent, the bicycle, is to share to some extent in the dreams of our ancestors and their great adventures. It takes an hour to fly the California Trail over the Utah and Nevada Deserts and the snow-capped Sierra Nevada, an hour in a plane with in-flight entertainment and lunch on a tray. On a bicycle, it was a sixteen-day struggle through snow, heat and blustering wind, but it was exhilarating cycling. I felt a part of that great wave of pioneers who had opened up the American West. Admittedly, I hadn't pushed a handcart across the deserts or fought with disease and Indians, but I'd toiled with all my belongings along that difficult road and glimpsed the magnitude of their achievement.

China is a mysterious land at the far end of the Eurasian continent, cut off from Europe by formidable deserts, the world's highest mountains and the secrecy of its rulers. The Silk Road is a name to conjure with. For a romantic traveller, the idea of cycling the Silk Road from the old Chinese capital of Xi'an was irresistible. Silk, spices, peacocks, jade, roses, heavenly horses – no other road in history had ever carried such precious wares. And no other road had been the route for such significant scientific and spiritual exchange. Discoveries in astronomy and mathematics, Buddhism, Islam, Christianity, gunpowder, paper and block-printing had all travelled this fabled highway in the plod of the camel trains and the scrips of the pilgrim monks.

Even the way we westerners discovered silk was exotic. It was the Romans who saw it first, in 53 BC, when they lost the Battle of Carrhae. They had advanced into the Middle East under Crassus, with no real opposition until they met the Parthians. Those superb mounted archers soon broke the Roman lines and threw the legions into disarray. Then they produced their ultimate weapon. They unfurled gigantic banners of red silk, which billowed out and filled the heavens, shimmering in the desert sun. The Roman horses panicked and the army was routed. The Romans had lost the battle, but they managed to obtain samples of this magical material, which the Parthians said they had got in exchange for an ostrich egg and some conjurers. It was the beginning of the Roman passion for silk. They never knew how it was made or where it came from, as they bought it through middlemen. Even when the secret of its production had leaked out in Byzantine times, the stuff produced in the West was inferior in quality and there was still a market for the delicate Chinese silk, which the Indians called 'woven wind'. It was the discovery of easier and safer sea routes to the East, not the failure of demand, which ended the glorious days of the Silk Road.

The Silk Road seemed to me to be the most magic of all the 'magic caskets' and I had never felt such keen anticipation as I felt on the morning I set out from Xi'an. I asked directions out of the city.

'You'll know you're on the Silk Road when you see the camels,' said an art student. 'They're so beautiful. I pass them every Sunday, when I go home to my parents for the day.'

With my imagination in overdrive, I cycled along West Avenue to the city walls and out through the Ming West Gate into the suburbs. It was the morning rush hour. I wove in and out of the flocks of workers on their heavy black bicycles. Their saddles were so low that their knees and feet stuck out sideways, and their cruising speed was about one-third of mine. They seemed to be drifting along in slow-motion, lost in their dreams.

Then I saw 'the beautiful camels'. There was a caravan of them on a grassy enclosure in the middle of the dual carriageway. They were laden with bales of silk and mounted by turbaned merchants shading their eyes with their hands as they scanned the far horizon. They were made of concrete! The shock brought me down to earth with a bang, but I took a few photographs just the same. The concrete caravan was an anticlimax, but it was still significant. It marked the spot where the Silk Road had issued from the original Tang West Gate to begin its remarkable journey. It was here that the real camels were loaded for their slow, arduous journey to the shores of the Mediterranean and the markets of the West.

The concrete camels were the first of many disappointments. The traders on today's Silk Road carried pots and pans, logs, television sets and contraband instead of exotic wares. The silk on sale in the markets was cheap and nasty, and the locals preferred the glittering nylon imported from Pakistan. The temples, burnt down in the madness of the Cultural Revolution, were gaudy reproductions. 'The Greatest Pass under Heaven', the Jiayuguan Fortress which marked the end of Imperial China and the start of the Gobi Desert, was lost in a factory suburb. The Great Wall along most of its length was nothing but lumps of fallen masonry and crumbling earthworks. The villagers wore grey suits instead of the quaint local costumes pictured in the guide-books. I was too early in the year to taste the melons of Hami, which are famous throughout Asia. I couldn't get a visa to cycle to Samarkand and Bokhara. In fact, the journey was one tedious plod – five months of mountain and desert with nothing more exciting than a distant sheep. It was not what I had expected to find in the magic casket. However, as the months passed by and my Chinese improved, I realised that the magic of the road lay not in silks and spices, but in sharing that very tedium with those for whom it was a way of life. Their tradition of hospitality to the travelling stranger stretched back through millennia and I felt privileged to be just another guest in their homes, another tiny drop in a timeless stream.

After China and Central Asia, I chose the branch of the Silk Road which led across Turkey from Doğubayazit on the Iranian border to Trabzon on the Black Sea. From there I took the ferry to Istanbul. More romantically, I sailed from Trebizond to Constantinople.

I'd visited Constantinople many times, but Trebizond was

still a dream city, glittering in the opulence of its palaces, its domes and towers rising through clouds of incense, as its jewelled Emperor processed to the sumptuous Church of Panaghia Chrysokephalos for Mass. For more than two centuries, under the Comnene Emperors, it had been one of the richest capitals in Asia Minor and I longed to see it.

The Empire of Trebizond was founded in 1204, when Constantinople was sacked by the Crusaders. Alexius Comnenus, a grandson of the Byzantine Emperor Andronicus I, escaped eastwards and with the help of his powerful aunt, Queen Thamar of Georgia, seized the port of Trebizond and the strip of coast from the mouth of the Phasis to Sinope. He proclaimed it an independent empire, sold trading concessions to the Venetians and later to the Genoese, then watched with delight as the Silk Road caravans wound their way through his city to take ship for Constantinople and the West. There were silver mines in the hills above; the coast was damp, warm and fertile; and there were so many fish in the Black Sea that the anchovies were said to throw themselves spontaneously onto the shore. It all came to an end in 1461 when the Emperor David Comnenus surrendered his crown and his narrow strip of Christian land to the unstoppable Ottoman Turks.

I was prepared for a bit of an anticlimax. No casket could be quite as magic as the jewelled one I'd created in my imagination. But when Shirley and I whizzed down the Zigana Pass to Trabzon, I wasn't expecting to find it quite so down-at-heel. Strangely enough, it still owed what little prosperity it had to Georgia – not to any formidable Aunt Thamar, but to the droves of beefy women whom the Turks called 'the Natashas'.

The Natashas arrived by sea every week and immediately began to shop. They were dressed in uniform black leather miniskirts, their hair was short and peroxide blonde and they had the torsos of prize-fighters. They shouldered their way through the crowds in the Russian market, towering above the stall-holders who were doing their best to bargain in Russian. Restaurants had their menus up in Russian and import-export firms advertised their rates in Cyrillic script. With my light brown hair and square face, I'm usually taken for a German abroad, so it was quite a novelty in Trabzon to be greeted in Russian and chased down the street with offers of bargain jeans, in bulk. The Natashas bought everything, from lollipops and Mars bars to wholesale quantities of pedal bins and pudding basins. But cheap clothes seemed to be their main interest, the jeans, T-shirts and heavy-duty long johns which they stuffed by the hundred into black plastic bin-liners. Just when it seemed that the cheaper hotels would burst with the loot, their ship returned to carry them home, and to bring the next wave of shoppers. The really enterprising Natashas carried on a double trade. They arrived empty-handed, worked as prostitutes for a while, then used their earnings to buy goods for Georgia's markets. Looking at all the tacky consumer goods which the Natashas bought made me realise how short of simply everything the former states of the USSR must be.

Of glorious Trebizond, only three churches survive, in different stages of decay, and the deserted ruin of the Monastery of Panaghia Soumela on its dizzy crag in the mountains. Trabzon today is a busy, drab provincial town, thriving on its Georgian traffic and obsessed with football (Trabzonspor is one of Turkey's top teams). Even the portrait bust of its greatest son is a disappointment. Suleiman the Magnificent, who was born in Trabzon, peers at his native town through rheumy eyes, a dodderer with a flowing white beard and one foot in the grave – a depressing memorial to one of the greatest rulers the world has ever seen.

Trabzon was simply not Trebizond. Fortunately, the two cities soon dissociated themselves in my mind, and I can still dream of the lamplight on the gold-encrusted mosaics of Hagia Sophia and bask in the splendour of the Comnenes. The Natashas have taken their sacks of long johns and disappeared.

On the Pacific islands, I hoped for a different sort of magic, the magic of landscape. Blue seas, coral reefs, white palm-fringed sands and vegetation as lushly tropical as the dreams of Douanier Rousseau. I found these delights in Tahiti and Moorea. They were dazzlingly beautiful islands, where the ocean teemed with fish and a plant had only to look at the rich soil to take root and flourish. I'd never seen such rampant vegetation or such magnificent tropical flowers. As Captain Cook remarked: 'In the article of food these people may almost be said to be exempt from the curse of our forefathers, scarcely can it be said that they earn their bread with the sweat of the brow; benevolent nature hath not only supplied them with necessaries, but with abundance of superfluities.'

Yet, when Nature was so lavish, the Tahitians were importing tinned and frozen foods and all the other trappings of western consumer society – and paying import duties of 54 per cent from the EEC and 80 per cent from elsewhere! The cost of living was devastatingly high and the islanders had become dependent on mass tourism and subventions from France.

Tahiti had lost its self-sufficiency and its innocence. It had become a tropical theme-park. I was greeted off the plane at 1 a.m. by a group of swaying, ukelele-playing islanders in vivid floral *pareos*, with garlands of leaves in their hair. The islanders sang for the tourists, did the menial work in hotels and survived on their own produce outside the cash economy, while expatriate French ran the administration, the army, the police and the lucrative travel business. It was a two-tier society, but the islanders were cheerful, indolent people, who seemed happy with their lot. The young dreamed of Paris, Miami and tourist dollars, while their elders harmonised together at the airport. Music was an integral part of their lives and the guitar, ukelele and close-harmony singing were still holding their own against western pop. It was one of the few relics of their lost paradise.

I don't often visit places which depend so heavily on mass tourism and I found the tourists on Tahiti unbelievable. They were almost parodies of themselves. As I was crossing the Pacific in the wake of Captain Cook, I cycled out one morning to Venus Point, to stand on the very spot from which he had observed the transit of Venus. There was a coffee-stall there and I was joined by a typical bunch: a mind-bendingly dull elderly couple on their way home to Cornwall from Melbourne, a pair of Geordie queers, four expletive-bandying Queenslanders and a myopic American male in a pale blue shell-suit and a mauve velvet beret.

Yet nothing could detract from the natural beauty of Tahiti and Moorea. Their beauty filled me with sadness for what they might have been. Even in Gauguin's day, there were tramcars, hotels and French administrative buildings, and I was surprised to see photographs of him in the Gauguin Museum, sitting on his verandah in a suit, while a Tahitian servant brought him coffee on a tray. It was a disappointment. I had imagined him really getting away from Parisian society and living with the islanders in their 'Nevermore' grass huts, not leading the pampered life of a colonial. But at least he would have eaten well. He would not have been reduced to today's diet of fast food and Coca Cola.

I followed Captain Cook on his voyage of discovery up the East Coast of Australia, he in *The Endeavour* and I on my Condor. It was a perilous coast for a navigator without a map, as his choice of names such as Cape Tribulation and Mount Sorrow clearly demonstrate. The Captain was often in a quandary. Should he keep as close as possible to the shore-line to produce useful charts, or should he sail further out in deeper waters, where it would be safer for his men? 'People will hardly admit of an excuse for a man leaving a coast unexplored he has once discovered,' he ruminated. 'He is then charged with timorousness and want of perseverance ... if, on the other hand, he boldly encounters all the dangers and obstacles he meets with, and is unfortunate enough not to succeed, he is then charged with temerity, and, perhaps, want of conduct.' A common dilemma, in many walks of life!

Sailing to and fro through gaps he found in the Barrier Reef, Cook made his cautious way up the coast to Cape York and the Torres Strait. I got as far as Cape York myself – not on my bicycle, as there were no roads up there, but on safari in a 'troopie'. I saw Possession Island, the small dot in the Torres Strait where Captain Cook 'once more hoisted English colours, and in the name of His Majesty King George III took possession of the whole eastern coast'. Then crossed over to Thursday Island.

I arrived to a celebration. It was the 120th anniversary of The Bringing of the Light to the islands of the Torres Strait by the

London Missionary Society. There was a procession round the town from the neat little Cathedral and a re-enactment on the Cathedral lawn of the arrival of the missionaries and their first meeting with islanders in tribal dress.

The Thursday Islanders were Polynesian and Melanesian by extraction, quite different in physical type and temperament from the Australian aborigines. They were huge women in vivid floral dresses and straw hats trimmed with flowers, and even huger men in floral shirts and sarongs. And they were all having a wonderfully carefree day. They reminded me of the Tahitians.

I went across to speak to the family in grass skirts, war paint and feathers, who had acted in the play. They looked so wild and terrifying, so outlandish, that I expected an exotic conversation.

I asked if it was a public holiday. 'Not bloody likely!' said the savage warrior. 'I had to take a sickie to come here.'

We were joined by the younger sister of the tribal matriarch. She was beautifully neat in her navy blue skirt, white blouse and court shoes, and she treated her feathered, grass-skirted sister to a stern ticking off.

'You look a real mess today! You should have worn black tights with that outfit.'

'I know. But I couldn't find them. I had to make do with these brown.'

What banal exchanges from a group of noble savages! Another illusion shattered.

Of all the 'dreamlike promises', the brand of tourism now dubbed 'ecological' is the most likely to disappoint. We approach it with such high expectations. 'A Linha Verde' (the Green Line), which begins about 50 km north of Salvador and runs parallel to the coast, a little inland, was billed as Brazil's first ecological highway. The pamphlets showed happy young people in an open-topped jeep, driving through cool green forest shade. When Katherine and I left the Coconut Highway to join it, we found a hideous asphalt gash with bare, churned-up soil on both sides, where the trees had been chopped down to make way for the tipper-trucks and had not been replanted. There was not a single café or filling station to provide a cold drink. The terrain was hilly, the vegetation poor scrub, there was no sign of human habitation and no wild life. 'Ecological' was the last way to describe such desolation and we could only suppose that the title had been artfully chosen to extract money from the World Bank.

In Leticia, I met a group of Germans who had just been on an 'ecotour' in the Amazon rainforest. It had culminated in a dinner of grilled crocodile in an Indian village. From their description of their night excursion in a canoe to lure the crocodiles with torches, it was evident that their 'ecotour' had been nothing but a crocodile-hunting expedition under a politically correct name. Cynics throughout South America are jumping on the ecological bandwagon for commercial gain and travellers with a serious concern for the environment should make careful enquiries before committing themselves to some of the expeditions on offer.

By this time, you may be wondering why I bother to travel at all, when romance is illusory and dreams so often fade. The answer lies in the adverb. Dreams *often* fade, but not always. And if one journey turns out to be a disappointment, the next one may well be that elusive magic casket.

Sometimes the magic takes me unawares. I cycled into Palos de la Frontera with modest expectations. I was following the explorers and conquistadors across Spain, and Palos was the small port from which Columbus set sail on 3 August 1492, on his first great voyage of discovery. A grand avenue of palm trees, La Avenida de las Americas, led me into the town. It was lined with plaques of *azulejos*, each a tribute from one of the states of South, Central and North America. I rode to the Church of San Jorge, with its famous *Virgen de los Milagros* (Virgin of Miracles), where Columbus had prayed before setting sail for the New World. He came out from San Jorge's dim interior and paused for a moment in the sunshine at the great West Door, the *Puerto de los Novios* (Door of the Bridegrooms). Then he led his crew down the broad flight of stone steps to the Rio Tinto, where the *Santa Maria*, the *Niña* and the *Pinta* were moored. The Rio Tinto has changed its course now and Columbus' actual embarkation point is a public garden, its centrepiece the Moorish fountain where he drew his fresh water supplies for the voyage. It was siesta time in Palos, and the church and garden were empty. Perhaps it was the heat, fatigue or lack of lunch, but I was suddenly there with Columbus, walking down the steps of San Jorge for that momentous voyage into the unknown. My flight of fancy didn't last long, but it was a moment of such exaltation that I thought I should take off like a skylark.

Palos de la Frontera shimmered with the romance of travel, like the Taj Mahal, the Gold Museum in Lima, Samarkand and the Hunza Valley. I'd dreamed of visiting all those places and they turned out to be every bit as evocative as I'd imagined.

Then there are travel's leaden caskets. Sometimes I'm bored with sightseeing. I drag myself dutifully to the next place in the guide-book, expecting nothing but tedium, and come away dazzled. The Mogao Caves near Dunhuang were like that.

I'd got as far as Anxi in my crossing of China. Anxi is the fork in the road, where the modern traveller chooses to skirt the dreaded Taklimakan Desert along its northern or southern rim. But in the great days of the silk trade, the fork lay 100 km to the east, at Dunhuang. There the Silk Road crossed the main track leading from Lhasa in Tibet northwards to Mongolia and southern Siberia, so caravans poured through Dunhuang from the four points of the compass, making it the wealthiest and most cosmopolitan of all the oasis cities. Once called 'the heart of Asia' its nickname was 'Little Peking'. But today it's an unimportant town, which would soon sink into the Gobi sands without the tourist attraction of the Mogao Caves, the Caves of a Hundred Buddhas.

Buddhism seems to have crossed the Himalayas from India to China in the first century AD and soon intrepid Chinese pilgrims were travelling the southern arm of the Silk Road through Dunhuang and Khotan to visit the sacred shrines in India and collect Buddhist manuscripts. In AD 366 a pilgrim monk named Lo Tsun was resting from the afternoon heat in a green valley near Dunhuang, when he had a vision of a thousand Buddhas seated in a cloud of glory. Overhanging the valley was a great cliff, riddled with caves, and Lo Tsun persuaded a rich pilgrim to have one of these caves painted and consecrated to the Buddha, to ensure his safe crossing of the Taklimakan Desert. It soon became the custom for every Buddhist who could afford it to have a cave carved or painted, either in supplication for a safe crossing or as a thank-offering for a safe arrival. This sacred work on the cliff face continued until the region turned to Islam in the thirteenth century. It represents a complete history of Chinese Buddhist art over an unbroken span of a thousand years.

I knew how important it was, but I still had to force myself to make the side-trip from Anxi. It was raining and I had a sore throat. I was sick of the desert and sick of China. I just wanted to cycle through it as fast as possible and I almost ducked out of Mogao Caves, to save myself three days. But Dunhuang cheered me up. There were more western tourists there than I'd seen since Xi'an and it was a great treat to be able to speak English again and stay in a really comfortable, well-run hotel. In theory, we like to be off the tourist track. But in practice, tourists bring competition and raise standards.

'No rip-off for foreigners. Same prices.' The notice caught my eye outside a pavement café, so I went in and ordered beef and tomatoes with delicious fried potatoes, my first for six weeks, and chatted with the proprietor. He also ran an unofficial minibus to the Caves ('same price for foreigners'). He fetched his parents out of the kitchen to meet this aged trans-China cyclist and we all sat under a café umbrella drinking Coke together in the afternoon lull. It was a typical Chinese family business, but this family was more innovative than most. The son out front spoke English to the tourists and charmed them into his minibus, while the parents in their aprons turned their woks to ham omelettes, chocolate pancakes and milk shakes, all astonishingly inedible fare to the Chinese. And together, they and their neighbours spelt the beginning of the end for Beijing's three-tier price-system. Competition was eating into it nicely in Dunhuang.

The next morning, I boarded his unofficial, flat-rate bus to the Mogao Caves. I was utterly bowled over. First there was the view of the giant honey-coloured cliff – a honeycomb almost a kilometre wide, carved from top to bottom with five hundred caves. Then there were the caves themselves, each one more brilliant than the last. The tempera paintings were still wonderfully fresh, the blues, greens and blacks as bright as the day they were painted. Above them were hundreds of tiny images of the seated Buddha, each with a gold-leaf halo. Some caves had statues of the Buddha carved out of the living rock, then covered with finely chiselled, painted terracotta, to give subtlety to the facial expressions and a sensuous feel to the garments. I can still close my eyes and see one huge reclining Buddha, blissfully at rest in the state of nirvana. Behind him stands a long row of disciples. The enlightened ones, who understand nirvana, are smiling at the Buddha's happiness, but the less advanced students are in tears, grieving over what they wrongly assume to be his death. Like the terracotta warriors, each statue is a portrait of an individual, the face carved with remarkable sensitivity to reflect the shades of spiritual enlightenment. Two of the shrines were a number of inter-connecting grottoes, soaring upwards to a height of 30 m to accommodate colossal standing Buddhas. I wandered up ramps and ladders, along balconies and rickety walkways, peering into cave after wonderful cave. They were absolutely stunning. They were without doubt the highlight of my three months in China and possibly the highlight of that entire circuit of the globe. And I almost gave them a miss!

Magic, as in romance, is easy to find. But magic, as in black and white, is more elusive. My one brush with it happened in Brazil, in Salvador, the home of *candomblé*.

In South America, magic is deep-rooted. You have only to look at the devotion on the faces of the Andean Indians to know that Christianity for them is more than a rational system of values. It's communion with the magical, with the power of the old gods who preceded Christianity and were given Christian trappings to dupe the Jesuits. The old and new, the unacceptable and the acceptable, have merged now into a religion of violent intensity. A pilgrimage to the Virgin of Guadalupe is an agonising crawl on hands and knees along burning roads. A visit to the market is a chance to spend rapt and tearful hours in the church before the Crucifix and the Virgin in her silver crown.

Brazil is more complex, a bubbling pot of religions and cults. It has the largest Catholic population and some of the most exuberant gold-encrusted Baroque in the world. But walk along Rio's Ipanema Beach at night and you will see the candles flickering in the sand and the votive offerings of flowers and fruit to Iemanjá, Queen of the Sea. The old Indian gods are still alive, but the powerful forces in the land are African.

When the Portuguese came to Brazil and began the large-scale cultivation of sugar-cane and tobacco, they found the local Indians a great disappointment. They were hunter-gatherers, who were so bad at regular, disciplined work, that the Portuguese had to import West Africans as slaves for the plantations. They were shipped across from Nigeria and Benin, bringing their religions with them, along with their spicy food and their drum-beat. When the colonists banned their gods, they simply gave them the names of Christian saints and continued to worship them in their disguises, in *candomblé* ceremonies.

When I was in Salvador, I particularly wanted to attend a ceremony at a *candomblé terreiro*, but didn't know how to go about it. Then fortune smiled on me. I was wandering through the cloisters of the Igreja São Francisco, when I was approached by a young man who offered me an invitation. (I learned later that the *Candomblistas* have a high regard for that particular church and often come to pray to St Francis and St Antony of Padua there.) He said he would send a van to my hotel in Itapoa to collect me and any others who wished to come.

That evening, Katherine and I set out for the *terreiro*, escorted by Sonny, a Project Trust volunteer who was teaching English in Recife. I was dressed in my best silk skirt for the occasion, with a black silk T-shirt. When we were halfway into Salvador and there was no time to go back and change, the driver suddenly announced that I must take off my blouse, as black was a negative colour and I couldn't wear it in the *terreiro*. Katherine and I both happened to be carrying scarves in our handbags, so we set about improvising. We had a hilarious time in the back of the minivan trying somehow to knot the two scarves into a respectable upper garment, watched by the bemused Sonny. The end result was decent, but it would certainly have won no prizes for fashion!

We reached downtown Salvador and drove down an almost perpendicular dirt road into what was clearly an African quarter of the city, an area into which we should certainly not have ventured alone at night. We pulled up in front of a tumbledown house and were led through a dark side alley into the back yard. This was the *terreiro*. At first sight, it was a cross between a Roman Catholic chapel and a fairground. It was covered over with a corrugated-iron roof and festooned with red and green paper streamers, narrow strips of white plastic, and cut-out cardboard goblets and fishes, sheathed in silver paper or coloured foil. Three white tiles were set in the concrete floor, one near the door and two in the centre of the yard. Fresh green leaves were scattered everywhere. Pictures of Jesus, the Virgin, St Jerome and his lion and St Antony of Padua hung in little shrines on corner tables. The main altar had five candles, a picture of Christ Crucified and two small statuettes, one of St George slaying the dragon and the other of a *gaucho* – the real object of worship at the heart of the ceremony. He was an African god, the King of Ketu in Benin, the son of Ogum, the protector of hunters.

We took our seats at the edge of the yard and the *terreiro* began to fill up with negroes. Then the nine participants in the ceremony filed in, one man in a white shirt and white trousers and eight women in long white robes. The solitary man prostrated himself to kiss each of the floor tiles in turn, then began to lead the eight women in an anti-clockwise dance round the central tiles to the beating of drums. The congregation clapped in time to the beat and chanted. The three drummers quickened their pace, the noise of the chanting mounted to a scream and the man in the centre began to stagger and reel. He had gone into a trance. The women supported him from the yard and he reappeared shortly afterwards, booted and spurred in *gaucho* dress, and smoking what looked like a normal fat cigar, but smelt of a substance quite different. He was now the god incarnate.

He circled the yard, kissing everyone, even us foreigners. Then he began to gallop around, whipping his imaginary horse like a child playing cowboys. It was a wild and staggeringly energetic dance. The drumbeat grew louder and faster, the chanting more intense and the atmosphere electric. One by one, the dancing women howled and went into trances themselves, smoking the special cigars and hurling their huge bodies around in abandon. We crept out two hours later, when there were upwards of eighty negroes cramming the *terreiro*, of all ages from toddlers up, and the drums and chanting had become terrifying in their intensity. In my rational mind, I didn't believe in the magic, but at some atavistic level it was still too disturbing for comfort.

There was a fiesta on in the streets of Salvador and Sonny, who was a Ugandan Indian in origin, slipped out of the van and melted joyfully into the coffee-coloured crowds. But it was no party for *gringas*, so Katherine and I went soberly back to our hotel and recovered from the evening's excitement with a plate of chips and a bottle of beer under the stars. The sky was deep blue velvet and the ocean sighed as the moon picked out the silver foam on its curling breakers. It was the sort of magic we were used to, the sort we could handle.

12 Lessons

Caelum non animum mutant qui trans mare currunt.
(Those who rush across the sea change their skies, not their souls).

Horace

Horace is one of my favourite poets and I often take him on my long journeys. But he is no traveller. For him, the tranquil delights of his farm near Licenza in the Sabine hills, his poetry, his library, his excellent wine cellar, his friends and the occasional dancing girl are all that a man could possibly desire. His one trip abroad, to study in Athens, was not a success. He was lured by Brutus into military action, for which he had no talent, fought ingloriously at the battle of Philippi and was glad to get back to Rome. If Greece was too much for him, he would certainly take a dim view of rushing across Chinese deserts in a bicycle-pannier!

Much as I love Horace, I disagree with him profoundly. Travel for me has been a change of soul. Or, to put it less poetically, travel has changed many of my attitudes. It has given me such a different perspective on life that I've almost become a new person.

Take possessions. When I cycled away from the champagne send-off on my first ride round the world, I was cycling away from an affluent lifestyle – a large headmistress' house in Suffolk, a London flat, an Alfa Romeo, suits from Hardy Amies and the best Italian shoes. My bicycle had two rear panniers and a handlebar bag. For the next fifteen months, everything I had in the world would be carried in those three bags. In one afternoon, I'd reduced my resources from easy abundance down to the bare essentials. It was 'downshifting' with a vengeance.

At first, I found it hard to manage, but little by little I got used to it. And a month or so into my ride, I realised what a liberation it was to be free of all those possessions. Possessions eat up our money and our time. They dominate our lives. We save up for them, struggle round the shops to find them; and when we've got them, we have to clean them, mend them, take them to be serviced, insure them and eventually buy a bigger house to put them in. All that effort and expense – and they're only things!

Since I started cycling, I've moved into a small flat in Central London and sold or given away the contents of my house. I don't run a car. I don't have a washing machine, a dish-washer or an electric toothbrush. I don't buy books, as my end of London has both public and university libraries. And with a park across the road, I don't need a garden. My aim is minimalism, but my existence is far from spartan. I live in comfort and eat and drink well, but I've rid my life of clutter and complicated equipment. I'm not quite as free in London as I am on my bicycle. I still have to take decisions on my wardrobe, whereas on my bicycle I carry one dress and that's the one I put on. But discarding unnecessary possessions has freed the time I used to spend on a host of petty chores. And as I own little of value, I can lock the door and pedal away without a care in the world.

Strangely, when I sat down to think of the new perspectives I'd gained from my travels, I found that they all began with the same letter. After possessions come priorities. I've cycled through some really desolate terrain – raw, windswept plateaux, icy mountain passes, and deserts which have never seen rain. I've crossed empty country, where I've had to cycle 200 km to reach the next habitation, and then it was only a filling-station in the middle of nowhere. These difficult journeys have put my priorities into order.

First comes water and second a safe place to spend the night. Food comes a poor third. Most westerners overeat and carry enough surplus fat to survive for a few days on short rations. But water and shelter are essential every day. I've always managed to find the water I needed, though in some parts of the world, where the tap water is untreated and the mineral water may be bottled straight from the local stream, I have to boil up supplies in advance with my electric water-heater. In the Third World, Coca Cola and Pepsi are safe to drink (neither of those two arch rivals could allow the other to make capital out of a contaminated batch). Tea is useful too, as the water and milk are both boiled. As a last resort, there are foul-tasting chemical purifiers.

I used to have an embarrassing social problem with water. When I cycle across deserts and desolate uplands, tribesmen and villagers often come over to meet me, carrying the most precious gift they have to offer – a cup of water. I used to offend them deeply by refusing it, but I knew that it would be madness to risk drinking such dirty water, even though I was sometimes running low. Then I had a brainwave. I now thank them most warmly for their gift, take a long draught from my own water bottle, then top it up with the water from their cup. As soon as I'm out of sight, I pop in a Puritab and in fifteen minutes I have a new supply of safe drinking water.

In some countries, finding a secure place to sleep is the problem which dominates my afternoons. I've slept in some very uncomfortable places, but if the door could be locked or barred, my bicycle and I were safe inside. Outside Europe, I carry my small tent, but I prefer not to use it. Quite apart from the discomfort of camping, I think it's courting danger for a lone woman to sleep out by the roadside. In towns I sleep in good hotels, but across country I've learned to appreciate whatever I can find, however rough. And I've learned to value the simple things we take for granted, like turning a tap and getting clean water.

I shall not dwell on poverty, though I have seen what it is to be desperately, heartbreakingly poor. One afternoon in India I saw four men ahead of me in the road. They were crouching down together in such a tight, intent little huddle that I couldn't work out what they were doing until I was almost on top of them. What I saw as I cycled by left me stunned. A lorry had spilt a puddle of oil and the four men were mopping it up with rags and squeezing it into small tins. For them, that puddle of oil was not just a tiresome traffic hazard. It was a thing of value, far too precious to be wasted. I thought of our throw-away society and I was ashamed.

Of all the countries I've visited, India is still, despite the economic advances of recent years, in a poverty-league of its own. But at least the sun shines and even the poorest beggar can enjoy his nap in the shade on a hot afternoon. His life is luxurious compared with that of the South American Indian high up in the Andes. I've seen Peruvian and Bolivian market women sitting on the pavements in the pouring rain, in temperatures not far above freezing. They have walked for hours over the mountains and all they have to sell is a dozen prickly pears. The rain streams down from their bowler hats and their skirts swirl in the water rushing through the gutters. Their children, barefoot and runny-nosed, sit impassively beside them, too wretched even to think of playing. With no electricity or heating in their huts, they can never feel warm and dry. Materially, they may be better off than the poorest of the sub-tropical Indians, but such cold poverty seems harder to bear.

Peace, my next lesson, was a difficult one to learn. In the end, I learned it from a Turk at a bus-stop in Antalya. I was rushing down the road one evening, anxious to get to the post office before it shut. As I flew by, the Turk asked me in English, 'Why are you so angry?' His question pulled me up sharply. I wasn't angry. I was simply in a hurry to get to the post office, but I'd worked myself up into such a state about it that the Turk took my anxiety for rage. I calmed down immediately. My letters were only letters to friends and the post from Turkey took five or six days anyway, so it was quite immaterial whether the letters went into the box that evening or the next morning. I stopped frowning and smiled at the man at the bus-stop.

In the West we make a virtue of being brisk and businesslike and rushing ourselves into coronaries. If there's no work to do, we invent it. The further East you go, the more peaceful and contented the people become. If there's no trade in the shop, they sit outside in the sun playing backgammon with their neighbours. They don't pretend to be busy, dusting the shelves or stocktaking. When I took them as my role models, I felt much more at peace with myself. I related better to the strangers I met and made friends more easily, simply by smiling and finding the time to talk. It's more of a challenge to stay peaceful in London, where life is fast and furious, but I still try to take things calmly and smile in the shops. I've often been grateful, on my solitary travels, for a kind word from a stranger, and who knows what solitary person may be standing next to me at the Sainsbury's check-out?

Of course, I could never stay peaceful without learning patience. There are so many frustrations for the traveller – red tape, telephones that don't work, post that doesn't arrive, unreliable trains, shifty rickshaw wallahs, hotels with clueless staff, people who say what they think you want to hear rather than what's correct, and people who are so laid-back that they've lost all sense of time. In self-defence, to keep my sanity, I've become so tolerant that I don't think I shall get agitated or impatient ever again. For a once brisk headmistress, this is a startling character change.

Providence has so far been kind to me. On one of my rides, I took the New Testament as my long read (in the Authorised Version, of course). Studying it in the light of my own experience, I was struck by the relevance of that well-known passage from St Luke's Gospel: 'Are not five sparrows sold for two farthings and not one of them is forgotten before God? But even the very hairs of your head are all numbered. Fear not therefore; ye are of more value than many sparrows.'

I've been in some very tight spots on my travels, alone on my bicycle in strange, sometimes dangerous places. But whenever the situation has seemed desperate, someone or something has always turned up. There have been many instances in this book. The wild dogs have given up the chase, the Chinese Police have relented, and the lights of a town have appeared in the distance, just as I was giving up hope.

I don't take unnecessary risks. I'm not a nervous traveller, but I'm not foolhardy either. The Lord helps those who help themselves, as the proverb says. I calculate the danger and proceed only if the odds are on the side of safety. But the unexpected sometimes happens, and what should have been a straightforward ride turns suddenly into a perilous situation. Panic sets in, and it's then that Providence, God or simply luck, according to your point of view, comes to the rescue. I still don't rely on it, but it's given me courage. Perhaps there is somone up there who keeps an eye on me?

On a less philosophical level, I've come to terms with poundage, my own. The first time I cycled round the world, I did it in one long, unbroken journey. All those months of unremitting physical effort reduced my weight by almost 13 kilos – and it didn't suit me. I looked scrawny and wrinkled, and I seemed to have lost most of my energy. So after years of trying to diet and lose weight, I changed my objective. As every one preferred me plumper, I had a wonderful time eating and drinking myself back into my old shape and I've never dieted since.

My last letter 'p' is the most important. I should never have embarked on my first solo trip around the world, had I not felt sure that 99.99 per cent of the world's people were kind, helpful and honest, and that the statistically negligible rogue, the one who always makes the headlines, was just as likely to cross my path in London as in Bangkok. In fact, I guessed that I should probably be safer out East, as our western society is more violent.

I was right to feel confident. I've been welcomed and cared for in every country, from China to Chile. I've been pampered in wealthy households and hospitably entertained by people who had virtually nothing to offer. I've even had money pressed on me by a small shopkeeper in Pakistan, whose entire stock I could have bought without denting my bank balance. He thought I must be poor as I was riding a bicycle! I've met only kindness on my travels and I've never once been threatened with violence.

On holiday, I move among the same sort of people I meet at home. They are people with the same standard of living and they view the world from a similar perspective to my own. On my bicycle, I pass through places the tourist never sees, places which I should never visit myself if I had a car to whisk me along to the next major city. Most of my travel lessons have been learned in these places, where people manage on very little because they have to, and because they have ingenuity. And where ingenuity fails, they accept their lack with patience. An empty beer bottle and a flat stone make just as good pastry as a rolling pin and a wooden board, and they cost nothing. Old car tyres make excellent rubber soles for shoes. And why buy a special bath for the baby when there's a large saucepan in the kitchen?

The first time I crossed real desert, the hotel porter brought me half a bucket of warm water. I took it into my shower room, where the tap was simply an ornament, and was amazed to discover how efficiently I could bathe in such a small quantity of water. A ladle was provided, so I started by scooping water over my head and giving myself a shampoo. The lather trickled down, followed by the rinsing water, and in no time at all I was transformed from a walking duststorm into a pale, spruce human being. I've since used the bucket and ladle system in small hotels throughout the East, in countries where water is a scarce resource, and I've come to feel uneasy in luxury hotels where the water flows freely. In Goa, I know that the villagers' taps are turned off in the holiday season and their fields go unwatered, so that tourists in the beach hotels can take unlimited showers. The same disaster occurs in Thailand. I've learned on my travels that all these baths we westerners wallow in are quite unnecessary, as it's easy to keep clean on half a bucket. It's a lesson we may all have to learn if the climate continues to change.

Water is only one of the resources we waste through our profligate, extravagant lifestyle. Which brings me back to possessions and to all the people around the world who have taught me how few of them we really need.

As Socrates once said, 'What a lot of things I can do without!'

Epilogue

Ah! que le monde est grand a la clarté des lampes!
Aux yeux du souvenir que le monde est petit!

Charles Baudelaire

S ouvenir-gathering is difficult on a bicycle. At the Fortress of Jiayuguan, just before I set out across the Gobi Desert, I bought a pink silk camel embroidered with blue and yellow flowers. He's a complicated little creature, with a green felt Chinese merchant on his back and tiny silk mice dangling from his toes. He hangs on the lampshade in my study, surveying me and my word processor. He's very light and he fitted comfortably into one of my panniers, along with a smooth green onyx apple that I bought in Rawalpindi and use as a paperweight. Those are the only tangible souvenirs of my ride and they are both as small as the world in the eyes of memory.

I had another memento, but that was only transient. When I arrived home, Julian came speeding round with a Karakoram cake, which he'd baked to celebrate my crossing. It was skilfully iced, with the Khūnjerāb Pass carved out in relief and the place-names painted in red cochineal. Inside was a very good cake, which is why that particular memento soon disappeared.

When I look at my camel and my onyx apple and reflect on my journey round the world, I'm only moderately happy. Warfare and visa problems left me with some very disappointing gaps. The one I most regret is the stretch of the Silk Road through the Fergana Valley to the great oasis cities of Samarkand, Bokhara and Khiva. In 1997, I went on a package tour of Uzbekistan. I could see that it was difficult cycling country. There were long desert crossings, few hotels, terrible food and alarming officials. But I would still rather have cycled to Timur's tomb in Samarkand and crossed the Oxus River on my own two wheels than peered at them through the windows of my air-conditioned coach.

The other gaping hole, also along the Silk Road, is Iran. I

tried to get a visa in Islamabad. The imposing marble halls of the Iranian Embassy were deserted, except for myself and one clerk who was lounging under a scowling portrait of Ayatollah Khomeini. He told me that I might possibly be granted a visa, but the Embassy was so busy that it would take at least four weeks to process my application. It was 49°C and humid in Islamabad, and the prospect of hanging about in that heat for a whole month was more than I could face, particularly as there was no guarantee that I should get the visa at the end of it. So I packed my panniers and flew to Turkey. Iran will have to wait until I have the time and patience to try again.

Ayatollahs and Kurds permitting, I shall cycle there some day. And I shall cycle the ancient roads of Iraq, once Saddam Hussein is toppled. Then there are the trade routes across Syria, and the spice routes, the amber routes, the jade routes, the silver routes and the routes of kings, priests and penitents. One route leads to another . . . and another . . . and another . . .

But first, Condor and I have a job to finish in India.

Appendix A
Bicycle Specifications

The sea-green Condor, which I rode from Rome to Jakarta:

Frame	Reynolds 531 twin-tube (mixte)
Wheels	Wolber rims, Shimano hubs, DT Alpina spokes
Gears	Shimano
Brakes	Shimano
Bars and stem	SR alloy touring randonneur
Headset	Shimano
Block	14–34
Seatpin	Shimano
Saddle	Brooks
Chain	Sedisport
Chainset	TA touring with gear ratios 36–48
Pedals	Shimano ATB
Tyres	Specialised Kevlar
Tubes	Madison Nutrak
Rack	Vetta alloy
Mudguards	Esge
Panniers	Karrimor
Bar bag	Karrimor Klik-Lok

Spares carried: 1 tyre, 2 inner tubes, 6 spokes, 1 gear cable, 1 brake cable, selection of nuts, bolts, screws and washers.
Tools: spanner, screwdriver, set of Allen keys, puncture repair kit, 2 valve adaptors.

The purple Kenhill Cube, which I bought in Beijing and rode to Rome:

Frame	Emmelle with crossbar
Gears	Shimano
Panniers	Karrimor Iberian
Bar bag	Karrimor Klik-Lok

Spares carried: None
Tools: As for Condor

This is a very short list, as there were few brand names and numbers to be found on the bicycle. I took a new set of panniers with me to Beijing, along with the tools. Spare parts were unavailable in China.

The bicycle served me faithfully on a very difficult ride. It has since been stolen in London.

Appendix B
Luggage Lists

A. Rome to Lisbon

Clothes

As it was winter, I travelled to Rome in corduroy trousers, ankle socks, trainers, a long-sleeved shirt, a lightweight pure wool jersey, an anorak and cycle mittens. This was my normal cycling gear.

I carried: waterproof trousers and sou'wester
woolly hat
silk balaclava
2 long-sleeved shirts
2 pairs socks
1 pair grey wool trousers
2 changes of underwear
1 long-sleeved silk vest
1 pair silk long johns
1 nightdress
1 large all-purpose cotton square
1 pair flat sandals, doubling as slippers
A Liberty's silk suit, with black silk T-shirt, black petticoat, black tights and high-heeled black sandals (for smart occasions)
Small black leather handbag

Medicines and Toiletries

1 course of Amoxycillin (a wide-spectrum antibiotic)
Aspirin, Senokot and Rennies
Savlon antiseptic cream
Cicatrin antibiotic powder
Canesten cream (for athlete's foot)
Anti-inflammatory gel (for muscle strains)
Selection of plasters
Cosmetics
1 tablet Roget et Gallet soap (my small luxury)
Clarins Sun Block (factor 25) for face
Ambre Solaire (factor 20) for arms and legs

Miscellaneous

Light down sleeping-bag
Thermarest sleeping-mat

Universal plug
Swiss army knife
Torch
Olympus AF-1 Camera and 5 slide films
Sewing kit
Nail file, clippers, tweezers
Writing pad, envelopes and 2 notebooks
Compass
Maps
Spanish pocket dictionary and phrase book
Stack of *Times* crosswords
Complete Works of Shakespeare

B. Salvador to Jakarta

Clothes

As I cycled to Heathrow in the English winter and arrived in Brazil in the middle of their summer, I wore an old fleece-lined tracksuit for the outward journey and an old long-sleeved shirt under my anorak. As soon as I reached Salvador, I changed into cotton trousers and a short-sleeved blouse and gave the tracksuit and winter shirt to the airport lavatory attendant, who was delighted with them.

I carried: Everything on the Rome to Lisbon list, except the grey wool trousers.
Additions: 2 short-sleeved blouses
Swimming costume and towel
I bought: 1 pair of white cotton trousers

Medicines and Toiletries

Everything on the Rome to Lisbon list
Additions: 30 Imodium capsules (for diarrhoea)
6 glycerin suppositories
200 Paludrine tablets (malaria prophylaxis)
100 Avoclor tablets (malaria prophylaxis)
1 malaria self-treatment kit from British Air clinic
2 Repel 100 mosquito sprays
Antihistamine cream
Prescription medicines for polymyalgia

Miscellaneous

Everything on the Rome to Lisbon list, except the Olympus camera and the works of Shakespeare.

Additions: Mosquito net
Electric boiler, mug, Nescafé and apple tea
Camping cutlery set
Padlock and chain (for dodgy hotel doors)
Pentax Espio 115 and 8 slide films
Portuguese pocket dictionary
South American Handbook
Lonely Planet (Brazil and Peru)
Don Quixote
6 editions of *Tough Puzzles*
I bought: The *Lonely Planet* guides to Australia and Indonesia in
Australia, together with the necessary maps.

C. Beijing to Rome

Clothes

I travelled to Beijing and cycled for the first two months in my winter
gear, as described in Rome to Lisbon. When the weather turned warm,
I left my corduroy trousers behind in a country inn for the cleaner.
I carried: Everything on the Rome to Lisbon list except the grey
wool trousers.
Additions: Black cotton trousers
Blue cotton trousers and blue silk shirt
Cream *shalwar kameez*
1 short-sleeved blouse
1 extra long-sleeved silk vest
1 extra pair silk long johns
1 thermal vest
Swimming costume and towel
Smog mask
I bought: Gloves and replacement trainers in China
Replacement cotton trousers, shirts and trainers in
Turkey

Medicines and Toiletries

Everything on the Salvador to Jakarta list, except the malaria
self-treatment kit and the Repel 100.

Miscellaneous

Everything on the Salvador to Jakarta list, except the mosquito net
and the books.

Additions: Space blanket
Tin opener
Travelling alarm clock
Polaroid camera and 30 shots
Mandarin phrase book
Turkish pocket dictionary
Lonely Planet China (relevant parts), *Pakistan and Karakoram Highway*
Odyssey Guide to the Silk Road
Horace's Odes
Poems of Matthew Arnold

I bought: A replacement camera battery, with great difficulty, and made a note never to travel without spares again!

Appendix C
Journey Logs

A. The Australian Outback. (Townsville to Darwin)

Day 1	Townsville – Mingela	105 km
	Overnight with friends	
2	Mingela – Charters Towers	62 km
	Backpackers' Hostel	
3	Charters Towers – Pentland	108 km
	Pentland Hotel	
4	Pentland – Prairie	99 km
	Prairie Hotel	
5	Prairie – Hughenden	45 km
	Grand Hotel	
6	Hughenden – Richmond	112 km
	Mud Hut Hotel	
7	Richmond – Julia Creek	144 km
	Gannons Hotel	
8	Julia Creek – Cloncurry	134 km
	Post Office Hotel	
9	Cloncurry – Mt Isa	118 km
	Overnight with friends	
10	Mt Isa – Yelvertoft Station	107 km
	Camping	
11	Yelvertoft Station – Camooweal	92 km
	Post Office Hotel	
12	Camooweal – Soudan Station	123 km
	Camping	
13	Soudan Stn – Barkly Homestead	142 km
	Barkly Homestead Motel	
14	Barkly Homestead – Rest Area	119 km
	Camping	
15	Rest Area – Three Ways	73 km
	Three Ways Roadhouse	
16	Three Ways – Renner Springs	134 km
	Renner Springs Desert Hotel	
17	Renner Springs – Elliott	92 km
	Elliott Hotel	
18	Elliott – Dunmarra	103 km
	Dunmarra Wayside Inn	
19	Dunmarra – Daly Waters	51 km
	Camping at Daly Waters Pub	

20	Daly Waters – Larrimah Wayside Inn	94 km	
21	Larrimah – Mataranka Mobil Caravan Park	68 km	
22	Mataranka – Katherine Victoria Lodge	109 km	
23	Katherine – Pine Creek Shell Roadhouse	90 km	
24	Pine Creek – Hayes Creek Wayside Inn	63 km	
25	Hayes Creek – Adelaide River Adelaide River Inn	49 km	
26	Adelaide River – Coolalinga Camping in Caravan Resort	86 km	
27	Coolalinga – Darwin Larrakeyah Lodge	34 km	

B. The Karakoram Highway. (Kashgar to Gilgit)

			Altitude
Day 1	Bus from Kashgar to Tashkurgan Tashkurgan Binguan	293 km	1335 m–3600 m
2	Tashkurgan – Dabdar Overnight in Tajik home	57 km	
3	Dabdar – Pirali Overnight with Chinese Army	38 km	
4	Pirali – Chinese Defence Post	31 km	
	Defence Post – Khūnjerāb Pass	5 km	4733 m
	Khūnjerāb Pass – Pakistan Border Post	17 km	
	Border Post – Dih Security Post Overnight in Security Post	35 km	3323 m
5	Dih – Sust Mountain Refuge Hotel	36 km	2700 m
6	Sust – Passu Shisper View Hotel	39 km	2400 m
7	Passu – Gulmit Marco Polo Inn	19 km	
8	Gulmit – Karimabad Hunza Lodge	38 km	
9	Karimabad – Gilgit Park Hotel	109 km	1500 m

Place Name Index

General Index

Note: *refers to entries in the place name index.